Springer Series on Ethics, Law, and Aging

Marshall B. Kapp, JD, MPH, Series Editor

Bonnie Brandl, MSW, * is the project coordinator for the National Clearinghouse on Abuse in Later Life, a project of the Wisconsin Coalition Against Domestic Violence. The National Clearinghouse on Abuse in Later Life provides technical assistance, training, and consultation on domestic abuse in later life. Ms. Brandl has worked with battered women and their children for more than 17 years. She has worked with the Wisconsin Coalition Against Domestic Violence for 14 years. Her published articles, manuals, and booklets on domestic abuse in later life have been distributed throughout the country. For the last nine years, she has presented at numerous national, regional, statewide, and local conferences on domestic violence and elder abuse. Ms. Brandl has a master's degree in social work from the University of Wisconsin-Madison. She currently lives near Boulder, Colorado, with her family.

Carmel Bitondo Dyer, MD, FACP, AGSF, graduated from Baylor College of Medicine in 1988. She is board certified in internal medicine and geriatrics and has been the director of the Geriatrics Program at the Harris County Hospital District since completing her postgraduate training in 1993. She is an associate professor of medicine at Baylor College of Medicine and is co-director of the Texas Elder Abuse and Mistreatment Institute, a collaborative effort of Baylor College of Medicine, the Harris County Hospital District, and the Texas Department of Protective and Regulatory Services. Her clinical interests include care of the elderly poor, elder mistreatment, dementia, delirium, depression, and geriatric assessment. Her research is in the area of elder neglect and the interdisciplinary approach to abused or neglected elders. She has made more than 100 presentations, including testimony before the U.S. Senate Finance Committee in 2002 on behalf of mistreated elders. Dr. Dyer is the principal investigator of a number of funded grants. In 2004, the Texas Elder Abuse and Mistreatment Institute received funding under the National Institute of Health's Roadmap Initiative to develop an interdisciplinary research consortium on elder self-neglect.

Candace J. Heisler, JD, served as a San Francisco assistant district attorney for more than 25 years before her retirement in 2002. As a prosecutor, she headed various units in the San Francisco District Attorney's Office including the Domestic Violence Unit, which oversaw the prosecution of domestic violence and elder abuse cases. She has edited four judicial curricula and a prosecution manual on domestic violence cases. She has authored a number of articles that have been published in *The Journal of Elder Abuse and Neglect* and in other publications. Ms. Heisler has developed courses on domestic violence and elder abuse for

California law enforcement, first-responders, and investigators. She also teaches courses in domestic violence and elder abuse for California law enforcement, victim witness program advocates, probation officers, domestic violence and elder abuse advocates and front-line workers, health care professionals, and prosecutors. She is a member of the California Violence Against Women STOP Task Force. Ms. Heisler has served on the Texas Medical Association Blue Ribbon Panel on Family Violence and on the National Committee for the Prevention of Elder Abuse. She has received many awards, including the California District Attorney's Association Career Achievement Award and the California Governor's Victim Services Award. Currently, Ms. Heisler is an assistant adjunct professor of law at the University of California's Hastings College of Law.

Joanne Marlatt Otto, MSW, has worked in the field of adult protective services for 25 years. She has an undergraduate degree in English from the State University of New York and a master's degree in social work from the University of Denver. From 1986 to 2000, she served as the program administrator of Adult Protection/Elder Rights Services with the Colorado State Department of Human Services. Since 2001, Ms. Otto has been the executive director of the National Adult Protective Services Association. In that role, she drafted language regarding adult protective services delivery for the Elder Justice Act. She also testified before the U.S. Senate Finance Committee on the need for federal protective services for elderly and disabled victims of abuse, exploitation, and neglect. Ms. Otto has published articles in *Victimization of the Elderly and Disabled, Generations,* and the *Public Policy and Aging Report.* She has made numerous presentations on elder and adult abuse, including to the National Institute on Aging, the Institute of Medicine, the U.S. Department of Justice, the American Geriatrics Society, and the FBI. Ms. Otto is the editor of *Victimization of the Elderly and Disabled* and is a partner in the National Center on Elder Abuse.

Lori A. Stiegel, JD,* is associate staff director of the American Bar Association Commission on Law and Aging in Washington. She has worked in the law and aging field at the local, state, and national levels since 1982, focusing on elder abuse since 1993. Ms. Stiegel was a member of the National Research Council Panel to Review Risk and Prevalence of Elder Abuse and Neglect and served on the National Committee for the Prevention of Elder Abuse Board of Directors from 1997 through 2004. Ms. Stiegel directs the commission's elder abuse grants, including its role as a partner in the National Center on Elder Abuse. She is the author of *Recommended Guidelines for State Courts Handling Cases Involving*

Elder Abuse and *Elder Abuse Fatality Review Teams: A Replication Manual*, as well as numerous articles and curricula for judges, court staff, lawyers, and professionals providing adult protective services, community corrections services, and victim services. She holds a B.A. from the University of Florida and a J.D. from the George Washington University National Law Center.

Randolph W. Thomas, MA, served for more than 24 years in the law enforcement profession. His experience encompasses patrol, investigations, planning and research, and, for more than 14 years, law enforcement training. He is a member of the South Carolina Adult Protection Coordinating Council and has served on a number of committees concerning elder abuse prevention. He is currently President of the National Committee for the Prevention of Elder Abuse and serves in an advisory capacity to the U.S. Department of Justice on the subject of elder abuse. He has been an adjunct professor at the University of South Carolina, Department of Criminology and Criminal Justice, in the areas of juvenile delinquency, crime prevention, and child abuse. He received his undergraduate degree in political science from Chaminade University and his master's degree in political science from the University of South Florida.

*The author is not speaking on behalf of her employer and the views expressed are her own and do not necessarily represent an official position of her employer.

Elder Abuse Detection and Intervention: A Collaborative Approach

Bonnie Brandl, MSW

Carmel Bitondo Dyer, MD, FACP, AGSF

Candace J. Heisler, JD

Joanne Marlatt Otto, MSW

Lori A. Stiegel, JD

Randolph W. Thomas, MA

SPRINGER PUBLISHING COMPANY

New York

We dedicate this book to the memory of Rosalie Wolf. We also dedicate this book to the front-line workers, law enforcement officers, prosecutors, health care providers, advocates, civil attorneys, and others who work with elder abuse victims on a daily basis. Their commitment to assisting victims and ending elder abuse inspires us.

Copyright © 2007 Springer Publishing Company, LLC

Springer Publishing Company, LLC
11 West 42nd Street
New York, NY 10036

Acquisitions Editor: Sheri W. Sussman
Managing Editor: Mary Ann McLaughlin
Production Editor: Emily Johnston
Cover design: Joanne E. Honigman
Composition: Apex Publishing

08   09   10/   5   4   3   2

Library of Congress Cataloging-in-Publication Data

Elder abuse detection and intervention : a collaborative approach /
  Bonnie Brandl ... [et al.].
    p. ; cm.
  Includes index.
  ISBN 0-8261-3114-X
  1. Older people—Abuse of—United States. 2. Older People—Abuse
  of—United States—Prevention. 3. Abused elderly—Services for—United States.
I. Brandl, Bonnie.
  HV6626.3.E458   2006
  362.6—dc22   2006018583

Printed in the United States of America by Edwards Brothers.

Contents

SECTION TWO: RESPONDING TO ELDER ABUSE

SECTION THREE: COLLABORATION

Preface

Everyone, including older people, deserves to live in peace and dignity. This generation of older Americans has achieved some amazing accomplishments. They have contributed to and lived through significant changes. Some lived through the Depression and the rapid economic changes that have occurred in the last 50 years. Others served in wars, such as World War I or II, the Korean War, or Vietnam. Some influenced art, music, or literature. Others were involved in changes in technology, medicine, or space travel.

However, most older people lived quiet lives raising families and participating in their communities. They come from a variety of racial, ethnic, economic, and religious backgrounds. These elders were mothers or fathers, sisters or brothers, and represent the rich heterogeneity seen in older people. Some elders were wealthy, some indigent; some had white- or blue-collar jobs. As younger adults, some chose to be homemakers or to be self-employed. Others were unable to work because of physical or mental health problems, and some were chronically unemployed. Some suffered trauma early in life or throughout their lives.

Most older people are loved and cherished, but too many are isolated in facilities or living in loneliness and fear in the community. Some elders become physically or emotionally hurt, and others lose their financial resources or suffer neglect or abandonment. Regardless of their background or societal contributions, every elder deserves to live safely and with dignity, and all deserve protection and intervention to stop abuse when it occurs.

Reported cases of elder abuse are increasing. Victims encounter multiple systems, and they are best served when professionals from these systems work together. It is the responsibility of these professionals to work collaboratively to enhance victim safety, hold abusers accountable, promote systemic change, and advocate for new policy initiatives and legislation, additional research and funding, and social change. This book provides the framework to begin and to build on multidisciplinary approaches at the local, state, and national levels toward ending elder abuse.

Introduction

Professionals in a variety of systems are encountering increasing numbers of older victims and their abusers. Health care professionals are identifying more older patients who have been harmed. Reports of elder abuse to Adult Protective Services (APS) and law enforcement are rising. More offenders are being prosecuted and held accountable than ever before. As the population percentile of older Americans increases, greater numbers of seniors who have been abused are contacting advocacy programs such as domestic violence and sexual assault organizations. Many older adults are turning to the civil justice system for remedies to abuse.

The increase in numbers of older victims seeking help raises the question: how many elders are being abused? Unfortunately, no one knows for sure. Too few surveys have been done in this area, and those that have been completed suffer from serious methodological problems. For example, the National Elder Abuse Incidence Study, conducted in 1998 under the auspices of the National Center on Elder Abuse, reported that 551,011 persons over age 60 experienced some form of abuse or neglect (National Center on Elder Abuse [NCEA], 1998). The study estimate of domestic elder abuse is significantly lower than previous estimates for many reasons. The study was not designed to determine how much elder abuse exists, but, rather, to look at the proportion of cases reported to APS versus the proportion of cases that actually exist (Cook-Daniels, 1999; Otto & Quinn, 1999). In addition, the sample size for the study was extremely small. Only 20 counties in 15 states were used. In each county only 12 to 13 agencies were included, and each agency had typically only four to six trained sentinels (individuals responsible for the initial data collection). Data were collected for only two months and were based on 1,498 actual cases (Cook-Daniels, 1999; Otto & Quinn, 1999). Moreover, the study did not assess abuse of older persons in long-term care facilities or other institutions.

Currently, no single national entity collects and analyzes elder abuse data from the various sources. Existing data are compiled from state APS programs, state Long-Term Care Ombudsman, regulatory agencies, and state Medicaid Fraud Control Units. One method used to determine the extent of the problem has been to look at data collected by APS agencies, because in most states, they are the primary responders to cases of elder abuse and abuse against vulnerable adults. For instance, the report titled *The 2004 Survey of State of Adult Protective Services: Abuse of Adults 60 Years of Age and Older* found that 565,747 reports of elder and adult abuse were made to APS in Fiscal Year (FY) 2003, a 19.7% increase from the 2000 Survey (472,813). Of this number, 32 states said that APS received a total of 253,426 reports on persons aged 60 and older. The majority of state APS programs serve vulnerable adults ages 18–59 in addition to people over 60. Because many states do not collect separate data on abuse victims age 60 and older, it is not possible to determine age-specific information from all 50 states, the territories, and the District of Columbia (Teaster, 2006).

A handful of smaller studies provide some information about the prevalence of the problem. In 1988, Pillemer and Finklehor, using a random sample method interviewing more than 2,000 older adults in Boston, estimated that between 701,000 and 1,093,560 older Americans are victims of abuse each year (Pillemer & Finklehor, 1988). These figures lead to estimates that 32 of every 1,000 elders in the United States were abused per year. Mouton, Rovi, Furniss, and Lasser (1999) found that 4.3% of the 257 women ages 50 and older who responded to a national health survey answered "yes" to questions about being currently in an abusive relationship. Harris (1996) reviewed the 1985 National Family Violence Resurvey and found that 5.8% of older couples had experienced domestic violence in the past year. Another study that examined APS records in Connecticut found that 1.6% of elders had been abused, neglected, or exploited over a nine-year period (Lachs, Williams, O'Brien, Hurst, & Horwitz, 1997). Hudson et al. (1999) found that 7.5% of surveyed elders had been abused at some point after turning age 65. In addition, Hudson and Carlson (1999) interviewed 917 people in North Carolina and found that 6.2% of adults stated that they had abused an elder.

Clearly, data and evidence from the field suggest that elder abuse is an increasingly serious problem in America. *But why focus a book on a collaborative or multidisciplinary response to elder abuse?* Each of the authors has been in his or her chosen field for more than 15 years. Several have witnessed elder abuse in their personal lives, often involving someone they cherish. Each of the authors has cases that haunt them—cases where their respective discipline failed an older victim.

For example, Helen was 72 years old when she came to the domestic violence shelter in 1983. All of the other residents were young women. To her dismay, Helen realized that she had been abused longer than any of the other residents had been alive. Helen stayed for two weeks before returning home, telling staff she didn't see any other options.

In another case, during her first night in a nursing home, Muryl, age 86, had all of her rings stripped from her fingers while she slept. The nursing home staff said that they had fallen off and been lost in the bedclothes. The rings were never found. Several days later Muryl's family reported the incident to the police. They were told that law enforcement did not respond to problems regarding lost possessions that occurred in nursing homes.

Through our professional experiences, each of us has found that the expertise, services, and resources of our respective disciplines were, on their own, inadequate to enhance the safety of older victims. Advocates cannot make arrests. Prosecutors cannot mend broken bones. Each of us began to look for others who were willing to collaborate to provide a wider array of options than any single system could provide.

Each of us has participated in multidisciplinary work on the local, state, and national level. We have struggled through the challenge of working with professionals who have different mandates and agendas, as well as celebrated successes that came from collaboration to promote victim safety and to hold abusers accountable.

The co-authors of this book are from adult protective services, law enforcement, prosecution, health care, advocacy, and civil justice. Writing this book forced us to form our own multidisciplinary team. We shared a common goal—to write a book promoting elder victim safety through collaboration. We agreed on an outline and a target audience. Then the conflicts began.

Like any newly formed team, we found ourselves needing to establish ground rules and deadlines. We reviewed each other's writing and were amazed to find so many different perspectives and viewpoints. We struggled to define elder abuse. Should self-neglect be included? What about crimes and consumer scams against older people? What about abuse in facilities? Where did domestic violence fit in? In the end, we found consensus on these issues, as described in Chapter 2.

As authors, we struggled with voice. In keeping with our respective disciplines, we differed on how formal or informal the tone should be. Which studies should be included, given the methodological problems with most of the existing research? How much technical detail versus broad concepts was appropriate?

We decided to let the experiences of victims speak for themselves through case examples. Many of the chapters in this text include case presentations to illustrate the major points. These cases are based on actual circumstances, but not on actual patients, victims, or clients, and many of the scenarios are composites of multiple cases. The names are fictitious and details about the lives of the victims have been eliminated; any similarity to an actual case is coincidental. However, elements of each example are based on elder abuse victims that we have encountered. First names were used for clarity, even though many seniors prefer to be addressed formally with their last name.

Language, including the use of jargon, was another source of contention. Should we use words such as *mistreatment, abuse, violence,* or *battering*? Are we talking about *victims, patients,* or *clients*? Is the harm caused by *abusers, offenders, perpetrators,* or *family members*?

In the end, we resolved these difficulties by allowing a voice for each author. Like any good multidisciplinary team, each member was encouraged to shine in her or his specialty area and, for that section, to use the language of that field. Other authors contributed additional text based on their expertise, providing further richness and depth.

Along the way, we recognized how much we still did not know about elder abuse. Too little research has been done. Studies are flawed. Too few resources and professionals are devoted to this issue. For the book to be more comprehensive, we wished we could have included additional authors with expertise in abuse in facilities, substance abuse, mental health, cultural competency, and a variety of other issues. Like any multidisciplinary team, we balanced the number of participants needed to get the job done versus having "too many cooks in the kitchen." We recognize that more could be said about some issues not fully addressed in this text.

One example of an issue we struggled with is abuse in long-term care facilities. The elder abuse field has historically separated the harm that occurs in the community (known as *domestic elder abuse*) from that which occurs in facilities, such as nursing homes, community-based residential facilities, or assisted living facilities (referred to as *institutional abuse*). Different systems of response were established; domestic elder abuse was generally considered the realm of APS (although some APS programs investigate suspected abuse in facilities), whereas regulatory agencies and Long-Term Care Ombudsman Programs dealt with institutional abuse. This distinction was logical in the early days, when the perception was that family members committed domestic elder abuse and facilities staff committed institutional abuse.

As the field has matured, however, perceptions about both forms of abuse have changed dramatically. Moreover, the systems of response have expanded and, to some extent, become less distinct. These changes have led many to believe that the line between domestic elder abuse and institutional elder abuse is largely artificial. The response to elder abuse should not depend on whether the roof over an older person's head is that of a private dwelling or a facility. In too many cases, that approach has meant that victims of abuse who live in facilities have not had the benefit of responses by the justice system, APS, and advocacy organizations, such as domestic violence or sexual assault programs. Although we recognize that facilities have legal responsibilities to protect their residents from abuse, we believe that the types of abuse committed and the types of perpetrators who commit them should determine the response. Therefore, as the parameters for this book were plotted, we felt strongly the need to address elder abuse that occurred in any location to encourage collaboration in both domestic and long-term care settings. To illustrate: if a nursing home resident is abused by her spouse or raped by an employee of the facility, then responses from regulatory, health care, APS, long term-care ombudsman, criminal justice, and civil justice systems are necessary. But assistance from the domestic violence or sexual assault systems is also appropriate. The victim in a nursing home needs the help those systems can provide as much as when the abuse or rape occurs under the roof of a private dwelling.

That said, the idea of writing about institutional abuse created a dilemma. Each of us had done some work on abuse in facilities, but our primary work had been devoted to domestic elder abuse. Consequently, the discussions of institutional abuse are not as comprehensive as the discussions about domestic elder abuse. It was decided, however, that narrowing the scope to domestic elder abuse was a disservice to many older victims and in direct conflict with the primary message about collaboration.

By listening to each author's unique perspectives, the team ultimately gained greater understanding and awareness. This is not the book any one of us could have written individually. It is stronger because of the multidisciplinary approach.

To illustrate that point, one of the authors found a six-piece puzzle. She gave each of her co-authors one puzzle piece. The puzzle pieces served to remind the group that working in isolation meant that each could see just one piece of the mosaic. Only when the pieces were put together could the group see the full picture.

This book is divided into five sections. Section One describes the historical context, definitions, and dynamics of elder abuse. Section Two focuses on responding to elder abuse, including identification, reporting, and the systems involved in elder abuse cases. Section Three focuses on collaboration by discussing the definitions and benefits, obstacles to success, informal practice-based responses, and team process. Accomplishing the work of the team is addressed in Section Four. These chapters illustrate how a multidisciplinary approach enhances case review, victim safety, abuser accountability, and system change. Finally, Section Five examines policy, legislation, research, and social change needed to work toward ending elder abuse.

REFERENCES

Cook-Daniels, L. (1999). Interpreting the National Elder Abuse Incidence Study. Victimization of the Elderly and Disabled, 2(1), 1–2.

Harris, S. (1996). For better or for worse: Spouse abuse grown old. Journal of Elder Abuse & Neglect, 8(1), 1–33.

Hudson, M., Beasley, C., Benedict, R., Carlson, J., Craig, B., & Mason, S. (1999). Elder abuse: Some African American views. Journal of Interpersonal Violence, 14(9), 915–939.

Lachs, M. S., Williams, C. S., O'Brien, S., Hurst, L., & Horowitz, R. (1997). Risk factors for reported elder abuse and neglect: A nine-year observational cohort study. The Gerontologist, 37, 469–474.

Mouton, C., Rovi, S., Furniss, K., & Lasser, N. (1999). The associations between health and domestic violence in older women: Results of a pilot study. Journal of Women's Health & Gender-Based Medicine, 1(9), 1173–1179.

National Center on Elder Abuse. (1998). National elder abuse incidence study. Washington, DC: Author.

Otto, J., & Quinn, K. (1999). The national elder abuse incidence study: An evaluation by the National Association of Adult Protective Service Administrators. Victimization of the Elderly and Disabled, 2(1), 4–15.

Pillemer, K., & Finkelhor, D. (1988). The prevalence of elder abuse: A random sample survey. The Gerontologist, 28, 51–57.

Teaster, P. (2006). The 2004 survey of adult protective services: Abuse of adults 60 years of age and older. Washington, DC: National Center on Elder Abuse.

Acknowledgments

Special thanks to my family—Rick, Lucas, and Travis—for their support and patience as I took time away from them to co-author this book. I am grateful to my parents and siblings, who taught me the benefits of a stable, loving family. I am also grateful to the numerous wonderful mentors who have encouraged, supported, and challenged me in this work. Special recognition goes to Jane Raymond and Tess Meuer. I want to express my gratitude to the staffs of the National Clearinghouse on Abuse in Later Life and of the Wisconsin Coalition Against Domestic Violence for all the amazing work they do on behalf of battered women and their children.

—Bonnie Brandl

I am grateful for the encouragement of my parents, Carmela and Salvatore Bitondo; the support of my mentors, Dr. Stephen Greenberg and Dr. David Hyman; and the love of my husband, Jim. Many thanks to the staff of the Texas Department of Family and Protective Services; our working relationship continues to be a most educational and enriching experience. I am indebted to the faculty, staff, and administration of the Baylor College of Medicine and of the Geriatrics Program at the Harris County Hospital District. It is a privilege to work beside these professionals as we strive to improve the lives of mistreated elderly patients.

—Carmel Bitondo Dyer

I wish to thank my parents, Betty and Dan; my brothers, Trey and Stan; and their families for their support over the years and during the writing of this book. Each has taught me that with a dream and hard work, anything is possible. I also want to thank my colleagues and friends at the San Francisco District Attorney's Office and at the police department for entrusting me for many years with these complex and remarkable cases.

To my many friends and colleagues who have helped me begin to understand the plight of abused elders and what I can do to improve their lives, I add special thanks. I hope this book reflects well on your guidance and advice. I also want to thank my co-authors for teaching me so much and making this dream of a book a reality.

—*Candace J. Heisler*

My participation in this project would not have been possible without the loving support of my husband, Jan, and my sons, Kevin and Ethan. Thank you for your patience and understanding for the many late dinners, lost weekends, and interrupted vacations. I also owe a great debt to the memory of my mother, Bertha Buckley Brown, who, through her own social work practice, set such high standards. Acknowledgment, as well, to all my colleagues at the National Adult Protective Services Association, whose knowledge and passion have contributed so much to my work and to the field of adult protective services.

—*Joanne Marlatt Otto*

My love and thanks to my parents, Eileen and Richard Stiegel, whose love and respect for their parents taught me by example. I am indebted to those clients of the Senior Advocacy Unit of Bay Area Legal Services in Tampa, Florida, who showed a young lawyer the terrible impact of elder abuse, although I wish they had not been in a position to do that. Thanks to my colleagues at the American Bar Association Commission on Law and Aging, who help support my work on elder abuse. I am grateful to my co-authors for their friendship and for their vision and commitment to improving the response to elder abuse.

—*Lori A. Stiegel*

I want to thank my wife, Charlotte, for her understanding and support on this project. I am grateful to my parents, Kathy and Walt, for teaching me how to age with dignity; to my children and grandchildren for showing me how to enjoy life; and to my friends in the law enforcement community for making my professional life interesting and rewarding.

—*Randolph W. Thomas*

SECTION ONE

Understanding Elder Abuse

Historical Context

Too often older Americans living in the community or in long-term care facilities (LTCF) are abused, exploited, and/or neglected. Relatives, partners or caregivers may steal money and treasured possessions. Lifelong partners who were abusive throughout the relationship continue their cruelty. Spouse/partners, adult children, and other family members or caregivers are the most common perpetrators of sexual assault and abuse (National Center on Elder Abuse, 1998). Seniors are told they are stupid or crazy, a common form of emotional abuse. Caregivers may neglect elders, leading to serious illness, harm, or death. Some older people do not, or are not able to, take care of themselves, a condition called self-neglect. In worse-case scenarios, older victims are killed by neglect, abuse, homicide, or homicide/suicide.

Reported cases of elder abuse are increasing. From 1986 to 1996, there was a steady increase in the reporting of domestic elder and vulnerable adult abuse nationwide, from 117,000 reports in 1986 to 293,000 reports in 1996. "This figure represents an increase of 150.4% since 1986" (National Center on Elder Abuse Web site). In 1998, the National Elder Abuse Incidence Study (NEAIS) suggested that only the tip of the iceberg of elder abuse cases are being identified (National Center on Elder Abuse, 1998). Two national studies of cases reported to Adult Protective Services (APS) in 2000 and 2004 that included both abuse of vulnerable adults and elder abuse found that during that period, there was a 19.7% increase in the number of elder/adult abuse reports in all 50 states, the District of Columbia, and three territories (Teaster, 2006).

Cases of elder abuse will continue to increase as Americans live longer. In the last 50 years, with advances in medical research, nutrition, health care, and modern conveniences, Americans are living longer than ever before and in greater numbers than previously experienced. Those numbers will continue to grow for at least the next several decades as the baby boomers age. In 2000, thirty five million people were older than age 60 in the United States. This is an additional 3.7 million people or 12% increase since 1990. Nearly 1 in 8 persons (12.4%) of the population is at least 65 years old. By 2030, the numbers of older Americans will more than double to 70 million. Those ages 85 and older will increase from 4.2 million in 2000 to 8.9 million in 2030 (U.S. Census Bureau, 2004). Seniors are more likely to live with a disability, which has been shown to be a risk factor for some elder abuse (Lachs, Williams, O'Brien, Hurst, & Horowitz, 1997).

The number of older Americans from a variety of ethnic backgrounds is also rapidly changing. Elder abuse crosses all racial, ethnic, religious, and economic lines. In 2000, minority elders were 16.4% of the elder population. The percentage of elders from minority populations is projected to increase to 25.4% by 2030. Between 1999 and 2030, some populations will increase more significantly than others: Caucasian (81%), Hispanic (328%), African American (131%), American Indian, Eskimo, Aleut (147%), and Asians and Pacific Islanders (285%). All minority populations will increase by 219% (U.S. Census Bureau, 2004). This increase in persons from a variety of racial and ethnic groups will impact the types of programming that will need to be created to effectively intervene in cases of elder abuse.

Even as the numbers increase, professionals also recognize that elder abuse cases are complex and diverse. Some older victims are healthy and mentally alert. Others suffer from a variety of health problems, as well as physical and cognitive disabilities. Victims and perpetrators come from various racial, ethnic, economic, and religious backgrounds. Older victims bring a range of generational, cultural, and spiritual values about what constitutes abuse and what help they will accept. Abuse can occur in long-term or new intimate partner relationships. Family members and caregivers may also be offenders. The abuse may have been going on for years or started recently. The cause of abuse may be due to an organic condition, poor care giving, or the desire to gain and maintain power and control over the victim.

Some elder abuse is a crime that calls for a response from the criminal justice system. In other situations, such as self-neglect, social service workers, physicians, and other health care workers are more likely to offer effective interventions. Abuse occurring in facilities has its own complexity, as the abuser may be a family member, staff member, volunteer, or another resident. A variety of governmental agencies may get involved in abuse occurring in facilities.

A collaborative response to elder abuse is required. Multiple disciplines must work together to ensure a seamless response to victims that promotes their safety and well-being. This book helps professionals and others to better understand the dynamics of elder abuse and methods that promote a collaborative response. Chapter 1 lays the groundwork for a collaborative approach by providing a brief history of the elder abuse field.

HISTORICAL CONTEXT

Family violence and sexual abuse, including abuse of older people, has been described in the literature for centuries. However, the naming and identification of child abuse, domestic violence, elder abuse, sexual assault, and abuse against people with disabilities and vulnerable adults are much more recent events. Child abuse was "discovered" in the 1960s by professionals working with victimized children. In the 1970s, both the sexual assault and battered women's movement emerged from grassroots efforts.

Although Burston identified the phenomenon of "granny battering" in a British medical journal (1975), elder abuse was barely acknowledged in the United States until 1978 (Bonnie & Wallace, 2003). Beginning in the 1980s, Congress focused increasing attention on elder abuse by holding a series of hearings and issuing several reports. It was not until February 2003, however, that a comprehensive federal response was initiated with the introduction of the Elder Justice Act by Senators Breaux and Hatch (Breaux & Hatch, 2002). The Act had not passed when the 108th Congress adjourned. It was reintroduced as S. 2010 by Senators Hatch and Lincoln in 2005 (Hatch & Lincoln, 2005).

Research on elder abuse has been scarce and underfunded. A few small studies were published in the 1980s and 1990s, but it was not until 1998 that the NEAIS was conducted by the National Center on Elder Abuse (NCEA) and Westat (National Center on Elder Abuse, 1998). Data from all 50 state Adult Protective Services programs, the District of Columbia, and Guam were collected in 2000 and again in 2004 (Teaster, 2006). In 2001, The National Academy of Sciences panel published "Elder Mistreatment: Abuse, Neglect and Exploitation in an Aging America" (Bonnie & Wallace, 2003). In 2001, the National Research Council Panel to Review Risk and Prevalence of Elder Abuse and Neglect reviewed and compiled a list of existing research in the field and called for more research in the field (Bonnie & Wallace, 2003). For a timeline of significant national events in the elder abuse field, see Appendix A.

The Federal Government's Response to Elder Abuse

The federal government has been slow to respond to elder abuse. Currently, not even one federal employee works exclusively on elder abuse issues (Breaux & Hatch, 2002). National funding on elder abuse is a fraction of all federal spending on abuse. "The federal government spends $153.5 million on programs directly addressing issues of elder abuse. In sharp contrast, the federal government spends $520 million on programs combating violence against women and $6.7 billion on child abuse prevention efforts. Of the $153.3 million spent directly on elder abuse prevention, $143.34 million is spent through the Department of Health and Human Services, with the remaining $10.16 million being spent on Department of Justice programs" (Anonymous, 2002, p. 16).

The Department of Health and Human Services provides funding and programming through the Social Services Block Grant (SSBG) program and the Older Americans Act. Social Service Block Grant funds are used to support APS agencies in less than half of the states nationwide. The Older Americans Act provides funding through the Administration on Aging for the Long Term Care Ombudsman Program, Prevention of Elder Abuse, Neglect and Exploitation Program, and the NCEA. Also housed in the Department of Health and Human Services is the National Institute on Aging, the Centers for Medicare and Medicaid Services, and the Office of the Inspector General. The National Institute on Aging conducts some research related to elder abuse. The Centers for Medicare and Medicaid Services contract with state agencies to survey nursing homes and respond to complaints about abuse and services. The Office of the Inspector General funds the Medicaid Fraud Control Units that exist in all but a few states to investigate and prosecute cases of patient abuse, neglect, and exploitation in nursing homes and, in some states, to also investigate complaints in other types of LTCF including assisted living facilities and board and care homes (Anonymous, 2002).

The Department of Justice provides funding through several of its entities, including the Office on Violence Against Women, Office for Victims of Crime, Bureau of Justice Assistance, and National Institute of Justice. Since 2002, the Office on Violence Against Women has provided grants to train law enforcement, prosecutors, and court personnel on elder abuse and abuse against people with disabilities. The Office for Victims of Crime has funded a number of elder abuse initiatives aimed at improving the response to older victims of abuse and exploitation. The Bureau of Justice Assistance has supported efforts to educate law enforcement officers and prosecutors about elder abuse, and the National Institute of Justice has provided grants for studies on medical forensic issues related to elder abuse.

Additional Responses to Elder Abuse

Many national organizations and statewide and local initiatives have been created to address the needs of victims, hold abusers accountable,

improve policies and practices, and raise professional and public aware-
ness. The primary national organization devoted to elder abuse issues is
the NCEA, which was first funded in 1989 through the Older Americans
Act by the Administration on Aging. Since 1998, the National Center on
Elder Abuse has been administered under the auspices of the National
Association of State Units on Aging with partners at the American Bar
Association Commission on Law and Aging, the Clearinghouse on Abuse
and Neglect of the Elderly at the University of Delaware, the National
Adult Protective Services Association, and the National Committee for
the Prevention of Elder Abuse. The mission of the NCEA is to "promote
understanding, knowledge sharing, and action on elder abuse, neglect."
Two other national projects worth noting are the National Clearinghouse
on Abuse in Later Life and the National Long Term Care Ombudsman
Resource Center. Both address a segment of elder abuse but are not
partners of the NCEA.

There are also some notable statewide and local elder abuse programs throughout the country. Some of these local and statewide efforts
are described in more detail later in the chapter. Many of these efforts
grew out of a specific discipline such as the aging network, health care, or
the criminal justice system; other projects use a collaborative model.

SYSTEMS' RESPONSES TO ELDER ABUSE

Over time a number of disciplines whose professionals are primary
responders to elder abuse victims began working on this issue. This section
describes the responses of the APS and elder abuse agencies, the criminal
justice system, health care, domestic violence and sexual assault movements, and the civil justice system. Addressing abuse in long-term care
facilities is also discussed. Historically, these systems have approached
cases of elder abuse using the expertise from their own disciplines but
have usually not worked collaboratively with professionals in other fields
to respond to older victims.

Adult Protective Services/Elder Abuse Agencies

APS is the principal public source of first response to reports of elder
and vulnerable adult abuse, neglect, and exploitation. (The definition of
vulnerable adult varies based on state statute but, in general, vulnerable
adults are persons 18 years and older who have physical or cognitive impairments that cause them to be unable to provide for their basic needs,
protect themselves, or report abuse.) APS programs are empowered by
states and local communities to accept and investigate reports of abuse,

neglect, and financial exploitation of elders and younger people with disabilities (Otto, 2002). The real impetus for states to provide APS came with the passage of Title XX of the Social Security Act in 1974. Broad language in the Act gave permission for states to use Social Services Block Grant (SSBG) funds for the protection of adults as well as children. By 1981, "all the states, in one way or another, noted that they had an office with responsibility to provide protective services to some segment of the population . . . providing such services to the needy even in the absence of authorizing legislation" (U.S. Congress 1981, p. 70). Absent federal direction on this issue, many states continued to adopt their own statutes for providing APS, which were usually delivered by state or local social service agencies (Otto, 2000). As state laws evolved, definitions became increasingly state specific, as did the programs. Currently, only six state APS laws do not have some sort of mandatory reporting requirement (Otto, 2000).

A continuing issue was the provision of protective services to self-neglecting persons with disabilities and elderly adults (Research Conference Recommendations, 1986). Researchers insisted that self-neglect was not a form of abuse, but APS practitioners recognized that self-neglecting adults made up the majority of their caseloads. Because the cases were complex and time-intensive, APS programs began to turn to other community agencies and to develop informal coalitions to meet the multiple needs of self-neglecting clients.

Criminal Justice System

The criminal justice system, and law enforcement in particular, has traditionally responded to calls relating to criminal conduct and community service functions, such as well-being checks. Responses to social problems, including family violence across the life span, were handled with little interaction with other systems. Historically, crimes against elders were dealt with by the criminal justice system, whereas elder abuse, neglect, and exploitation by family members in the home setting were seen as social service problems. "It became apparent in the last decade that although elder abuse was a public welfare matter and later taken over as an aging issue, it could also be viewed as a crime. Today, police officers, prosecutors, and health and social service providers realize that they all have an important role to play in preventing victimization of elders whether perpetrated by strangers or family members" (Wolf, 2000a, p. 1). Previously, where legal interventions were sought, civil, not criminal, courts were used.

Prosecutors have typically been reactive. They addressed cases that were investigated and presented by law enforcement, rather than initiating and conducting investigations of family violence matters. It is not surprising that when few arrests for domestic violence and elder abuse were made, few prosecutions were initiated. Adding to the limited response, there was little training provided to criminal justice professionals on the investigation and prosecution of elder abuse cases. When victims declined to prosecute or wanted to drop charges, many agencies did not proceed. Many cases, including situations in which the victim had dementia or simply was believed to be confused, were not investigated or prosecuted. There were no specialized victim support services for older victims or specialized investigation or prosecution units.

Significant changes have occurred over the last decade in some communities. These new responses tend to be localized, although the National District Attorney's Association has now adopted a position that:

> given the numerous agencies and individuals that are involved with elders on a daily basis, the National District Attorneys Association recognizes that a multidisciplinary approach to prosecuting elder abuses cases should be considered. Individuals and agencies from the medical and financial fields, public health, service providers, and law enforcement should be involved, as appropriate, in a team effort to investigate, prevent, and prosecute elder abuse crimes. In order for the multidisciplinary approach to be successful, prosecutors must take a leadership role in these teams. (National District Attorneys Association, 1977)

Its research arm, the American Prosecutors Research Institute, APRI, has begun to develop information and research on national prosecution promising practices.

In various communities, specialized investigative and prosecution units have been established (NDAA, 2003). Some prosecutors' offices, such as San Diego, California; San Francisco, California; Seattle, Washington; and Cook County, Illinois, have established specialized elder abuse units. These units often have one prosecutor who works with a victim throughout the case, a process called "vertical prosecution." Training curricula and programs have been developed. Specialized victim advocates operate in some locations to serve elder crime victims (Heisler & Stiegel, 2002). Increased numbers of arrests and prosecutions are also occurring.

Civil Justice

The civil justice system handles an array of legal remedies that may be used to protect an older person from elder abuse or to respond to an elder who has already been victimized. These include claims for compensation due to harm or to recover financial losses resulting from abuse, neglect, or exploitation; restraining orders or injunctions; divorce or separation; guardianship or conservatorship; mental health commitments; and attempts to undo a will, deed, contract, or other type of transaction because of fraud or undue influence.

There is not a large body of case law on elder abuse. Decisions relating to guardianships and conservatorships are not categorized as elder abuse cases. Other civil actions and remedies have either not been used, or not recognized or classified as elder abuse cases. Most civil legal decisions and verdicts are not documented in case law reports and therefore do not become a part of the body of case law precedent on which other lawyers rely in building subsequent cases (Stiegel, 2000).

Elder abuse victims usually do not turn to the civil justice system for a variety of reasons. These include reluctance to take legal action; practical problems such as difficulty traveling to or accessing a lawyer's office or courthouse, or the lack of understanding that there are civil legal remedies available; difficulty of proving elder abuse cases; the cost of bringing civil legal cases to court, and the challenges to obtaining and then actually collecting a recovery that exceeds the legal costs; the slow pace and customary delays of the civil legal process; and a lack of knowledge about and sensitivity to elder abuse victims by judges and other court personnel.

There are some sources of civil legal assistance for victims that may help to prevent victimization. Every community is expected to have a free government-sponsored legal services program for persons over age 60, as well as a legal services or legal aid program for persons with low incomes and few assets. Depending on funding and priorities, these programs may be able to help older persons avoid or respond to victimization. State or local bar associations may run volunteer lawyer programs that can provide similar services. Lawyers who work in law firms and charge for their services can also help older persons with civil matters related to elder abuse.

An increasing number of elder abuse cases, particularly those regarding nursing home abuses, are being heard and reported by the civil courts. This change is due to growing awareness by victims and their family members, new laws, increased training of lawyers and other professionals about old and new civil legal remedies, training of judges about elder abuse, and a growing recognition that elder abuse is a legal, as well as a social and health problem (Stiegel, 2000).

Medical Response to Elder Abuse

The medical response to elder abuse has been slow in coming. From the late 1970s, when Burston referred to "granny-bashing" in a *Lancet* article, to the 1990s, physicians contributed little to the medical literature. Most considered it strictly a social problem and not within the purview of medicine. Awareness increased as social scientists began to perform more rigorous studies of the issue. A few academic centers around the United States now have active elder abuse research programs. Most of the published data are from epidemiologic analyses or descriptive clinical studies (Alpert, Tonkin, Seeherman, & Holtz, 1998; Hendricks-Matthews, 1997).

The inclusion of elder abuse in medical curricula has been inconsistent. A recent National Research Council report called for all health professional schools to educate their trainees about the issue of family violence, including elder abuse (Bonnie & Wallace, 2003). A recent report by the Institute of Medicine called for all health professional schools to educate their trainees about the issue of family violence, including elder abuse (Institute of Medicine, 2002). Four academic programs in different locales across the United States have started providing elder abuse training in the field with APS workers for professionals from a variety of disciplines (Heath, Dyer, Kerzner, Mosqueda, & Murphy, 2002).

Physicians and nurses have been providing clinical care to victims of elder abuse for years. When they recognize it, physicians generally consult with social workers to develop intervention plans. Geriatric teams have applied interdisciplinary geriatric assessment and intervention to victims of elder abuse as they do for other vulnerable elders.

Domestic Violence and Sexual Assault Movements

In the late 1980s, the connection was being made between domestic violence and elder abuse. In Wisconsin, the Department of Health and Family Services held a landmark conference bringing together participants from domestic violence and APS in 1988. In 1992, the American Association of Retired Persons (AARP) sponsored a national forum to address the needs of older abused women. As a result of this forum, AARP provided funding to the Wisconsin Coalition Against Domestic Violence (WCADV) to produce a document on the needs of older battered women and a directory of services. From 1994 to 1996, the United State Administration on Aging funded six national demonstration projects to examine the specific needs of older abused women and methods of collaboration to improve responses. In 1999, the WCADV received funding from the U.S. Department of Justice, Office on Violence Against Women, to open the National Clearinghouse on Abuse in Later Life. In 2000, the Violence Against Women Act provided grants to train law enforcement, prosecutors, and court personnel on elder abuse and abuse against persons with disabilities.

During the last decade, an expanded framework for understanding the dynamics of elder abuse emerged that recognized the presence of power and control dynamics in many cases. Domestic violence advocates recognized that existing services were not tailored to meet the needs of older abused women. In some communities, domestic violence programs hired elder abuse specialists and created older abused women's support groups. These programs are still scattered throughout the country, but modest improvements have been made in the availability of specialized services for older abused women. In other communities, such as Phoenix and San Francisco, abuse in later life programs have been created and sustained through the aging field. A national survey found more than 100 programs across the country that focus on abuse in later life and 34 support groups for older abused women (National Clearinghouse on Abuse in Later Life, 2003). Although some agencies working with people with disabilities have begun creating programs for victims of abuse, few of these services have been designed for older victims.

More recently, sexual assault programs have also begun to look at elder sexual abuse and to create written materials and services for older victims. The Wisconsin Coalition Against Sexual Assault has created several materials including a video on sexual abuse in later life.

The Response to Elder Abuse in Long-Term Care Facilities

The problem of elder abuse in nursing homes and other LTCF (referred to as "institutional abuse") has elicited attention from Congress, government agencies, the media, and advocacy organizations since Senator Frank Moss's seminal hearings in the 1960s (Anonymous, 2002). Like elder abuse occurring in the community, institutional abuse is underreported (U.S. General Accounting Office, 2002), and the extent of the problem is largely unknown (Anonymous, 2002).

LTCF residents may be physically or mentally incapable of reporting abuse. They or their family members and other visitors may fear that reports will result in increased abuse or retaliation. Even when reports are made, regulatory, investigatory, and advocacy agencies responses have often been inadequate (U.S. General Accounting Office, 2002).

Congressional hearings, government studies, advocacy by residents' family members, and media attention have led to significant changes in the response to institutional abuse. These developments include the creation of the Long Term Care Ombudsman Program, which provides advocacy for LTCF residents regardless of age and the establishment of the National Citizens Coalition for Nursing Home Reform. Ombudsman programs and other agencies have developed and implemented training programs for LTCF direct care and administrative staff (Menio & Keller, 2000).

Responses to abuse in facilities have varied. Some states, including Georgia, have developed statutory reform initiatives. Efforts have been made to strengthen the regulatory process at the state and federal levels. The number of personal injury lawsuits for nursing home abuse has exploded, and it is now common to see lawyers specializing in nursing home abuse cases. Medicaid Fraud Control Units have been established in almost every state to investigate and prosecute abuse and exploitation in nursing homes, and their jurisdiction has expanded to include assisted living facilities. The U.S. Department of Justice established its Nursing Home Initiative, which supported federal and state criminal and civil actions against long-term care facilities through education of prosecutors, law enforcement officers, staff of APS and Long Term Care Ombudsman Program, and regulatory personnel, as well as through the development of state working groups composed of those professionals (Office of Justice Programs, 2000).

Multidisciplinary Approaches to Elder Abuse

Historically, systemic responses to elder abuse were not collaborative and often involved only a few systems that did not communicate effectively with each other. As professionals' understanding of the complexity of elder abuse has increased, more programs throughout the country are responding to elder abuse using a multidisciplinary approach that will be described and promoted throughout the remainder of this book. Some highlights of multidisciplinary approaches to elder abuse are described in this section.

Wisconsin, Oregon, Texas, and Louisiana have developed successful collaborative statewide efforts. Throughout the 1990s, Wisconsin formed a collaborative effort with the Department of Health and Family Services, Wisconsin Coalition Against Domestic Violence, Wisconsin Coalition Against Sexual Assault, the Coalition of Wisconsin Aging Groups, and others to focus on domestic violence and sexual assault in later life. In 1994, a task force in Oregon worked with and trained bank personnel to identify financial exploitation (Anonymous, 2002). The Texas Department of Protective and Regulatory Services created a public awareness campaign titled "Not Forgotten." The U.S. Department of Justice's Nursing Home Initiative has produced successful working groups in Louisiana and Virginia to identify and respond to substandard care in nursing homes (Anonymous, 2002).

Local multidisciplinary teams have been working together for many years. The Greater Cleveland Roundtable has focused on domestic abuse in late life. The San Francisco Consortium staffed by the Institute on Aging works to "protect and maintain the health, independence, and safety of elders by providing a comprehensive range of services to vulnerable seniors aimed at preventing or responding to abuse or neglect" (Institute on Aging Web site, 2004). In Phoenix, Arizona, the Maricopa Elder Abuse Prevention Alliance was created in 1993 and now has approximately 100 professionals from a variety of disciplines working together on elder abuse and domestic abuse in later life (Area Agency on Aging, 2002). Both local efforts address elder abuse and have specific programming on domestic abuse in later life.

Several criminal justice initiatives are worth noting. A specialized law enforcement unit was established in Fresno, and specialized elder abuse units in both law enforcement and prosecution have been created in San Francisco, Ventura County, San Diego, and Los Angeles. Elder service officers focusing specifically on elder abuse exist in Cook County, Illinois (Chicago), Hillsborough County, Florida (Tampa), and the state of Louisiana. Louisiana has legislation that requires the designation of an elder abuse prosecutor in each judicial district, as well (Heisler & Stiegel, 2002). There are also TRIADs active throughout the country. TRIAD stands for the three sectors of a community that partner to keep seniors safe from crime: public safety, criminal justice, and seniors.

Specialized teams have been developed to address financial exploitation. These teams (often called Financial Abuse Specialist Teams or FAST) provide expert consultation and training to protective services and other professionals in cases of elder financial exploitation and assist in recovering or preventing further loss of assets. They also provide education and training on elder financial abuse. The Los Angeles FAST was convened in 1993 to combat elder financial abuse in Los Angeles County (Bernatz, Aziz, & Mosqueda, 2001). The Los Angeles FAST and similar teams across the country work closely with bank personnel to gather information and secure assets. Mental health specialists train team members to administer assessments to determine whether the older person is a victim of undue influence or has diminished capacity. Law enforcement officers train personnel on team members' legal rights and protections in disclosing information to investigators regarding suspected exploitation (U.S. Departments of Justice and Health and Human Services, 2000).

Medical response teams have also been created in several communities including Houston, Texas, and Orange County, California, to respond in a multidisciplinary manner to elder abuse. In the mid-1990s, several academic centers collaborated with protective service specialists, civil and/or criminal lawyers, police officers, and victim advocates to form specialized interdisciplinary geriatric assessment and intervention teams. The first formal medical response team began at the Beth Israel

Hospital in Boston, Massachusetts, in the 1980s. The purpose of this hospital-based team was to provide consultation and support to hospital staff, assist in a multidimensional evaluation of older victims of mistreatment, and develop treatment plans (Matlaw & Spence, 1994). In New York City, another hospital-based team was formed at Mount Sinai Hospital in 1998. This team serves hospitalized victims and assists them with counseling and other supportive services (Kahan & Paris, 2003).

In 1995, a geriatric medicine interdisciplinary team at Baylor College of Medicine, Houston, Texas, began collaborating with the APS of Texas and later became know as the Texas Elder Abuse and Mistreatment Institute (Dyer, Hyman, Pavlik, Murphy, & Gleason, 1999). Also in the mid-1990s, a similar team was established at the University of California, Irvine, called the Vulnerable Adult Specialist Team. Other academic medical centers, including the Robert Wood Johnson Medical School in New Jersey and the Hennepin Medical, Center, Minnesota, have also forged alliances with APS (Heath et al., 2002).

Since 2001, the elder abuse field has begun to develop fatality review teams, borrowing a concept that has been used successfully in the child abuse and domestic violence fields. The broad goal of elder abuse fatality review teams is to examine deaths caused by or related to elder abuse to improve the systems that respond to victims and prevent similar deaths in the future. There are currently eight elder abuse fatality review teams, which are located in Houston, Texas; Maine (statewide team); Orange County, California; Pima County, Arizona; Pulaski County, Arkansas; and Sacramento, San Diego, and San Francisco, California. Several other states and communities are in the process of establishing teams.

A multidisciplinary response is also beneficial in facility cases. Because LTCF administrators generally have a sense of when they will be surveyed and thus can prepare, a few states have developed collaborative projects such as Florida's "Operation Spot Check" or California's "Operation Guardian" to conduct random, unannounced inspections of LTCF.

As is evident in the discussion in this chapter, the elder abuse field is growing, and research and programming are emerging. The naming and identifying of elder abuse are relatively recent occurrences. Too little research has been done to grasp the prevalence and incidence of elder abuse. Congress and the federal government have touched on elder abuse but have failed to address the problem in any meaningful way. Yet, the work in the field on the local, state, and national levels has been impressive given the limited resources. Through the efforts of numerous dedicated professionals from a variety of disciplines, awareness of elder abuse and the development of promising practices and specialized programming increased significantly within the last decade.

Early efforts to respond to older victims used a "silo" approach, in which each discipline responded to cases, without working with others. Throughout the last decade, however, a multidisciplinary response is emerging and is now considered best practice. The next two chapters focus on defining and understanding the dynamics of elder abuse in order to lay a foundation for a multidisciplinary response.

CHAPTER TWO

Defining Elder Abuse

INTRODUCTION

Practitioners, researchers, and policymakers have struggled with the definition of elder abuse for years. The federal government has not established a nationally recognized definition of elder abuse (Bonnie & Wallace, 2003). Studies use different definitions depending on what was studied and when and where the study was completed. The ages of victims and forms of abuse included in legal definitions vary from state to state. Older people, professionals, and community members may have different interpretations of what constitutes abuse. Studies show that members of different racial and ethnic groups have significantly different perceptions about what behavior constitutes elder abuse (Anetzberger, 1998; Hudson & Carlson, 1999; Moon, 2000). Professional lexicons define the forms of elder abuse based on the conventions that exist within the respective fields. Prosecutors, law enforcement officers, advocates, protective service specialists, and health care providers use terms that make sense in their professional circles as defined by specific roles and tasks. For example, a protective service specialist may handle a case of physical abuse, whereas law enforcement will refer to the same case as assault. Absence of a universally accepted definition of elder abuse can lead to difficulties collaborating on research, training, prevention strategies, and interventions.

For the purposes of this book, elder abuse includes the following:

- Physical, sexual, or emotional abuse; financial exploitation; neglect; or abandonment of an adult age 60 or older, who lives either in the community or a long-term care facility, perpetrated by a person in an ongoing "relationship of trust" with the victim. Relationships of trust can include familial-like situations and/or persons who have authority to assist an elder with financial, health, or legal decisions or are responsible to provide care (such as staff in a facility). Familial "relationships of trust" include those between spouses or partners, family members, and some caregivers who become like family. In many of these familial cases, the older individual may or may not be in need of assistance or care, the abuse is generally a pattern of behaviors over a period of time, and the victim may want to maintain the relationship and protect the abuser. Another category of "relationship of trust" includes persons with legal responsibility to make legal, health, or financial decisions for the victim, or persons who have a fiduciary or legal responsibility for a victim. In many of these situations, the victim is unaware the abuse or financial exploitation is occurring or may have been unduly influenced to believe the abuser is acting in his/her best interest. Relationships of trust also include caregivers who have taken on the responsibility of providing care for an older person who is unable to take care of or protect himself or herself.

- Self-neglect (because these cases represent a significant portion of the Adult Protective Services [APS] workload).
- Sexual assault, theft, or financial exploitation that is committed against a long-term care facility resident by anyone, including staff, another resident, a visitor, or a stranger who enters the facility unlawfully (because of the facility's legal responsibility to protect its residents from harm).

The term *elder abuse* is used generically throughout the book to include these concepts unless otherwise indicated.

Some state laws define elder abuse more broadly than does this book. Other state laws define it more narrowly. Some professionals label any crime against older people as elder abuse. They argue that in many circumstances, seniors are targeted for specific crimes, especially telemarketing frauds, sweepstakes, and repair scams. These crimes may have a significant negative impact on the victim, but they are beyond the scope of this book. In general, crimes committed by strangers are handled primarily by the criminal or civil justice systems and not by the other systems discussed in this book. Additionally, the lack of a relationship based on love, family ties, societal expectations, or trust between the victim and perpetrator means that victims may be more willing to get help, report the crime, and assist with prosecution.

For this book, the hallmark of elder abuse—what distinguishes it from crimes committed against older persons by strangers—is that victims and society may experience a unique sense of betrayal when the perpetrator is someone with whom they have an ongoing committed partnership, familial or other type of trust relationship. Victims may choose not to report, may hinder the investigation, or may recant. A wife may be afraid that if she reports the abuse she will be forced to divorce her husband of 52 years. A father may fear that his son will be arrested and go to prison if the financial exploitation is discovered. These victims may sabotage efforts to hold the abuser accountable because they are afraid of retaliation, living alone, or losing their independence; they may also fear what will happen to the perpetrator. In addition, the community is betrayed when a person who takes on the responsibility of caring for or making decisions for an older person uses that position of power to abuse, neglect, or exploit the elder. A victim of elder abuse may have greater needs than a victim of crime by a stranger, and these needs may necessitate that more systems work collaboratively to offer remedies and support.

This chapter addresses the "who, what, when, where, and why" of elder abuse. It elaborates on the definition of elder abuse as used in this book and highlights issues related to the (1) age of the victim, (2) health and functional status of the victim, (3) gender of the victim and perpetrator, (4) residence of the victim, (5) relationship between the victim and perpetrator, and (6) forms of abuse.

AGE

There is no universally accepted definition of the age at which a person becomes an elder. Definitions of "elder" vary from program to program, system to system, and state to state. For example, a person becomes eligible for federally supported aging services at age 60. Domestic violence and sexual assault programs for seniors often include persons 50 years or older. Some states enhance criminal penalties for crimes committed against a person who is age 65 or older. This text refers to persons over the age of 60 as elders because that is the age used by the federal Older Americans Act to trigger eligibility for aging services that may be of benefit to victims of elder abuse.

Adult Protective Services (APS) program eligibility criteria vary throughout the country. Some APS programs serve vulnerable adults (persons age 18 to 59 who are dependent or unable to care for or protect themselves or report abuse) and older victims age 60 or 65 and older. Other APS state statutes define their service population as exclusively vulnerable adults. In these states, anyone age 18 and older who meets the legal definition of a vulnerable adult (based on state statute) is eligible. Many older people, however, are not vulnerable adults. They do not have physical or cognitive disabilities that impair their ability to protect themselves or to ask for help.

These older individuals, typically victims of domestic violence, may be victims of elder abuse but may not be eligible for APS services. In some states, APS programs only serve older adults. Some of those states also require the older person to be vulnerable, but others simply use an age criterion.

HEALTH AND FUNCTIONAL STATUS OF THE VICTIM

Some elder abuse victims are in good health and have no cognitive impairments. For example, many older abused women are active and fit; however, other elder abuse victims suffer from some health-related problems or physical or cognitive disabilities. Some elder abuse victims have significant impairments that make them susceptible to abuse and unlikely to report.

Certain health changes are associated with age. These changes occur in the heart, lungs, kidneys, bladder, stomach, and intestines, irrespective of disease. These health changes usually do not affect function, and most elders are able to adapt; however, some age-related changes affect function and threaten independence. For instance, after approximately age 40, visual accommodation declines and most people need corrective lenses to read books and menus. The lens also thickens and becomes yellow, permitting less light to reach nerves in the eyes that transmit images to the brain. Hearing decreases after approximately age 50; deficits can range from very mild to severe. Muscle strength and mass decline by 50% between the ages of 20 and 70 years. This can result in gait imbalance, decreased mobility, and falls (Abrams, Beers, Berkow, & Fletcher, 1995).

A host of medical diseases that particularly afflict elders can lead to functional decline. These include diseases of the lungs, such as emphysema; heart disease, such as coronary insufficiency or congestive heart failure; kidney failure; and osteoarthritis. Any disease, such as cancer, that progressively robs the individual of strength or results in malnutrition leads to increased vulnerability.

Both dementia and depression are independent risk factors for elder mistreatment. There is a high prevalence of depression and dementia in elder abuse and neglect (Dyer, Pavlik, Murphy, & Hyman, 2000). Psychosis in old age is most often associated with dementia and depression and can lead to significant functional deterioration.

Furthermore, loss of executive functioning can prevent elders from seeking medical care or extracting themselves from an abusive or exploitive situation. In many instances, the elder can verbalize a desired outcome, but cannot perform the actions required to reach the goal. Loss of executive function may be a significant cause of self-neglect.

As noted in the previous section, many APS programs use health or functional status as a criterion for service eligibility. Statutory language defining these criteria varies tremendously. Some states use health criteria, indicating that APS may serve persons who have a disease or physical condition, such as mental retardation, cerebral palsy, brain damage, or substance abuse. Some states use functional status, such as the lack of decision-making capacity or an inability to provide care for or to protect oneself. Some states use a combination of health and functional status, and some states simply use legal or residential status, declaring that persons are eligible for APS services if they have had a guardian appointed to act for them or if they reside in a long-term care facility.

GENDER

Research indicates that gender matters in terms of the forms of elder abuse experienced by victims. While women make up the majority of elder abuse victims, older men are also harmed (Crichton, Bond, Harvey, & Ristock, 1999; Dunlop, Rothman, Condon, Herbert, & Martinez, 2000; Greenberg, McKibben, & Raymond, 1990; Lachs et al., 1997; Lithwick, Beaulieu, Gravel, & Straka, 1999; NCEA, 1998; Otiniano et al., 1998; Ramsey-Klawsnik, 1991; Teaster & Nerenberg, 2000; Vladescu, Eveleigh, Ploeg, & Patterson, 1999). Some data suggest that women are the victims in approximately two-thirds of reported cases of elder abuse (NCEA, n.d.). Women are more likely than men to be victims of neglect, or of emotional, physical, or financial abuse, but men are more likely to be abandoned (NCEA, 1998).

Two studies completed more than a decade ago using the Conflict Tactics Scale found more male victims than female victims of physical abuse (Pillemer, 1986; Podnieks, 1992a, 1992b). The results of these studies are questionable, however, because the Conflict Tactics Scale does not differentiate between levels of physical violence. For example, "throwing a brick at one's partner is considered just as dangerous as tossing a pair of socks" (Zorza, 2001, p. 83). Whether an action was taken to harm another person or was in self-defense is not taken into account. The scale also does not recognize which party may be living in fear or has changed his or her lifestyle as a result of the abuse (Zorza, 2001). Men who reported being hit or having something thrown at them indicated that they were not afraid of their partner and had not changed their lives (e.g., given up a job or schooling, went to a shelter) because they were afraid. Battered women typically described living in fear of future incidents and changing their lives to accommodate the abuser. Pillemer

(1986), an author of one of the these two elder abuse studies, acknowledged that women suffered significantly more injuries than men (6% of males vs. 57% of women), and that abused "women were almost twice as likely as the abused men to be 'very upset' by the abuse."

Most studies have found the majority of perpetrators to be male (Brownell, Berman, & Slamone, 1999; Crichton et al., 1999; Lithwick et al., 1999; NCEA, 1998). Overall, men were more often the perpetrators in substantiated cases of physical and emotional abuse, financial exploitation and abandonment. Women, on the other hand, were more likely to be perpetrators of neglect (NEAIS, 1998, p. 7). Elder sexual assault victims are overwhelmingly female and the perpetrators male (Holt, 1993; Ramsey-Klawsnik, 1991, 1993b). Of the cases reviewed, only older men (not women) perpetrated homicide-suicide in later life (Cohen, 1998).

RESIDENCE: ABUSE OCCURS AT HOME

Some may think of elder abuse as occurring only in nursing homes, but elder abuse is not limited to facilities. Most elder abuse occurs in private homes in the community rather than in institutional settings (Kosberg & Nahmiash, 1996). As discussed in the introduction, the same forms of abuse that are seen in the community are also seen in facilities, and this text generally does not draw a distinction between domestic and institutional abuse unless otherwise indicated.

RELATIONSHIP BETWEEN VICTIM AND ABUSER

This book focuses on elder abuse in situations in which the victim has an ongoing relationship of trust with the perpetrator. "Trust relationship" has been defined as "a care giving relationship or other familial, social, or professional relationship where a person bears or has assumed responsibility for protecting the interests of the older person or where expectations of care or protection arise by law or social convention" (Bonnie & Wallace, 2003, p. 39). Thus, a trust relationship may include that between a victim and his or her spouse or partner, adult child or other family member, or a paid or volunteer caregiver. Trust relationships also include those with fiduciaries who have an obligation to act in the older person's best interests, including guardians or conservators, agents under a power of attorney, lawyers, accountants, financial advisers, or other trusted persons.

Spouse/partner relationships can take a variety of forms. Spousal or partner relationships may be long term, for example, marriages that have lasted 40 years or more. Another scenario is a new relationship, often following the death of, or divorce from, a previous partner. The abuse could be occurring throughout the relationship or may be relatively new. Abuse can occur in any relationship, regardless of the sexual identity of the victim or perpetrator.

Other family members may also abuse, neglect, and exploit older individuals. Adult children may physically assault or sexually abuse their parents. In other situations, the adult children financially exploit their parents by stealing money or possessions. Grandchildren, siblings, and other family members may also engage in abusive behaviors. In some instances, the family member is providing care for the older person. In other situations, the older person is healthy and competent, and it is the family member who is financially or emotionally dependent on the victim.

Caregivers may be family members, hired professionals, friends, neighbors, or volunteers. Most care of elders is provided in a loving, caring fashion and without abuse. But, unfortunately, in some cases, caregivers use their position to harm the older person. A caregiver is defined as a person who bears or has assumed responsibility for providing care or living assistance to an adult in need of such care or assistance (Bonnie & Wallace, 2003).

Caregivers may also be the victims of abuse perpetrated by the care recipient. For example, an older woman who was abused throughout her marriage may now provide care for her husband. He may continue to be abusive even if he is ill or frail. Her husband may yell at her, hit her with his cane, or throw plates of food at her as she tries to provide care (Phillips, de Ardon, & Briones, 2000).

FORMS OF ELDER ABUSE

Regardless of the relationship between the victim and the abuser, many of the forms of abuse are similar. Specific legal definitions describing forms of abuse vary from state to state. In general, the seven main types of elder abuse include physical abuse, sexual abuse, emotional abuse, financial exploitation, neglect, self-neglect, and abandonment. Given the array of definitions in the field, this section highlights these forms of abuse using definitions created by the National Center on Elder Abuse The definition for self-neglect was developed by the National Adult Protective Services Association and was adopted by the American Public Welfare Association. Definitions, signs to look for, and a case example are provided for every category of abuse.

Research shows that in most cases of abuse, multiple tactics are used against the victim (Greenberg et al., 1990; Podnieks, 1992a, 1992b). For example, Anetzberger (1998) found that 89.7% of the time, psychological abuse was accompanied by other types of abuse.

Physical Abuse

> Physical abuse is defined as the use of physical force that may result in bodily injury, physical pain, or impairment. "Physical abuse may include, but is not limited to, such acts of violence as striking (with or without an object), hitting, beating, pushing, shoving, shaking, slapping, kicking, pinching and burning. In addition, inappropriate use of drugs and physical restraints, force-feeding, and physical punishment of any kind also are examples of physical abuse." (NCEA, n.d.)

The ultimate form of physical abuse is homicide. Some cases of so-called sweetheart scams, in which the perpetrator, generally a younger woman, befriends a lonely elderly male, marries him, and then gets control of his assets, may end in the victim's death. Sometimes medications, including heart medication, are manipulated resulting in premature death. Such matters can be staged to look like natural deaths and can be difficult to identify and classify. Investigations may not occur at all because the death is not recognized as homicide (Dyer, Connolly, & McFeely, 2003).

In an emerging area of research, elder homicide-suicides have been studied. Researchers have estimated that there are between 1,000 and 1,500 such cases annually in the United States. The incidence rates are higher in the population age 55 and above (Malphurs & Cohen, 2001). A total of 83% involve spouses and intimate partners (Cohen, 1998, 2000).

One-third of all cases involve couples with histories of domestic violence. All involve an overvalued attachment of the perpetrator to the victim and a desire to maintain the integrity of the relationship when threatened with separation or dissolution. That separation or dissolution may be due to a change in health status of either partner, an anticipated end to the relationship, or a pending move to a hospital or nursing home by one party. There is a high incidence of untreated and undetected psychiatric problems, especially depression (Cohen, 1998, 2000). (For more information on strangulation, homicide, or homicide/suicide, see Chapter 10.)

An Example of Physical Abuse

Denise was 73 years old and frail. She was widowed and lived on Social Security plus a small pension. Her son George was in his mid-40s and had a long history of bipolar disorder. He had been

TABLE 2.1   Signs and Symptoms of Physical Abuse Include, but Are Not Limited to:

- Bruises, black eyes, welts, lacerations, and rope marks
- Bone fractures, broken bones, and skull fractures
- Open wounds, cuts, punctures, untreated injuries in various stages of healing
- Sprains, dislocations, and internal injuries/bleeding
- Broken eyeglasses/frames, physical signs of being subjected to punishment, and signs of being restrained
- Laboratory findings of medication overdose or under-use of prescribed drugs
- An elder's report of being hit, slapped, kicked, or mistreated
- An elder's sudden change in behavior
- The caregiver's refusal to allow visitors to see an elder alone
- Changes in speaking, breathing, or swallowing that may be the result of strangulation

living in an outpatient mental health facility, but was evicted after he stopped taking his medication and started drinking. After his eviction, he moved in with his mother.

Every month when Denise's Social Security check arrived, he would take it. If Denise refused to sign it over to him, he would beat her and lock her in a closet. On more than one occasion, he left her in the closet for more than 24 hours.

An Example of Homicide/Suicide

Bennie and June had been married for almost 50 years. Neighbors and friends described them as a loving couple who had "had their share of problems" over the years, usually when they had been drinking. They had one son, Jim, who lived nearby. After calling his parents repeatedly for several days, Jim went to their home and found June lying in bed in a pool of blood. Her skull was crushed and she was dead. It appeared that she had been beaten to death with a full bottle of wine. Jim found Bennie's body in the garage. He had killed himself with a shotgun.

Sexual Abuse

For the purposes of this book, sexual abuse is defined as non-consensual sexual contact of any kind with an elderly person. Sexual contact with any person incapable of giving consent is also considered sexual abuse. It includes, but is not limited to, unwanted touching, and all types of sexual assault or battery, such as rape, sodomy, coerced nudity, and sexually explicit photographing. (NCEA, n.d.)

When committed by persons known to the elder victim, sexual abuse can begin with covert actions, such as inappropriate remarks and threats; progress to forcing the elder to watch pornographic materials or listen to explicit sexual accounts, and escalate into sexualized kissing and fondling, oral-genital contact, digital penetration, rape, and rape by foreign object. Attacking victims' genitals with blows or weapons is sexual abuse. Coerced or forced sexual activity that the victim does not want, such as forced sexual activity when seniors are exhausted, ill, or asleep, is considered sexual assault. In some cases, there may be exploitation, such as prostituting or swapping a helpless victim, or sadistic and ritualistic acts (Ramsey-Klawsnik, 1991). Sexual abuse constitutes less than 1% of all forms of elder abuse (Tatara, 1993). In 1992, approximately 20,040 women over age 50 were sexually assaulted (Dombo, 1995).

Sexual abuse in facility settings or involving caregivers can include unwarranted, intrusive, or painful procedures that occur during bathing or cleansing of the victim's genitals or rectal area. The application or insertion of creams, ointments, thermometers, enemas, catheters, fingers, soap, washcloths, or other objects into bodily orifices, when not medically prescribed or not necessary for the health and well-being of the individual, is also sexual abuse. Institutions that deny residents protection against sexually transmitted diseases also commit sexual abuse.

Perpetrators of elder sexual assault fall into four categories: (1) strangers or acquaintances; (2) caregivers; (3) family members, including spouses and intimate partners, other relatives, and adult sons; and (4) fellow residents in a residential care setting (Mouton, Roji, Furniss, & Lasser, 1999; Muram, Miller, & Cutler, 1992; Pittaway & Westhues, 1993; Ramsey-Klawsnik, 1991; Teaster & Nerenberg, 2000).

TABLE 2.2   Signs and Symptoms of Sexual Abuse Include, but Are Not Limited to:

- Bruises around the breasts or genital area
- Unexplained venereal disease or genital infections
- Unexplained vaginal or anal bleeding
- Torn, stained, or bloody underclothing
- An elder's report of being sexually assaulted or raped (NCEA, n.d.)

Although only a few studies have examined elder sexual assault, nearly all the victims studied were women, and all but one identified perpetrator were male. Research indicates that being healthy and active, married, or living in an institution does not protect older women from being sexually abused. In three studies deriving data primarily from reported cases, identified victims were overwhelmingly impaired: 80% of the victims in the Burgess, Dowdell, and Prentky study (2000) used a wheelchair or were bedridden and 60% had dementia; 80.9% of the victims in the Teaster and Nerenberg study (2000) lived in a nursing home and fewer than a quarter could walk without assistance; and 71% of the victims in the Ramsey-Klawsnik research (1991) were classified as "totally dependent" or functioning "very poorly" or "poorly."

An Example of Sexual Abuse

Gladys was 101 years old and lived in a nursing home. Her son-in-law was observed having sexual contact with her. Although Gladys acknowledged that the sexual contact was occurring, she did not want it reported. Her son-in-law had told her that he would hurt her daughter (his wife) if she did not consent. Trying to protect her daughter, who was also a resident at the nursing home, Gladys never told anyone about the abuse. Law enforcement was not contacted and the facility staff was uncertain about how to respond.

Many of the sexual abuse cases had witnesses: 76.2% of the cases in the Teaster and Nerenberg (2000) study, and nearly one-third of the cases in both the Burgess et al. (2000) and Ramsey-Klawsnik (1991) studies. Burgess et al. (2000) pointed out that although many victims did report their assaults, those who could not often displayed trauma-related behavior that staff could be trained to identify as possible signals of sexual assault.

Psychological or Emotional Abuse

Emotional or psychological abuse is defined as the infliction of anguish, pain, or distress through verbal or nonverbal acts. Emotional or psychological abuse includes, but is not limited to, verbal assaults, insults, threats, intimidation, humiliation, and harassment. In addition, treating an older person like an infant; isolating an elderly person from his or her family, friends or regular activities; giving an older person the "silent treatment"; and enforcing social isolation are examples of emotional and psychological abuse. (NCEA, n.d.)

Psychological abuse can result in depression, nervous disorders, fearfulness, physical illness, and even suicide (Moskowitz, 2003; U.S. Senate Special Commission on Aging, 1991). Psychological abuse includes repeated verbal attacks against the victim's worth as an individual or in his or her role as a parent, family member, friend, co-worker, or community member. Abusers often humiliate their victims in front of family members, friends, or strangers. They repeatedly claim that victims are crazy, incompetent, and unable "to do anything right." Victims of psychological abuse are treated like servants or children, and the perpetrator makes all decisions.

Other techniques that perpetrators use to psychologically abuse their victims include threatening placement in a long-term care facility, hiding or destroying important documents, or threatening to call immigration authorities or to lie about the victim's immigration status. Threats of violence and harm can be directed at the victim, other family members, property, prized possessions, pets, or service animals. Some abusers use intimidation through screaming, driving recklessly, stalking, or putting the victim under surveillance.

Perpetrators often have identified victims' strengths and vulnerabilities and use both against them. For victims who cherish pets, the abuser may harm or threaten to hurt the animals. Victims who love their grandchildren may find that the relationship is sabotaged and manipulated by an abuser who makes ugly remarks or limits contact. Older persons with strong spiritual or religious beliefs may have artifacts such as Bibles, rosaries, or items used for tribal ceremonies destroyed.

Offenders may also inflict harm by targeting a victim's limitations. Verbal attacks often emphasize the victim's vulnerabilities, such as reading or language abilities, physical size, disabilities, immigration status, or sexual orientation. A perpetrator may speak intentionally softly to a woman who is hard of hearing. A female caregiver may leave a male victim undressed in a public location to humiliate him. Glasses, dentures, walkers, or canes may be destroyed. Abusers may use too much or too little medication to cause confusion or inflict pain. Perpetrators of psychological abuse often use sleep deprivation or withhold fluids or food to undercut the victim's sense of reality.

Finally, a primary tactic used by abusers is isolation. Tactics can include controlling all of the victim's time, activities, and contact with others or interrupting the victim's social or support networks by feigning jealousy or monopolizing the victim's time and attention. Abusers often distort reality by lying or withholding information, especially about help and support. Offenders may speak for the victim without their consent and intercept communications from caseworkers and other potential

TABLE 2.3   Signs and Symptoms of Emotional/Psychological Abuse Include, but Are Not Limited to:

- Being emotionally upset or agitated
- Being extremely withdrawn and noncommunicative or nonresponsive
- Unusual behavior usually attributed to dementia (e.g., sucking, biting, rocking)
- An elder's report of being verbally or emotionally mistreated (NCEA, n.d.)

helpers. Family members and friends may be cut off from victims because the abuser refuses to allow contact or relay information. Some offenders behave badly or are abusive to family and friends, which results in a decline or cessation of visits with the victim. Other loved ones may get misinformation about illnesses or be told that the victim no longer wants to see anyone else. Victims who do not speak English or fear deportation may end up extremely isolated. Some abusers move to rural or isolated communities, far from supportive friends and family, to keep a victim away from others.

Psychological abuse often leads to, or accompanies, other forms of abuse. The presence of psychological abuse is a strong indicator that other forms of abuse also are occurring.

An Example of Psychological Abuse

During the course of her marriage, Rosita didn't trust herself to make decisions. She considered herself forgetful because she frequently lost or imagined things. For example, one day a potholder she had purchased on her honeymoon with Jose disappeared from the wall and was replaced by a calendar. When she asked Jose, he said the calendar had been there all along. Six months later a gift from her mother disappeared. Jose told her that he was worried about her and that she needed to get more rest. He suggested that he take over the checkbook because she couldn't be trusted with money. Over the years, more items disappeared and Rosita turned more responsibility over to Jose. She gave him the car keys and allowed him to make all the major decisions. When Jose hit her, she knew he was right, that no one would believe her because she was unstable. When Jose died, Rosita began cleaning the house to sell it. Upstairs in the attic she found a box full of all the items that had been "lost" over the years. Jose had intentionally taken them and hidden them from her to undermine her confidence and convince her that she was unstable.

Financial or Material Exploitation

> Financial or material exploitation is defined as the illegal or improper use of an elder's funds, property, or assets. Examples include, but are not limited to, cashing an elderly person's checks without authorization or permission; forging an older person's signature; misusing or stealing an older person's money or possessions; coercing or deceiving an older person into signing any document (e.g., contracts or will); and the improper use of conservatorship, guardianship, or power of attorney. (NCEA, n.d.)

A number of elders become victims of financial exploitation simply because they lack capacity and are unable to participate in their own decision making. Those who do have decision-making capacity or who have diminished capacity are sometimes subject to undue influence. Undue influence undermines the free-will element of consent. It is the misuse of one's role and power to exploit the trust, dependency, and fear of another to deceptively gain control over that person's decision making (Nerenberg, 1996; Nievod, 1992; Quinn, 2000, 2001; Singer, 1992). It can also manifest in the suspect's manipulation of the elder based on a relationship between the two (Blum, 1999).

TABLE 2.4   Signs and Symptoms of Financial or Material Exploitation Include, but Are Not Limited to:

- Sudden changes in bank account or banking practice, including an unexplained withdrawal of large sums of money by a person accompanying the elder
- Inclusion of additional names on an elder's bank signature card
- Unauthorized withdrawal of funds using the elder's ATM card
- Abrupt changes in a will or other financial documents
- Unexplained disappearance of funds or valuable possessions
- Substandard care being provided or bills unpaid despite the availability of adequate financial resources
- Discovery of an elder's signature being forged for financial transactions or for the titles of his/her possessions
- Sudden appearance of previously uninvolved relatives claiming their rights to an elder's affairs and possessions
- Mail redirected to a new location
- New relationship in elder's life
- Unexplained sudden transfer of assets to a family member or someone outside the family
- Provision of unnecessary services
- An elder's report of financial exploitation (NCEA, n.d.)

An Example of Exploitation

James was an 87-year-old man who had been residing in a licensed residential care facility for two years. Mary Ann, one of his caregivers, was a 28-year-old licensed nursing assistant. James' only living family member was a nephew, Roger, who held his power of attorney for finances and health care. James was on good terms with his nephew, but he did not visit very often. James was a congenial gentleman with congestive heart failure who was quite lonely. He had significant savings and kept both his checkbook and savings passbook in his room.

During the course of his stay at the residential facility, Mary Ann befriended him. Over a period of about 14 months, he gave Mary Ann several "gifts" of money, as well as a "loan" to help her out of difficult financial problems. Although the facility had strict rules prohibiting acceptance of gifts, this policy was ignored. In the fall of 2000, James was hospitalized for several days. In his absence, Mary Ann took his checkbook and wrote five checks for more than $10,000, making them out to herself and her boyfriend. Approximately six weeks after a report to APS and law enforcement resulted in an investigation, James died. Roger said that his uncle was "heartbroken" about the incident because he had trusted Mary Ann and cared for her and her young daughter a great deal.

Neglect

Neglect is defined as the refusal or failure to fulfill any part of a person's obligations or duties to an elder. Neglect may also include failure of a person who has fiduciary responsibilities to provide care for an elder (e.g., pay for necessary home care services), or the failure on the part of an in-home service provider to provide necessary care. Neglect typically means the refusal or failure to provide an elderly person with such life necessities as food, water, clothing, shelter, personal hygiene, medicine, comfort, personal safety, and other essentials included in an implied or agreed-upon responsibility to an elder. (NCEA, n.d.)

TABLE 2.5 Signs and Symptoms of Neglect Include, but Are Not Limited to:

- Dehydration, malnutrition, untreated bed sores, and poor personal hygiene
- Unattended or untreated health problems
- Hazardous or unsafe living conditions or arrangements (e.g., improper wiring, no heat, or no running water)
- Unsanitary and unclean living conditions (e.g., dirt, fleas or lice on the person, soiled bedding, fecal/urine smell, inadequate clothing)
- An elder's report of being mistreated (NCEA, n.d.)

A critical issue in neglect cases is determining whether an individual had a legal responsibility to provide care. A duty to provide support or care is usually based on an established relationship, contractual responsibility, statute, or actual assumption of care. Sometimes jurisdictions have enacted specific laws detailing these legal duties. Other states, rather than passing specific laws, impose well-established legal duties from other states or from English law dating to when the United States was formed. Common law duties may be embodied in law (LaFave & Scott, 1986). An example is the requirement that spouses support one another for the duration of the relationship (Moskowitz, 2001). Paid caregivers have a contractual duty to provide appropriate care for the duration of the contract. The question of whether an individual is a caregiver depends on the facts of the situation and the laws and court decisions in the state where the problem occurred. In an often-cited case in California, the court ruled that criminal liability for neglect rests only with actual care providers and persons who have a direct duty to control the behavior of someone who is abusing or neglecting an elder (*People v. Heitzman,* 9 Cal. 4th 189, 37 Cal. Rptr. 2d 236, 886 P. 2d 1229 [1994]).

An Example of Caregiver Neglect

Nellie, an 82-year-old woman, was brought to the emergency room because "a bone was sticking out of her leg." The patient had Alzheimer's disease and had fractured her hip six months earlier. After hip surgery, she had spent three months in rehabilitation and received further therapy at home. One month before Nellie's admission to the hospital, home health agency notes revealed that she had been walking and following commands. Nellie presented to the hospital writhing in pain. She was emaciated and resembled a concentration camp survivor. She was moaning and incoherent. She had eight bedsores in multiple sites, many of them covered with black scabs. Her femur was fractured and yellow-splintered bone was extruding from a swollen wound just above the knee. There was copious bloody discharge from the fracture site. The patient had a fever; subsequent studies showed that bacteria were growing in her blood. She had lice in her hair and on her body. Her son was her primary caregiver and had power of attorney. He was a salesman and, while he worked, he had hired a woman to care for his mother. He was unsure about when the bone was first sticking out of her leg. He requested that she be deemed a "do not resuscitate case."

Self-Neglect

> Self-neglect is defined as an adult's inability, due to physical or mental impairment or diminished capacity, to perform essential self-care tasks including: (a) obtaining essential food, clothing, shelter, and medical care; (b) obtaining goods and services necessary to maintain physical health, mental health, emotional well-being, and general safety; and (c) managing one's own financial affairs. Choice of lifestyle or living arrangements is not, in itself, evidence of self-neglect. (National Association of Adult Protective Service Administrators, 1991)

Self-neglect is a condition in which the older person is no longer willing or able to provide basic care for himself or herself. Experts in the field argue for and against the inclusion of self-neglect as a type of elder abuse. There are no perpetrators in cases of self-neglect and no one to prosecute; however, self-neglect cases are the ones most commonly reported to APS. Self-neglect is seen in combination with other forms of elder abuse (Pavlik, Hyman, Festa, & Dyer, 2001). It is more commonly associated with underlying medical disease states that may be amenable to intervention by medical professionals. In addition, self-neglectors often put themselves, other persons, and their pets at risk of harm. In all, 37 states include self-neglect in their elder abuse statutes. Many interdisciplinary teams encounter self-neglect or focus on this issue.

TABLE 2.6 Signs and Symptoms of Self-Neglect Include, but Are Not Limited to:

- Chronic disease, cognitive impairment, mental illness, physical impairment, and/or substance abuse that is often untreated
- Malnourished and/or dehydrated
- Isolated, lives alone, paranoid, often refuses access to home
- Victim appears dirty, not dressed appropriately for the weather
- Exterior of home poorly maintained, littered with discarded items and weeds
- Stacks of unpaid bills, utilities have been shut off
- Interior of home is filled with trash, garbage, feces, urine
- Multiple animals, often in poor health or dead
- Insect or vermin infestation
- Rotting food (Duke, 1991)

An Example of Self-Neglect

Harold was a 68-year-old alcoholic living in a room above a bar. He was no longer able to walk around the neighborhood due to a sore leg. His landlady called Adult Protective Services (APS) because the stench emanating from his room was so bad that she thought he had died. The landlady reported that he appeared to have lost a significant amount of weight. The APS investigator found Harold living in a small corner of his room by the door. The rest of the room was crammed from floor to ceiling with newspapers, rags, garbage, and human waste.

Harold appeared to be confused. His right leg was gangrenous from ankle to knee. Police arranged for his involuntary transport to the hospital because of his deteriorating mental and physical condition. After two weeks in the hospital, Harold refused to allow the surgeon to amputate his leg and he left the hospital against medical advice. The assigned visiting nurse reported that Harold was noncompliant with aide services, treatment, and medications. He objected to the cost of the antibiotics he desperately needed. She also reported that Harold was experiencing delusions and hallucinations, but refused to be readmitted to the hospital.

Abandonment

Abandonment is defined as the desertion of an older person by an individual who has assumed responsibility for providing care for an elder, or by a person with physical custody of an elder.

TABLE 2.7 Signs and Symptoms of Abandonment Include, but Are Not Limited to:

- The desertion of an elder at a hospital, a nursing facility, or other similar institution
- The desertion of an elder at a shopping center or other public location
- An elder's own report of being abandoned (NCEA, n.d.)

An Example of Abandonment

A very confused older man got off a cross-county bus in Denver, Colorado. Someone in San Diego had purchased a one-way ticket for him and put him on the bus with a paper bag containing some food and a change of underwear. The man had Alzheimer's disease. He did not remember his name and had no money and no identification.

CONCLUSION

Before working collaboratively on interventions, prevention strategies, training, or research, professionals must establish a clear working definition of elder abuse. Given the various definitions currently in the field, this task is not as simple as it might seem. Professionals will need to discuss and agree on the components described in this chapter such as age, health, and functional status, gender, residence, relationship between victim and offender, and forms of abuse to determine what will be included in a multidisciplinary response.

This chapter focused on the "who, what, when, where, and why" of elder abuse. Chapter 3 addresses why elder abuse occurs and why victims remain in relationships with perpetrators. Chapter 4 lists indicators of abuse, building on the definitions provided in this chapter, to assist professionals in recognizing various forms of abuse.

CHAPTER THREE

Dynamics of Elder Abuse

When social phenomena have long traditions in society and short scientific histories, the initial theories derived to explain their existence are often blends of tradition, social myth, conventional wisdom, folklore, and the best fit that theoreticians and clinicians can make with the existing scientific knowledge at the time. In the search for remedies, assumptions are made and concepts are borrowed from other areas; some fit, but many do not. Such has been the case with elder abuse. Although, [while] many theoretical explanations for elder abuse have been suggested and accepted, few have been subjected to the rigor of empirical testing. (Phillips, 1986, p. 87)

Understanding the dynamics of elder abuse is crucial to identifying and using effective interventions. Professionals will respond to elder abuse based on the framework they use to analyze the situation. Too often, professionals get mired in their own experiences and belief systems and are unable to recognize and assess elder abuse. Some professionals will use only one framework to explain elder abuse, with the result that victims who do not fit the model will not be identified. Using a limited framework narrows the number of victims who will be identified and expands the number of victims who may be misassessed. Elder abuse is multifaceted and there are multiple causation factors and models. Understanding the relationship between victims and offenders is necessary to developing an effective plan toward prevention.

The primary question discussed in this chapter is "why?"

- Why does elder abuse, including sexual abuse, financial exploitation, abuse in facilities, and self-neglect occur?

- Why does an older person who is being harmed maintain a relationship with the abuser?

Unfortunately, the answers to these questions are not simple.

WHY DOES ELDER ABUSE OCCUR?

A variety of hypotheses have been explored over the years to explain elder abuse: (1) caregiver stress/excessive demands, (2) victim characteristics, (3) perpetrator characteristics, (4) transgenerational issues, (5) social exchange theory, and 6) power and control dynamics. In addition, the unique dynamics of sexual abuse in later life, financial exploitation, abuse in facilities, and self-neglect are discussed in more detail.

Caregiver Stress/Excessive Demands

Josie took care of her mother. She also worked full time and had a family of her own. When her mother was demanding and Josie felt overwhelmed, she yelled at her mother, and once she hit her. Josie loved her mother and wanted to provide good care. She simply could not manage all the stress in her life.

Most caregivers are compassionate and provide good support and care; however, caregiving can be hard work and, at times, stressful. Given the challenges that sometimes occur when providing care for an older person, the notion that caregivers can be pushed past their limits resonates with professionals and community members. Therefore when several studies in the 1980s suggested that caregiver stress was a primary cause of elder abuse (Montgomery, 1989; Steinmetz, 1988), this theory was generally accepted without question. The caregiver stress theory suggests that overwhelmed caregivers, burdened by the demands of providing care, may at times harm the older, frail person in their care. The theory was simple and attractive. Older adults, like children, were seen as in need of protection. Early interventions focused on reducing the stress of the caregiver through case management and other social services. Priority was given to the needs of the caregiver, not the victim.

The problem is that more recent studies have not supported caregiver stress as a primary cause of elder abuse (Godkin, Wolf, & Pillemer, 1989; Phillips, de Ardon, & Brione, 2000; Pillemer & Finkelhor, 1988, 1989; Reis & Nahmiash, 1997, 1998). Studies indicate that caregiver stress can lead to abuse in a limited number of cases (Ramsey-Klawsnik,

2000), but "notwithstanding the popular image of abuse arising from dependent victims and stressed caregivers, evidence is accumulating that neither caregiver stress levels nor victim levels of dependence may be core factors leading to elder abuse" (Wolf, 2000b, p. 9). In many cases, the victim is more functionally independent than the perpetrator (Pillemer & Finkelhor, 1989; Reis & Nahmiash, 1997, 1998; Seaver, 1996; Wolf & Pillemer, 1997). In fact, studies found the dynamics of abuse in later life to be similar to those experienced by younger battered women (Harris, 1996; Pillemer & Finkelhor, 1988).

Unfortunately, too many professionals and policymakers continue to believe that elder abuse is primarily caused by caregiver stress or poor family communication. This inaccurate analysis can lead to the following fundamental errors:

- Inaccurate assessments by professionals, who focus on identifying the vulnerable adult as the first step of their investigation. For example, an older battered woman may now be more physically capable than her husband, who physically abused her for years. She may be the primary caregiver. If she responds to his threats by locking him in a room to protect herself, an Adult Protective Services (APS) worker looking at vulnerability may initially determine that the husband is a vulnerable adult and the spouse is guilty of confinement. Without an assessment that involves interviewing the wife to learn about the history of domestic violence, the wife could be seen as the perpetrator (Bergeron, 2001). Focusing on caregiver stress fails to acknowledge that some victims of elder abuse are healthy and do not require care or that there are cases where the caregiver is the victim and the care receiver is the perpetrator (Phillips et al., 2000).
- Too often services, prevention strategies, interventions, and policies are designed to help families and caregivers reduce stress and improve communication. These practices may lead to a calmer caregiver or family member, but they may do nothing to make the victim safer when the dynamics of abuse are rooted in power and control. Caregiver stress is often an excuse, not an explanation, for abuse. Everyone lives with stress; few respond by harming older individuals.
- Reducing stress and improving communication are seen as the job of social services. When abuse is labeled as mistreatment and not a crime, criminal justice remedies are not considered. Abusers are not held accountable for their behavior or challenged on their sense of entitlement, which enables them to mistreat older persons.

- Stress reduction techniques may encourage the victim to "try harder" to be less difficult to care for. This implies that the victim is to blame for the abusive behavior. Often victims already believe that they are to blame (based on what abusers have repeatedly told them). This message supports the batterer by suggesting that some responsibility for the abuse lies with the victim. Victims may stay in unsafe situations longer, trying to fix the relationship rather than focus on their own safety needs (Brandl, 2000).

Victim Characteristics or Behaviors

Ada, age 87, has lived in Manor Care Nursing Home for the last three years. Ada came from a background of wealth and privilege. She ordered the nursing home staff around as if they were her personal servants, sometimes berating and slapping them. One of the aides, Marsha, sometimes hit her back, saying, "She deserved it."

Some researchers have looked for victim characteristics or behaviors that may have led to the abusive behavior. The tendency in the past was to consider elders as dependent, vulnerable, and in need of protection. Blaming the victim was very much a part of the original (but flawed) construction of elder abuse as a manifestation of caregiver stress. This characterization[,] buttressed by societal prejudice against the aged and aging, had the effect of making old people into "legitimate or deserving" victims. (Wolf, 2000b, p. 9)

Researchers have examined victim behaviors, such as blaming others, being manipulative, or having poor social skills, but have not found evidence to support these as common victim characteristics.

Some commonalities do exist among elder abuse victims, although they are by no means predictors. Several studies noted that high percentages of victims lived with their abusers (Godkin, Wolf, & Pillemer, 1989; Greenberg, McKibben, & Raymond, 1990; Lachs, Williams, O'Brien, Hurst, & Horowitz, 1997; Lachs et al., 1997; Pillemer & Finkelhor, 1988; Seaver, 1996; Vladescu et al., 1999). Victims experience common reactions to trauma, such as depression, a wish to end their lives, unhappiness, or shame or guilt (Anetzberger, 1998; Le, 1997; NCEA, 1998; Older Women's Network, 1998; Pillemer & Finkelhor, 1988; Podnieks, 1992a; Reis & Nahmiash, 1997, 1998). Physical or cognitive impairments are also common, although by no means universal (Godkin et al., 1989; Greenberg et al., 1990; Lachs, Williams, O'Brien, Hurst, & Horowitz, 1997; Lithwick et al., 1999; NCEA, 1998; Pillemer & Finkelhor, 1988, 1989; Podnieks,

1992a; Ramsey-Klawsnik, 1991; Reis & Nahmiash, 1997, 1998; Seaver, 1996; Teaster & Nerenberg, 2000). Whether victims become depressed or impaired as a result of the abuse or whether depressed or impaired elders are more susceptible to being abused is unclear.

In contrast to studies that looked for characteristics to blame the victim, several studies identified the strengths and survival skills of victims (Podnieks, 1992b; Seaver, 1996). Podnieks (1992b, p. 59) stated there is "strong evidence of adaptive strengths and hardiness of victims." Seaver (1996, p. 19) notes that these women "have been eager to learn, use resources well, and respond enthusiastically to the idea that they deserve more peaceful lives."

Current data suggest that no single profile of an elder abuse victim exists (Pillemer & Finkelhor, 1989; Seaver, 1996). Looking at abuser characteristics is a more powerful predictor than victim characteristics (Pillemer & Finkelhor, 1989).

Perpetrator Characteristics

Henry, age 49, moved back in with his mother, Agnes, age 78, after he lost his janitorial job. He was suspicious of others, had no friends or outside activities, and depended on his mother's financial support. He started hitting her and threatening to have her put in a nursing home when she did not give him her Social Security check.

A few studies have examined common traits among abusers of elders. Some found that a significant number of abusers suffer some form of impairment (Brownell et al., 1999; Cohen, 1998; Godkin et al., 1989; Greenberg et al., 1990; Lachs et al., 1997; Pillemer & Finkelhor, 1989; Reis & Nahmiash, 1997, 1998; Seaver, 1996). These impairments included substance abuse, mental illness and depression, and cognitive impairments.

Research also indicated that the abusers tended to be dependent on their victims for housing, transportation, and sometimes for care (Brownell et al., 1999; Pillemer & Finkelhor, 1989; Seaver, 1996; Wolf & Pillemer, 1997). Financial dependency of adult children also seems to be a key factor (Godkin et al., 1989; Greenberg et al., 1990; Pillemer & Finkelhor, 1989; Reis & Nahmiash, 1998; Seaver, 1996; Wolf & Pillemer, 1997). Some research also suggests that abusers have problems with relationships, may be more isolated, and lack social supports (Godkin et al., 1989; Reis & Nahmiash, 1997). Brown (1989) suggests that abusers with personal problems may be more physically abusive.

Intergenerational or Transgenerational Violence

Ellen's father physically and sexually assaulted her as a child. When her father became ill, Ellen grudgingly took responsibility for his care. Sometimes she refused to bathe him or feed him. Occasionally, she treated him roughly, causing bruises on his arms and back.

Intergenerational abuse is often considered as a possible cause of family violence in later life. This theory postulates that adults who were abused as children may retaliate against their aging parents (Gelles, 1983; Hickey, 1979; Steinmetz, 1977; Straus, Gelles, & Steinmetz, 1980). These interactions are a pattern of learned behaviors that teach an abused child to become an abusive parent (Hickey & Douglass, 1981). Another aspect of this theory is that the abuse is committed for revenge in retaliation for actual or perceived childhood abuse by the elderly relative (Rathbone-McCuan & Hashimi, 1982). Currently, not enough research exists to support or rule out this theory. Two studies indicate that intergenerational transmission of violence is not an inevitable process, but that it may be a factor in some cases (Korbin, Anetzberger, & Austin, 1995; Podnieks, 1992b).

Social Exchange Theory

Glenda, age 43, has never dated. She lives with her father, Arthur, who is now 82. She says that she will never have a relationship with a man as long as her father is alive. She shops, cooks, and cleans for him. In return, she expects him to be happy and grateful. Whenever he expresses sadness at the loss of Renee, his wife of 54 years, Glenda yells at him, shouting that he ought to appreciate all that she does, and that if he doesn't, she might as well put him in a nursing home.

Another theory that has been explored is that of social exchange. Social interactions involve the exchange of rewards and punishments between persons. People seek to maximize rewards and minimize punishments. Rewards include exchanges of sentiments, resources, and services. Punishment involves exchanging negative sentiments, withholding resources, and delivering punishing behaviors (Gelles, 1983). "We provide resources to others because we receive them in return" (Ansello, 1996, p. 16).

According to Pillemer (1986), social exchange theory helps to explain child abuse, domestic violence, and elder abuse. The victim is dependent on the aggressor for care (rewards). The aggressor believes that the victim is not reciprocating with equal rewards. The abuser has control of the rewards, and there are no consequences for his abusive behavior (punishment). The abuser believes that the personal rewards he derives from the exchange are too little when compared to what he is giving the victim, and, therefore, he is entitled to impose punishment on the victim. When the abuser is more dependent on the victim than the victim is on the abuser, the abuse arises from the abuser's resentment of his or her powerlessness. Without resources for a normal exchange, the abuser uses the resources of control and violence (Pillemer, 1986). Workers from APS often encounter situations that appear to be social exchanges gone wrong. Although typically they do not label the interactions as such, it is a familiar dynamic.

Power and Control Dynamics

Some studies have found that family violence in later life often involves an abuser who uses a pattern of coercive acts to control, dominate, or punish the victim. These dynamics are similar to those experienced by younger battered women (Harris, 1996; Pillemer & Finkelhor, 1988). When abusers believe they are entitled to "run the show," they will use any means necessary to get their needs met. Abusers feel their actions are justified and that they have a right to control their victims. Perpetrators often believe they deserve unquestioned obedience from the victim (Schechter, 1987).

The sense of entitlement that abusers feel may originate from a variety of belief systems. An older man may believe that he is the designated head of the household and, as such, can set and enforce the rules. He may have been battering his wife for the past 50 years to "keep her in line." Adult children may not value older people and may believe that they are entitled to treat their parents poorly or to take their money or possessions. An adult son may order his mother to do the laundry, cook his meals, and turn over her Social Security check. If she doesn't, he may threaten her or hit her. A caregiver may see her role as keeping the older person from harm by feeding, bathing, and assisting that person, but do so in an abusive manner as a way of maintaining control. The way that people characterize elders can impact elder abuse. Negative perceptions and distortions about older adults can create abusive situations. When physically and cognitively impaired elders are perceived as less valuable to society, there is an increased potential for abuse (Viano, 1980).

Organic Basis for Challenging or Aggressive Behavior

In some situations, a person who was previously nonviolent becomes abusive as a result of physical changes. These changes may be the result of delirium, in which case the behavior may respond to medical treatment. Or the changes may be the result of dementia or an injury to the brain. In either case, the aggressor does not intend to harm others, is unaware that he is doing so, and is unable to modify his behavior by himself. The most likely indicator of these situations is a marked and sudden change in the aggressor's behavior.

Typologies of Elder Abusers

Dr. Holly Ramsey-Klawsnik identified a typology of elder abuse offenders in the 1990s. She postulated five types of abusers: (1) the overwhelmed, (2) the impaired, (3) the narcissistic, (4) the domineering or bullying, and (5) the sadistic. Overwhelmed offenders are well-intended caregivers who are unable to meet the demands of providing care. Impaired caregivers have problems that render them unable to provide appropriate care. They may have physical or mental illness, advanced age, or frailty or developmental disabilities. These caregivers are doing the best they can but are unable to provide adequate care. Often they are unaware that their care is harmful (Ramsey-Klawsnik, 2000).

Narcissistic individuals are motivated by anticipated gain. They are concerned with meeting their own needs and often see the older person's vulnerable state as an opportunity to receive income or possessions. Domineering or bullying offenders feel justified in using any method necessary to get what they want. They misuse relationships and positions of trust or use power to exert control over others. Sadistic offenders "derive feelings of power and importance by humiliating, terrifying, and harming others." They often feel sexual arousal or pleasure in seeing someone else's pain and fear (Ramsey-Klawsnik, 2000, p. 20).

This analysis of elder abuse offenders has guided the field to acknowledge that a range of explanations is possible to explain the behavior of perpetrators. In addition, there are unique dynamics that occur with sexual abuse, financial exploitation, abuse in facilities, and self-neglect.

WHY SPECIFIC FORMS OF ELDER ABUSE OCCUR

Consent

Before discussing the dynamics of sexual abuse and financial exploitation, it is important to address the issue of consent, as it significantly impacts both of those forms of abuse. The legal definition of consent for entering into a financial transaction, making a gift, or agreeing to sexual contact generally requires that a person be able to understand the transaction or activity, be able to make judgments about it, and decide if it is something he or she wants. More specifically, consent requires that a person act freely and voluntarily, not under the effects of threats, force, duress, or promises; that the person has knowledge of the true nature of the transaction, could consult third parties if desired, and had access to all pertinent information, and had the legal capacity to make a choice. Passivity is not consent. Consent requires free will and positive cooperation in the matter at hand.

Why Do Sexual Abuse and Assault Occur in Later Life?

As discussed earlier, elder sexual assault is a complex phenomenon that involves abuse by family members and others. Stranger rapes in later life, although rare, do occur. In these cases, the victim does not know the perpetrator. The offender often breaks into the senior's home and sexually assaults the victim. Although sexual assaults by strangers are crimes and important to acknowledge, they are beyond the scope of this book. This book focuses on sexual assaults that occur in relationships of trust or to victims living in facilities where there is a duty to protect. Examples of this category are attacks by facilities' staff members and resident-on-resident assaults.

Most elder sexual assault occurs within relationships. Sometimes sexual abuse is part of the constellation of physical, emotional, financial, and other forms of abuse that perpetrators use to gain and maintain power and control over their intimate partners. Such abuse occurs in long-term marriages or in new intimate relationships. It is linked to the abuser's sense of entitlement to sexual contact with his spouse or partner at any time. Female or male victims in these relationships, often unaware of spousal rape laws, may feel they are required to comply (Ramsey-Klawsnik, 2003). In other situations, the victim may have cognitive disabilities and may not be able to consent to sexual contact. However, the spouse or partner may feel entitled to continue the sexual relationship, even though the person is no longer able to communicate whether or not sexual contact is desired. Some sexual abuse between partners may be related to the abuser's failing health and the progression of a disease such as dementia. This is organic-based violence, rather than sexual assault grounded in the need for power and control. Sexual abuse in same-sex couples can also fit into any of these same categories.

Incestuous elder sexual assault also occurs. Adult children, grandchildren, or siblings may be the perpetrators. Most often an adult son abuses his mother, although assaults by daughters on their mothers do occasionally occur. The adult children-perpetrators often have mental health or substance abuse problems, or both. They are often dependent on their parent for food, clothing, shelter, and spending money. "As the parent becomes increasingly elderly and ill, she becomes more and more available to her poorly functioning offspring as a potential victim. It is not unusual to find a pattern of multifaceted abuse" (Ramsey-Klawsnik, 2003, p. 50).

In facilities, caregivers or volunteers may take sexual advantage of a vulnerable patient. Residents may be sexually assaulted by other residents. In some cases, the resident who is a perpetrator may have dementia and may be acting out in sexually inappropriate ways. In other situations, the resident is a sexual predator, who may now be living in a nursing home and may be continuing a lifelong pattern of sexual violence.

According to Ramsey-Klawsnik (2003), some perpetrators have domineering or bullying personalities; others are sadistic and derive pleasure and satisfaction from inflicting pain and humiliation. Domineering and sadistic offenders engage in chronic, multifaceted, and continuing abuse. They are attracted to their elderly victims because of the victims' perceived vulnerability.

Just as there are variations in relationships, there is no single motivation or "profile" for all perpetrators. Most rapists, at least those from outside the family unit, are thought to be power or anger rapists. The power rapist typically chooses victims who are in his same age group and usually uses minimal physical force to overcome the victim's resistance. This rapist believes he is entitled to the contact or uses the assault to resolve feelings of sexual inadequacy by proving he cannot be refused (Larkin, 2001).

In contrast, the anger rapist seeks to express anger, rage, and contempt for the victim. He will use overwhelming and debilitating force to gain immediate control (Hagan, 2001). Violence is often well beyond that necessary to overcome resistance. This type of rapist seeks victims who are available and vulnerable; their age and social group are unimportant. Anger rapists typically are retaliating against authority figures that the victim is believed to represent or extracting pleasure from the victim's suffering (Larkin, 2001). These rapists may well have criminal histories for assault, including domestic violence.

Rapists seek to reduce their identification and detection by selecting vulnerable individuals (Hagan, 2001; Ramsey-Klawsnik, 1996). Elderly victims, especially those in facilities, are attractive targets. Offenders frequently select persons they know or with whom they have an intimate relationship as their victims, believing that these victims will not report the abuse or, if they do report, will not be believed (Hagan, 2001; Ramsey-Klawsnik, 2003).

Why Does Financial Exploitation Occur?

In the 1990s, financial exploitation of elders was labeled "the crime of the '90s" (The old being increasingly bilked, 1991). From 1994 to 2000, the amount of financial exploitation reported to APS increased by 61% (Otto, 2002). Financial abuse of elders occurs because, as bank robber Willy Sutton said about banks, "That's where the money is" (Sutton, 1976). Persons in the United States over the age of 50 own 70% of the nation's private wealth (Dychtwald & Flower, 1990). This wealth is often in the form of savings or real estate. Adults ages 65 or older control 70% of funds deposited in financial institutions (Hafemeister, 2003). Financial exploitation occurs because of greed. Someone, often a family member or a new acquaintance, realizes that the elder has assets and finds ways to tap into them. Sometimes family members assume that they are entitled to an older relative's assets and do not want to wait for the elder to die to claim what they think is rightfully theirs. Often the elder will be pressured into signing over real estate that has been fully paid for and represents his or her entire life savings. Once the deed has been transferred, the elder may find that he or she has lost not only the assets, but his or her home. Promises of life care are rescinded and the elder may either become homeless or end up in a long-term care facility at public expense.

Undue influence may play a role in financial exploitation, sexual assault, and abuse. Undue influence is the misuse of one's role and power to exploit the trust, dependency, and fear of another to deceptively gain control over that person's decision making (Nerenberg, 1996; Nievod, 1992; Quinn, 2000, 2001; Singer, 1992). It can also be the result of the abuser's manipulation of the elder stemming from a relationship between the two (Blum, 1999). Undue influence undermines the free-will element of consent, which was described in the previous section.

Professionals often confront situations in which an elder appears to have entered into an agreement or transaction that is not in his or her best interest. It is not uncommon for the elder to have suffered a significant financial loss or acted against his or her apparent best interest. The elder may admit that he or she agreed to do what was done. Careful evaluation of the circumstances may reveal that the elder was taken advantage of, denied important information, isolated, and rushed to act. Rather than an exercise of free will, the circumstances reflect manipulation through the use of undue influence.

When an elder agrees to a course of action, such as a financial transaction, gift, or consent to sexual contact, based on undue influence there is no legal consent and the agreement is void. Undue influence, however, is difficult to identify because it involves a process rather than a single act or event (Nerenberg, 2000c).

Perpetrators use a variety of techniques to gain control of the victim's decision making, including isolating the victim, creating dependency, and inducing fear and mistrust of others. Perpetrators threaten victims and urge them to make decisions quickly and without advice from others (Johnson, 2003). The perpetrator courts and befriends the elder, gaining his trust and cutting him off from friends, family, and sources of information. The abuser then induces the elder's dependency and creates a siege mentality in which the victim is left believing that no one except the abuser cares about him. Everyone else is portrayed as wanting the elder's assets and as abandoning him. The victim is rendered fearful and is subsequently easily manipulated (Quinn, 2000).

Blum (1999) offers another model for assessing the presence of undue influence. Five elements must be present including isolation of the victim from pertinent social contacts or information, creation of victim dependence on the perpetrator, emotional manipulation of the victim, the victim's acquiescence, and the resulting loss.

Persons who are mentally competent and persons with diminished capacity to consent are equally susceptible. High-risk factors include physical illness, cognitive and emotional impairments, dementia, memory loss, and isolation (Quinn, 2000). Persons experiencing significant life transitions, such as the death of a spouse or other loved one, are also vulnerable to undue influence (Nievod, 1992). Cognitive decline, sensory losses, and nutritional deficits increase susceptibility to undue influence (Johnson, 2003).

Why Does Abuse in Facilities Occur?

Institutional abuse is often an invisible problem. Older patients in long-term care facilities may be the most "invisible, voiceless, and dependent population in society" (Kosberg & Nahmiash, 1996, p. 34). Getting to the "why" and "what happened" can be even more complicated in facility cases, because there are more people involved—some who live or work at the facility, some who are visiting, and some who are involved in the investigation. For the purposes of this book, the perpetrator can be a family member, staff person, volunteer, stranger, or another resident. Cover-up of the abuse by the facility to avoid lawsuits or negative media attention can make understanding what happened even more difficult than in cases of domestic elder abuse.

Family members who have been abusive in the past may continue the pattern when the elderly person is placed in long-term care. A son might continue his verbal abuse of his mother; a husband may insist that he has the right to continue to have sexual relations with his wife, even though she now lacks the capacity to give consent. A daughter may take the patient's Social Security check for her own use and not pay for her mother's care.

Facility staff has easy access to people who are very frail and who may be unable to call for help. Some staff workers are abusive out of frustration—they lack the training to know how to handle difficult patients. Others may abuse patients in retaliation for the perception that they are underpaid and overworked by the facility administration. Others may have a past history, particularly of sexual abuse, which they repeat at each new facility. One study found that abusive staff persons are more likely than nonabusive staff to have negative attitudes about elders, to have emotional problems, and to view the work place as stressful (Pillemer & Moore, 1988).

Resident-on-resident abuse occurs for a number of reasons. Usually it is a combination of a patient who lacks impulse control, a lack of staff supervision, and inappropriate programming. In some facilities, the client mix is the problem. Younger persons with mental illness or traumatic brain injuries are housed with frail elderly people with dementia. Convicted sexual predators who have multiple health problems may be placed by the court in a long-term care facility that also provides care for vulnerable elderly persons.

Unfortunately, some long-term care facilities still look on situations of elder abuse as internal matters, and they conduct their own investigation using facility staff not trained in investigative procedures. Evidence of wrong-doing by staff is sometimes covered up or destroyed, or the alleged perpetrator is fired, but no reports are made to regulators, APS, law enforcement agencies, or the Long Term Care Ombudsman program. This practice allows perpetrators to move from one facility to another, where they continue to prey on vulnerable patients. This disregard for victims' rights may be labeled institutional or systemic abuse. It occurs when systems created by society to provide care and protection fail to fulfill their responsibilities.

Why Does Self-Neglect Occur?

Self-neglectors are usually isolated and living in squalor. Many have not had a medical evaluation in years; often they have an undiagnosed medical or mental illness. They are likely to refuse services and have questionable functional and decision-making abilities (Otto, 2002). More than 93% of self-neglecting elders had some difficulty caring for themselves, and of that group, one-third were totally unable to care for themselves. Thus, there appears to be a strong correlation between self-neglect and the ability to care for oneself, a finding that is not surprising (NCEA, 1998).

According to the National Center on Elder Abuse, the largest percentage of self-neglecting elders are age 80 or older (NCEA, 1998). Analysis of data from Texas showed that 90% of all the self-neglectors reported in one-year's time were over the age of 65. National Center on Elder Abuse data showed that three-quarters of the self-neglecting elders were White, with the next largest group identified as African American (NCEA, 1998).

Numerous studies have shown a correlation between self-neglect and medical or mental illness (Dyer & Goins, 2000; Lachs, Williams, O'Brien, Pillemer, & Charlson, 1998; NCEA, 1998). The most common illnesses are dementia, depression, psychosis, alcohol abuse, and loss of executive function. Alcoholism is thought to be a significant contributor to the etiology of self-neglect among older adults. Affected individuals can suffer from malnutrition, develop chronic health problems, acquire unintentional injuries, become depressed, neglect their health care needs, and isolate themselves from friends and family. Alcoholism in elders often is not diagnosed in medical settings, because the patient's erratic and self-neglecting behavior is attributed to the effects of medical conditions (Blondell, 1999). The inclusion of medical personnel on elder abuse teams has helped to identify these issues, as few APS workers have formal psychiatric or medical training.

A qualitative study of 30 clients categorized as self-neglectors by APS explored the factors contributing to this particular form of abuse. The study examined interpersonal problems, such as relationship failures, being abandoned by significant others at a time of need, betrayal, domestic violence, poor relationships with parents, and family estrangement. The study found a number of turning points—significant moments in the self-neglecting elder that he or she perceived as life changing and that contributed to the self-neglect. Among these were the death of significant others (including a pet), health crises, forced relocation, and abandonment. "Significant negative events may raise identity questions or may lead to loss of identity" (Bozinovski, 1995, p. 278) resulting in the radical change in the way the self is organized. "Turning points have significant implications for identity, personal control, situational definitions, and for continuity of self" (Bozinovski, 1995, p. 279).

The majority (52.9%) of substantiated cases reported to state or local APS involved self-neglect (Teaster, 2006, p. 5). These cases are complex and time-consuming, and present multiple challenges to practitioners. A number of these cases appear to have no perpetrator other than the self-neglecting person. On closer examination, however, many cases of self-neglect contain layers of other forms of abuse, some of which, particularly domestic and family violence, have occurred over much of the victims' lifetimes (Bozinovski, 1995).

Because the cases are complex and time intensive, other community agencies either refuse to get involved, or do so only briefly, and turn to APS for help (Otto, 2002). The issue of self-neglect is intimately tied to the self-neglector's right to self-determination, and this is the most complicated factor for professionals who receive these reports. Three-fourths of substantiated self-neglecting elders were either sometimes or often confused, but almost one-fourth were not confused (NCEA, 1998). This 25% of self-neglecting elders poses the greatest challenges to professionals who intervene. These are the self-neglectors who often repeatedly refuse services, even when they are living in dangerous or deplorable situations. Yet, because of their ability to make informed choices, they are not appropriate for court-ordered imposition of guardianship actions and involuntary services.

A critical factor in the substantiation and intervention in self-neglect cases is the person's right to self-determination, which is ultimately tied to the capacity to consent. Persons with capacity have the right to make foolish choices. A college student with papers and books piled floor to ceiling does not require medical, social service, or legal intervention. Currently, the gold standard for determining capacity to consent is a psychiatric interview, which must be performed by a physician. Reliable capacity screening tools are not available for field administration by law enforcement or protective service personnel.

Although physicians and protective service specialists often see clients who refuse assistance, a national survey showed that less than 10% of adult protection clients received services without their consent, and that all states made vigorous efforts to protect clients' rights. "The focus is not on serving adults against their will, but rather on assuring that the critical services are not denied because the adult in need lacks capacity to consent to receive essential services" (National Association of Adult Protective Services Administrators, 1993, p. 25).

Uncovering why a person is self-neglecting is a complex puzzle of which many of the pieces still are missing. A recent study of hoarding behavior published in the *American Journal of Psychiatry* found that "compulsive hoarding and saving symptoms, found in many patients with obsessive-compulsive disorder, are part of a discrete clinical syndrome that includes indecisiveness, disorganization, perfectionism, procrastination, and avoidance" (Saxena et al., 2004, p. 1). The study concluded that one cause of hoarding behavior may be due to unusual metabolic reactions to glucose in the brain (Saxena et al., 2004). Other theories to explain self-neglecting behavior are that these individuals are trying to maintain continuity in their perception of self (Bozinovski, 1995); that they are depressed (NCEA, 1998); that they have some form of mental illness or substance abuse, dementia, or other medical condition that makes them incapable of appropriate self-care (Dyer & Goins, 2000); or that they have been prior victims of family violence (Bozinovski, 1995). Until more research is done in this area, the puzzle of why people neglect themselves may remain incomplete.

WHY DOES AN OLDER PERSON WHO IS BEING HARMED MAINTAIN A RELATIONSHIP WITH THE ABUSER?

Most victims who have a relationship of trust with their abusers have conflicted feelings about intervention. Victims do not want to be abused, neglected, or exploited. In many cases, the victim wants the abuse to end, but also wants to maintain a relationship with the abuser in a safe, nonthreatening manner. The familial or caregiving relationship often has many benefits during the times the abuse is not occurring. The victim may still love the family member abuser and may have valid reasons for trying to preserve the relationship or protect the person.

Spouses or life partners may have been together for many years. The victim may value the longevity of the relationship. Cultural, spiritual, or generational values may make divorce or separation unthinkable. Memories, shared friends, family and home, and fear of being alone may be contributing factors. Adult children and grandchildren may apply pressure to keep the couple together.

Parents face unique challenges when deciding how to deal with abusers who are their adult children. The parents often want to try harder to help their children. They may resist interventions that may result in their children being arrested, institutionalized, or living on the streets.

Victims abused by caregivers may fear being left alone or without a caregiver if they report the abuse. They often appreciate some qualities of the caregiver or sympathize with them. Sometimes victims fear that the caregiver will retaliate or that they will be institutionalized if they report.

Victims face difficult decisions as they decide how to proceed after being abused. Many times the choices available to them are limited or not realistic or reasonable. Victims weigh three levels of concern as they analyze their options and determine their next steps. They look at their own values and internal messages about what options they are willing to consider. Victims also experience abuser-generated risks: the repercussions of making decisions to leave or separate from an abuser (Davies & Lyon, 1998). They also examine systemic barriers: do programs and services exist that are useful in enhancing their safety? This section highlights some of the obstacles victims face, often in combination, noting victims' beliefs, abuser tactics, and systemic barriers. Table 3.1 illustrates these dynamics for older battered women abused by a spouse/partner or adult child.

In addition, specific barriers exist for many victims. Victims often face multiple obstacles as they make decisions about their relationships with their abusers. Barriers to living free from abuse can include fear;

financial realities; cultural, generational, and religious values; and health status.

Victims may fear retaliation. The most dangerous time for victims can be while they are separating from the abuser or getting help from friends, family, or professionals. Victims may be stalked, seriously harmed, or killed. Some victims may fear being alone or further isolated. Some fear hiring new caregivers or going to live in a nursing home.

Financial realities impact the choices available to victims. Many victims face the choice of living with abuse or in poverty. Abusers may have

TABLE 3.1 Obstacles Faced by Some Older Victims of Abuse

Victim Beliefs/Concerns	Abuser's Message to Victim	Societal Message About Victims
I am not a victim of abuse.	I am not abusive. You are clumsy and forgetful.	Older people are not victims of abuse.
It's my fault.	Everything that happens to you is your fault.	She should be able to control him better.
I want to stay with my husband/ adult child.	It's your job to be a wife /mother and to take care of the house and me.	"Good" wives/mothers stay with their families.
I don't know who to call for help.	No one will believe you or help you. They will know you are crazy/incompetent.	Services for older people don't exist because they don't get abused.
I'm afraid to call for help.	I'll kill you if you tell anyone I hurt you. You don't have the right to leave.	Abuse in later life isn't really dangerous.
I want to keep my house, my belongings, and my current lifestyle.	Everything is mine.	If the abuse were real, she would just leave.
If I have to leave, where will I live and how will I pay for rent and other expenses?	If you leave, it will be with the clothes on your back. I'll make sure you don't get anything.	She can live independently if the abuse is really serious. Other older women do. It's too bad she didn't work when she was younger so she would have some money of her own.
I'm concerned about my health and/or my abuser's health.	If you leave, I will take your name off the insurance policy.	She is responsible for taking care of her ill spouse/partner or adult child.

(continued)

TABLE 3.1 *(continued)*

Victim Beliefs/Concerns	Abuser's Message to Victim	Societal Message About Victims
	It is your job to take care of me. You're my wife/mother.	
I want to be in a relationship (wife/mother). I like the role of wife/mother.	You are nobody without me.	"Good" wives/mothers stay with their families.
I want to be part of my community—visit my family and friends.	If you leave, I will tell everyone it is your fault. They will believe me—not you. Nobody will want you if you're not with me.	This is a private, family squabble. We don't want to know anything or get involved. (Brandl, 2000)

stolen assets and property or threatened to take everything. Some victims may not be aware of their family resources or what they are entitled to claim if they separate or divorce. Victims requiring medical care may be concerned about health care coverage or the cost of assistance. In communities with long waiting lists for financial programs or for affordable housing, victims may feel they have no options but to continue contact with their abuser.

Older victims from various racial and ethnic backgrounds may define abusive behavior differently (Anetzberger, 1998; Hudson & Carlson, 1999). Cultural norms also differ about the role of parents continuing to provide support (emotional or financial) to grown children (Brown, 1989; Griffin, 1994; Sanchez, 1999). In some cultures, older women are taught to depend on family members; when there is abuse, they may not want to act against deeply rooted traditions. In some cultural groups, a negative stigma may be attached to a woman who lives alone or who goes to a nursing home. Abusers may take advantage of a victim's connection to a community to force her to maintain the relationship. For example, some older victims may be coerced to stay with their abuser to avoid being ostracized by their community.

Immigrants may fear deportation for themselves, their spouse/partner, or other family member (whether they are here legally or illegally). In some cases, an abusive family member may have sponsored the older person and now may wield the threat of deportation. Many immigrants do not speak English or do not speak it very well. They may have difficulty getting a job or may not be eligible for Social Security benefits or pensions that would give them some financial independence. Even social services may not be equipped to provide help to older battered immigrants.

Religious values often play an important role in the lives of older people. Some older people believe that their religious teachings mandate that they stay in their abusive marriage. For other victims, the fear of losing their church, synagogue, or faith- or spirituality-based friends and community make considering leaving their abuser difficult (especially for partners of religious leaders, pastors, rabbis, etc.).

Victims who live in rural areas may experience greater isolation. Dimah and Dimah (2003) found that rural elder abuse victims experience more physical and emotional abuse, and more deprivation (willful denial of a vulnerable adult's needs, such as medical care, therapeutic device, food, or shelter) than urban victims. Neighbors may live miles away and services may not be available in their county. Their abuser may be friends with or related to prominent town members, like the sheriff and the judge. Trained professionals and services may be hours away from the elders' homes. Farmers may be unable to leave crops or livestock or pets. Transportation is a significant barrier. If the caregiver is an abuser, it may be difficult to find a different caregiver or facility.

Older gay, lesbian, bisexual, and transgender persons may fear ending a relationship and being "outed" at work or to family and friends. They may feel afraid to talk with clergy, counselors, or others about their relationship and the abuse. Some may be unwilling to contact law enforcement because of past negative experiences. As they make decisions about staying with or leaving their partner, they may encounter legal and financial barriers, such as the lack of rights to a pension or Social Security benefit (Cook-Daniels, 1997).

Health problems can create obstacles to living free from abuse. Victims of long-term abuse may experience numerous physical and mental health conditions as a direct result of the abuse. They may have permanent injuries that require ongoing care. Chronic pain or undiagnosed illnesses may be the result of years of stress and trauma. Staying with an abuser may seem a more inviting option than asking strangers to provide care or moving to an institution. Keeping the same caregiver or staying in the same facility may seem less frightening than making a major change. Abusers often use the threat that "no one else will provide care for you" to make victims feel trapped. Because caregivers and quality facilities are difficult to obtain in some communities, the thought of situations becoming worse with change is often a fear.

Health problems of the abuser also impact victims' decisions. Some victims who are planning to leave or have left, stay or return if the abuser becomes critically ill or acquires a disability. Many older women feel it is their responsibility to care for a spouse/partner or adult child in need.

They may believe the threat of physical abuse is reduced because of the abuser's frail condition (even though this often isn't true).

Victims with disabilities, substance abusers, and victims with mental illness may run into additional barriers. Authorities may have trouble understanding them, may not believe their account, or may think that they would not be credible witnesses for legal proceedings. They may have trouble finding services that deal with the trauma and victimization, in addition to their disability, chemical dependency, or mental illness. Some of these victims, such as those with brain injuries, dementia, or cognitive disabilities, may have trouble retaining information that will assist them with safety planning and taking the next steps. Professionals may become frustrated because they do not know how to offer helpful interventions.

Persons living in facilities also face barriers to living free from abuse. Some victims may have hoped the nursing home or residential setting would provide safety from an abusive spouse/partner, only to find that the abuse (particularly sexual) continues. A spouse/partner, adult child, or grandchild may harm the victim during a visit onsite or offsite. Staff or other residents may be perpetrators. Too often, staff in nursing homes and other institutions are not trained to look for signs of abuse and neglect, especially by family members.

Systemic Barriers

Victims of abuse may have tried to get help before, without success. They may be concerned for their safety and for the safety of others. Some victims want to stay in their own home but make the abuse stop.

For their protection, the abuser's safety, or because they are not ready for change, victims may:

- Protect the abuser.
- Remain silent.
- Ask worker to leave and/or refuse services.
- Try to avoid police intervention and the arrest of the abuser.
- Minimize abuse and deny abuse occurs.
- Blame themselves for the abuse (e.g., "If I had gotten dinner done on time" or "If I had not gotten my haircut today, he wouldn't be mad at me now.").
- Look to the abuser to answer questions.
- Ask for help and then change their mind.
- Recant.
- Cancel or miss appointments.
- Not follow through on "the plan."
- Talk fondly of the abuser's good qualities.

- Make statements like "He won't like that," or "I don't think she'll let me do that" (Brandl, 2000).

When victims are ready for a change, the systems designed to help them often fail. Restraining or protective orders may be ignored. Emergency shelters may not be accessible. An older victim may go to the domestic violence shelter only to find that no one her age is a resident, staff, or volunteer. An older victim may find it financially impossible to leave. Some victims find it difficult or impossible to get health insurance. Affordable housing may be nonexistent or require signing up on waiting lists that are several years long. If the victim was receiving care from the abuser, it may be difficult to find a quality caregiver. These and other problems create insurmountable setbacks for victims.

Many older victims of abuse have tried on their own to make the abuse end or have reached out to others for help. Many victims are truly survivors, having figured out strategies to stay alive through years of abuse. The reasons older victims remain in relationships with abusers are often a combination of many of the topics discussed in this section. Too often, older victims face difficult or impossible choices as they make decisions about what to do. In many cases, they are making these decisions alone, without help from friends, family, or professionals because they are too embarrassed or ashamed to ask for help. Sometimes they may not even be aware that they are being abused or that help is available.

CONCLUSION

Elder abuse is complex. There are many causes for abuse and as many reasons why victims choose to remain in relationships with their abusers. Understanding the dynamics of elder abuse is critical for professionals working with victims and perpetrators and for those participating in a multidisciplinary response.

A common mistake made by many professionals is to try to make elder abuse cases fit into one framework based on their personal and professional experience. Some professionals believe that elder abuse is primarily a private family matter and that it does not require the involvement of any professionals. Others believe the root cause of most elder abuse is dysfunctional family dynamics and caregiver stress. These professionals suggest that a social service response is appropriate in most cases. Those working in criminal justice recognize that elder abuse is often criminal behavior. Domestic violence and sexual assault advocates acknowledge the similarity between the experiences of younger and older victims.

To best meet the needs of victims, professionals are encouraged to start by gathering information from the victim when possible. In addition, professionals should examine the physical evidence to determine what kind of abuse happened and why. A multidisciplinary approach will help professionals to avoid the missteps of assuming that the abuse is based on one causation theory and of offering remedies that may be inappropriate for the victim. In all cases, blaming the victim for the abuse is inappropriate. Understanding the complexity of elder abuse will help professionals work together more effectively. Section Two discusses ways to help elder abuse victims, including individual strategies, systemic responses, and a multidisciplinary approach illustrated through case examples.

Responding to Elder Abuse

CHAPTER FOUR

Identification and Reporting

How are elder abuse cases identified so that victims can receive assistance and perpetrators can be held accountable? A few older people ask for help for themselves by calling 911, law enforcement, Adult Protective Services (APS), or an advocacy organization. In the majority of elder abuse or neglect cases, however, someone else, such as a family member, friend, or neighbor, reports the abuse. Sometimes the report is made by a professional who has regular contact with the older person, such as a banker, home health nurse, Meals-on-Wheels volunteer, beautician, barber, meter reader, or postal worker. Community and faith-based organizations hold regular events for older members, and their staff may also identify abuse and report. Doctors and other health care providers also have an opportunity to identify abuse through universal screening, during physical examinations, or in an emergency room setting.

Some victims may seek services directly from an advocacy organization or initiate remedies from the civil justice system rather than having an investigation conducted. Victims or caring family members may contact a domestic violence or sexual assault program for services. Persons living in facilities may talk with an ombudsman. Civil remedies may include protective orders, divorce, or conservatorships. Advocates from all of these agencies can provide information, referrals, and ongoing support for victims.

Even with all the possibilities described here for identifying elder abuse, many situations in which older persons are being harmed are missed or ignored by family members, neighbors, friends, and professionals. Before a collaborative response can be implemented, elder abuse cases must be identified. Professionals and community members need to learn common behavioral indicators and signs of abuse. Many victims are afraid, embarrassed, or ashamed to tell anyone about the abuse. Others will drop hints that are too often ignored or misinterpreted. In other cases, the signs will be changes in the behavior or appearance of the victim. Sometimes it is the behavior of a perpetrator that indicates a potential problem.

IDENTIFYING ELDER ABUSE

Victim Says That Harm Is Occurring

An indicator that is often discounted occurs when the older person says that he or she is being harmed. In some cases, victims, especially those who are living in facilities or who have cognitive disabilities, are not seen as credible reporters, and their statements about being afraid are dismissed. In general, if an older person reports being harmed by someone, contacting APS or law enforcement should be considered. Those professionals can thoroughly investigate the accusations. In some cases, persons who report events that cannot be accurate (e.g., being abducted by aliens) may, in fact, be victims of actual abuse, as offenders often choose victims who may not be credible reporters.

In other circumstances, the victim may have medical or mental health conditions that cause delusions and there may be no abuse occurring. Sometimes the reporter was a victim of sexual assault or abuse earlier in life and now may be reliving the traumatic experience, and is confused about when and where the abuse actually occurred. Rather than simply dismissing the elder's account as not credible, it is important to have a professional investigate the allegation.

Behavioral Indicators of Abuse: Victims and Perpetrators

In other situations, victims will not report abuse directly, but will drop hints, offer coded disclosures, or display behavioral indicators that are worth exploring. Behavioral signs from victims can be new or may have been present for a long time, especially in cases of domestic violence that has been occurring for many years. Listed in Table 4.1 are possible behavioral indicators of abuse by potential victims and abusers. Most or all of the indicators need *not* be present for abuse to be occurring. One or two indicators may warrant further questioning and investigation. Some victims will not display any of the behaviors on the chart, yet still are being harmed. Often there is a correlation between the victim's behavior and that of the perpetrator. If any of the behavioral or other signs are present from either column of Table 4.1, it is time to ask questions, offer information to the potential victim, and make a report to law enforcement, APS, or regulatory agencies.

Perpetrator's Behaviors

Abusers do not fit one mold. Some abusers may appear angry and defensive to anyone with whom they come in contact. They may attempt to threaten, belittle, manipulate, or intimidate helpers. Others threaten to sue those who try to help the victim. Some abusers may be respected and powerful leaders in their communities, church, or professions. Many are funny, entertaining, charming, and charismatic. But to the victims, and behind closed doors, their behavior may be the opposite of their public

TABLE 4.1 Victim/Abuser Behaviors

A Victim May	An Abuser May
Have injuries that do not match the explanation of how they occurred	Minimize or deny the victim's injuries or complaints
	Attempt to convince others that the victim is incompetent or crazy
Have repeated "accidental injuries"	Blame the victim for being clumsy or difficult
Appear isolated	Physically assault or threaten violence against the victim or victim's family, friends, pets, or the worker
	Isolate the victim, prevent outside activities and contacts
	Threaten or harass the victim
	Stalk the victim
	Have a history of mental illness
Say they are, or hint at being, afraid	Act overly attentive toward the victim
Give coded communications about what is occurring	Act lovingly and compassionately to the victim in other people's presence
Consider or attempt suicide	Consider or attempt suicide
Have a history of alcohol or drug abuse (including prescription drugs)	Have a history of alcohol or drug abuse
Present as a "difficult" client	Refuse to allow an interview with the victim to take place without being present
	Speak on behalf of the victim, not allow the victim to participate in the interview
Have vague, chronic, nonspecific complaints	Say that the victim is incompetent, unhealthy, or crazy

(continued)

TABLE 4.1 *(continued)*

A Victim May	An Abuser May
Be emotionally and/or financially dependent on the abuser	Be emotionally and/or financially dependent on the victim
Miss appointments	Cancel the victim's appointments or refuse to provide transportation
Delay seeking medical help	Take the victim to different doctors, hospitals, and pharmacies to cover up abuse
	Refuse to purchase prescriptions, medical supplies, and/or assistive devices
Exhibit depression (mild or severe)	Turn family members against the victim
	Talk about the victim as if he or she is not there or not a person (dehumanize victim)
Exhibit evidence of effects of stress and trauma	Exhibit evidence of effects of stress and trauma

persona. These "Dr. Jekyll and Mr. Hyde" personalities can be deceiving. Charming abusers fool too many friends, family, and professionals.

INDICATORS OF ELDER ABUSE

Investigators often learn of elder abuse long after it has occurred, making a comprehensive investigation difficult. Situations of possible abuse must be identified and reported promptly to law enforcement, APS, or the appropriate regulatory agency. This section discusses the forms of abuse described in Chapter 2 using case examples. In many cases, multiple forms of abuse coexist. The cases illustrate possible scenarios for each form of abuse. Each section also describes which individuals or professionals might be most likely to notice each form of abuse, as well as some common signs and indicators.

Examples of Physical Abuse

Svetlana moved to the United States 40 years ago to marry Igor. Because he kept her captive in her own home, she did not learn to speak much English. Igor beat Svetlana, pushed her down the stairs, and broke her leg. He strangled her several times until she passed out. Igor told her that if anyone found out about the abuse, she would be deported to Russia because her paperwork had not been completed when she moved to the United States.

Enrique lived in Sunny Meadows Nursing Home. At night, the aide tied him to his bed so he would not get up to use the bathroom. One staff person regularly threw food at him when he ate too slowly. The nurse who usually cared for him slapped him and threatened to call his family if he complained.

Who Might Identify Physical Abuse?

Anyone with close and regular contact with an older person might identify physical abuse. Health care providers are often in the best position to notice physical abuse because they are the people most likely to see the victim unclothed. Sometimes family members or friends see bruises or other marks indicating abuse. Dentists see bruising on the patient's face, neck, and mouth. Beauticians see injuries to the face and scalp. Other professionals from the faith community or aging services may also recognize signs of physical abuse. Because clothing and/or bedclothes may cover injuries or signs of physical harm, if abuse is suspected and it is appropriate, the victim should be asked if he or she is willing to remove a garment to reveal any signs of injury.

Signs and Indicators of Physical Abuse Include, but Are Not Limited to, the Following:

- Fractures of bones or skull
- Welts, lacerations, rope marks
- Bite marks
- Burns (unusual location, type, or shape similar to an object, such as an iron or cigarette burn)
- Bruises with shapes similar to an object, like a belt or fingers, bilateral on upper arms from holding or shaking, clustered on trunk from repeated shaking, finger marks on neck
- Overuse or underuse of medications
- Untreated injuries
- Internal injuries

Strangulation is a form of physical abuse that is often undetected. First-responders often do not observe injuries on the victim. Specifically, in 85% of cases there were either no external injuries or injuries so minor as to be difficult to see and photograph. Perhaps because of the absence of visible injuries, cases that do not result in death or are not obviously serious have been discounted as insignificant, akin to a slap or scratch, or based on unreliable or false allegations. Few victims present at emergency departments and when they do, at times medical practitioners underevaluate the situation and dismiss the patients as intoxicated, hyperventilating, or hysterical (McClane, Strack, & Hawley, 2001).

Common indicators of strangulation include neck pain, soreness, tiny scratch marks or dots (petechial hemorrhages) from broken capillaries, raspy voice, difficulty swallowing, light-headedness or head rushes, fainting and unconsciousness, red eyes (bursting of blood vessels in the sclera of the eye), ligature marks in cases where ligatures were used, and loss of control of bodily functions resulting in involuntary urination and defecation (Strack, McClane, & Hawley, 2001). Most strangulation injuries are internal and are located in the neck and throat. Common indicators include changes in breathing, voice, and swallowing. Less common indicators are restlessness and hostility shortly after assaults, changes in personality, and psychiatric illness on a longer-term basis.

Sexual Abuse

An Example of Sexual Abuse

After a neighbor's report, APS found Abigail, age 78, in her home. She was bedridden and sleeping on a urine-soaked cot. She was brought to the hospital by law enforcement. While she was in the hospital, her adult son visited her regularly. Staff described him as "creepy" and would cover their nametags when they saw him coming to avoid having to deal with him. A night nurse walked in and found Abigail's son with his head between his mother's legs. He said he was "cleaning his mother" because staff members were not doing it properly.

Who Might Learn About Sexual Abuse?

The signs of sexual abuse are more difficult to recognize owing to the private nature of the contact and the shame and fear victims often face. Health care professionals are those most likely to identify sexual abuse, either during routine physical examinations or while providing personal care. Victims themselves may provide clues to family and friends through coded communications, such as "I don't like those movies my son makes me watch."

Signs and Indicators of Sexual Abuse Include, but Are Not Limited to, the Following:

- Difficulty in walking or sitting
- Pain or itching in genital area
- Unexplained venereal disease or genital infections
- Bruises around the breasts, inner thighs, or genital area
- Unexplained vaginal or anal bleeding
- Torn, stained, or bloody underclothing

Emotional Abuse

Examples of Fearful Behavior

Ellie separated from her husband of 52 years and moved into her own apartment. After her move, she met her friends at the senior center and attended Mass regularly. Sometimes she noticed her husband's car parked outside her building and near the church. She saw footprints leading to her bedroom window. She found her beloved pet cat dead on her front doorstep. She suspected that her husband was stalking her.

Denzel lived in a nursing home. His sister came to visit him every week and made fun of him. She told him that he was stupid and crazy. She made fun of his hearing loss by saying things quietly and then laughing at him when he misunderstood her.

Susan and Gail had been in an intimate relationship for two years. Both were in their early 60s. Susan had not told her children or employer that she was a lesbian. Gail threatened to disclose their relationship if Susan did not give her money to go drinking.

Who Might Identify Emotional Abuse?

Emotional abuse is sometimes difficult to identify. It is often overlooked or discounted, as it leaves no visible marks, is difficult to define, and is usually not criminal conduct. Family members or friends may witness examples of emotional abuse. Abusers often appear charming in front of others; victims may minimize the extent of the abuse. Mental health professionals and health care providers may see signs of emotional or physical problems that cannot be explained and may infer that emotional abuse is occurring. If not confronted and stopped, emotional abuse can escalate to physical abuse that may have a lethal outcome.

Signs and Indicators of Emotional Abuse Include, but Are Not Limited to, the Following:

- Emotional upset or agitation
- Depression or suicidal ideation
- Hypervigilance when in the presence of the abuser
- Withdrawn and noncommunicative or nonresponsive behaviors
- Unusual behavior that is usually attributed to dementia (e.g., sucking, biting, rocking, crying)
- Signs of self-mutilation

Financial Exploitation

Examples of Financial Exploitation

Anita and TJ lived together for 43 years. TJ had been an elder on the tribal council for the past five years. Two years ago, their youngest son, Marlin, moved in with them after his divorce. Marlin worked at the local casino, but drank and gambled away most of his salary. He threatened to hurt his mother and destroy his father's reputation at the tribal council if they did not give him money.

Alex was married for 53 years. His wife died six months ago. Alex lived a frugal lifestyle and had saved almost half a million dollars. Tina, age 32, met Alex at church. She befriended him and offered to move in with him and help around the house. In exchange, she asked him to write large checks to her to pay for her mother's medical expenses and other "necessities."

Missy was 89 and had Alzheimer's disease. During the last three months, Missy's caregiver, Michelle, took her to the bank to cash several checks for $1,000, which Missy then handed over to Michelle. In addition, Michelle took some of Missy's valuable jewelry, saying that the jewels were a gift to her from Missy.

Who Might Identify Financial Exploitation?

Family members may identify financial exploitation when they find bills unpaid or valuables missing, or when the elder suddenly has a new best friend or romantic interest. Bank personnel are in the unique position of monitoring an elder's spending habits and may notice changes in spending patterns. Attorneys may be asked to make unusual changes to wills and property deeds. Health care providers or others may also notice that a person with adequate resources no longer seems to have enough money to meet his or her daily expenses. Substance abuse or mental health professionals may learn about financial exploitation from sessions with perpetrators or victims.

Signs and Indicators of Financial Exploitation Include, but Are Not Limited to, the Following:

- Sudden changes in bank account or banking practice, including an unexplained withdrawal of large sums of money
- Abrupt changes in a will or other financial documents
- Unexplained disappearance of funds or valuable possessions
- Substandard care being provided or bills unpaid despite the availability of adequate financial resources
- Unexplained sudden transfer of assets or title to real estate
- Extraordinary interest by family member or "new friend" in older person's assets
- Completion of a legal document or transaction that the elder does not understand or was rushed to complete

Neglect

Examples of Neglect

Susan, age 87, was bedridden as a result of severe arthritis. She needed help getting to her walker and getting around the house. She also needed meals prepared for her. Henry, her husband, provided care for her because he did not want to pay anyone to help them. He fed his wife only when he felt like it. Some days he gave her medication and other days he did not in order to save money. When she whined too much, he would overmedicate her to "stop her nagging."

Anthony has been bedridden for more than a year with advanced dementia. He required full-time care. His sons moved into his home to provide care. Instead, they did not feed him appropriate foods, assist him with toileting, or turn him in bed. As a result, Anthony developed many pressure ulcers that went untreated, resulting in massive infections and ultimately, his death.

Who Might Identify Neglect?

Neighbors, family members, health care providers, or other professionals often identify neglect in the home. Neighbors or family members may notice changes in the appearance, health, or hygiene of an older person or see deterioration of the condition of the elder's residence or property. Physicians and other health care professionals may see untreated medical conditions or note missed appointments. Pharmacists might see that prescriptions are not being filled regularly. Representative payees and guardians may notice that the care by hired caregivers is not adequate to meet the patient's medical needs.

Signs and Indicators of Neglect Include, but Are Not Limited to, the Following:

- Dehydration
- Malnutrition
- Hyperthermia or hypothermia
- Hazardous or unsafe living condition/arrangements
- Inadequate or inappropriate clothing
- Absence of eyeglasses, hearing aids, dentures, or prostheses
- Unexpected or unexplained deterioration of health
- Untreated decubitus ulcers and other health conditions
- Failure to thrive
- Lack of routine medical care and/or medications

ABUSE AND NEGLECT IN LONG-TERM CARE FACILITIES

An Example of Facility Abuse

At age 96, Charles was living in a nursing home. He was in the last stage of Alzheimer's disease, was totally bedridden, and could not feed or toilet himself. When his daughter visited him, she often found him lying in his own excrement. He had deep decubitis ulcers on his tailbone and heels, as well as bruises around his mouth.

Sign and Indicators of Abuse and Neglect in Long-term Care Facilities Include, but Are Not Limited to, the Following:

- Inappropriate use of restraints
- Injuries that do not match the explanation of how they occurred
- Untreated injuries or illnesses
- Overmedication
- Severe weight loss without intervention
- Disappearance of personal items, such as false teeth, hearing aids, money, and mementos

Who Might Identify Abuse or Neglect in Long-term Care Facilities?

Family members are usually the first people to identify the abuse and neglect of long-term care patients. Ombudsmen who make regular visits to nursing homes are in a position to see ongoing problems with patient care. Regulatory agency staff may also become aware of poor quality institutional care. The state attorney general's office may identify Medicare fraud relating to patient abuse or neglect. Business employees may see a confused older adult wandering about their premises.

Abandonment

An Example of Abandonment

APS was called because Felipe, age 63, was abandoned by his son Carlos at a local motel. Carlos did not pay his father's motel bill, but continued to cash his Social Security checks. A medical team was called to see Felipe. He had uncontrolled hypertension and muscle weakness on his right side, with permanent shortening of his muscles. He had a mild dementia, but severe depression. He also had a history of seizures and right-sided paralysis due to a stroke. He was completely unable to care for himself. He has a caring brother and sister-in-law, but his son had denied him access to all other family members.

Who Might Identify Abandonment?

Abandonment is most likely to be identified by hospital staff when a patient is left at the emergency room. In addition, family members may come forward when an older relative suddenly disappears from his or her place of residence.

Signs and Indicators of Abandonment Include, but Are Not Limited to, the Following:

- A cognitively-impaired patient is left in the hospital emergency room without caregiver contact information
- Victim is put on a bus with a one-way ticket to another town or state
- Victim is left at a public building, such as a mall, city hall, or police department

Self-Neglect

An Example of Self-Neglect

Roberta lived alone in a house that was falling apart. The front porch sagged, the windows were broken, and the yard was filled with trash. She kept to herself, spending most of her time inside caring for her many cats and dogs. The house was filled with old newspapers and the floors were covered with excrement. In the summertime, neighbors complained of the smell coming from the house.

Elder self-neglect occurs frequently, but is largely hidden. Self-neglecting elders tend to be withdrawn from society, live alone, and do not use traditional services. They often suffer from a variety of untreated medical conditions, many of which would respond to treatment. Their mortality rate is two times that of persons who have not been reported to protective services (Lachs, Williams, O'Brien, Pillemer, & Charlson, 1998). What began as an independent lifestyle may often deteriorate over time into a reclusive and marginal existence. Victims may live in situations that range from untidy surroundings to absolute squalor. It is sometimes difficult to differentiate between an eccentric lifestyle and one that poses an immediate danger to the elder and or other people.

Who Might Identify Self-Neglect

A neighbor is usually the first person to make a report based on the bizarre behavior of the elder or the rundown appearance of the elder's living situation. Mail carriers and utilities personnel may also report. Public health officers or code enforcement officials may be asked to condemn the residence. Animal control may respond to reports of multiple animals that lack appropriate care.

Signs and Indicators of Self-Neglect Include, but Are Not Limited to, the Following:

- Trash in unkempt yards, strong odors coming from the house
- Many pets, often in poor health
- Dirty appearance, add or inappropriate dress
- Withdrawn, depressed, or hostile behaviors
- Isolated, lives alone
- Hazardous or unsafe living condition/arrangements, abundance of trash, animals, vermin, insects in and around the victim's home
- Absence of eyeglasses, hearing aids, dentures, or prostheses

- Unexpected or unexplained deterioration of health
- Untreated health conditions, lack of routine medical care and/or medications

Sometimes it is not possible to gain entrance into a self-neglector's home. Well-meaning attempts to do so are seldom successful and may result in increased withdrawal on the part of the elderly person.

Self-neglectors sometimes present in hospital emergency rooms because of health crises. Older people who have suffered recent severe health problems or trauma, been the target of crimes, or suffered multiple losses also may be at risk of becoming self-neglectors, especially if there are not support services available. It is often difficult to convince them to accept services, and it may take weeks or months to build sufficiently trusting relationships for them to do so.

Asking About Abuse

To gather information about what has occurred, the professional needs to ask some initial questions. Effective interviews with older people, victims of abuse, and people with disabilities require skill, patience, and creativity. In general, victims of abuse respond best to someone who has taken the time to build a rapport. Asking general questions leading to more specific ones is often a useful strategy. A private place for the interview, out of view and earshot of the abuser, is generally most effective. Questions to elicit information from an older person about abuse could include:

- How is your social life? When was the last time you went out with friends or family?
- Who makes decisions at your house? Who decides how your money is spent?
- How are things going with your spouse/partner, caregiver, or adult child?
- Is there someone in your family who has emotional or drinking or drug problems?
- Are there strangers coming in and out of your home without your permission?
- Are you afraid? Has anyone made you feel uncomfortable?
- Have you ever been hit, kicked, or hurt in any way?
- Does anyone threaten you or force you to do things you do not want to do?
- Have you ever been forced to do sexual acts you did not wish to do?
- Is any of this going on now?

ADDITIONAL GUIDELINES FOR EFFECTIVE INTERVIEWING

Cultural, generational, and other values may impact the quality of the interview and the information that is gathered. Members of some cultural groups may be more willing to report abuse or talk to professionals about family problems than others (Moon & Benton, 2000; Sanchez, 1999; Tomita, 1999). Many older persons may be uncomfortable talking about personal or private matters with strangers. They may fear that younger professionals will impose their own generational values about divorce or women's roles, and judge their decisions. They may also fear that the admission of an abusive situation will result in their placement in a nursing home. Or they may simply not define what is occurring to them as abuse. They may say, "Harry has always had a bad temper," or "That's just the way our family talks to each other."

Interviewing People With Disabilities

Effective interviewers:

- Do not assume that a person with a disability has a cognitive limitation or is not telling the truth.
- Treat adults as adults, regardless of any disabilities they may have.
- Work with specialists in disabilities fields to gain information about communication barriers, successful interviewing techniques, and information about assistive technology for persons who cannot otherwise communicate (e.g., using pictures/diagrams for people with speech impairments).
- Look and speak directly to the person being interviewed, rather than at the interpreter or others in the room.
- Use simple language when communicating with a person with a cognitive disability. Avoid "confusing" questions about time, sequences, or reasons for behavior or abstractions.
- Use a sign language interpreter if the individual is deaf or hard of hearing and is familiar with sign language.
- Take their time and do not rush the interview.
- Use open-ended questions and nonleading questions whenever possible (Baladerian, 2004).

REPORTING/REFERRING ELDER ABUSE

After suspected abuse has been identified, the next step is responding. This section discusses how individuals can make reports or referrals to professionals who can focus on safety, support, and services for victims.

Elder abuse is underreported. The lack of reporting has negative consequences for victims in the community and in institutions. There are many reasons for not reporting, including fear of increased abuse or retaliation, social stigma or lack of whistleblower protections, ignorance about when and how to report, and belief that reporting will not improve the situation. Anecdotal evidence suggests that victims and families are reluctant to report abuse when it occurs in the home, as well as in institutional settings. Unless there is someone willing to step forward and make a report, the abuse is likely to continue and may eventually prove fatal.

After recognizing possible abuse, sometimes it is difficult to decide what to do next. Many people are concerned about bringing up possible abuse for fear of violating the privacy of the victim and the family. Many victims, however, have indicated that they are looking for help and appreciate kind, thoughtful questioning, and information.

In life-threatening situations or other emergencies, calls can be made to 911 or emergency services to get an immediate response from law enforcement, emergency medical treatment services, or paramedics. Life-threatening situations include physical or sexual assault in progress, as well as threats with weapons. Emergency situations include criminal acts in progress, and situations where there is an immediate and significant threat of loss of assets.

In nonthreatening situations, reports can be made directly to law enforcement if a crime is suspected. Depending on the local practice, these calls may go to 911 or to nonemergency law enforcement numbers. Law enforcement agencies may dispatch sworn or civilian personnel to take an in-person report or may take information over the telephone. They may mail out a report form to the caller. Depending on the information conveyed in the report, however taken, an investigation may then be conducted.

A report can also be made to social services by contacting APS, or by looking in the phone book under government agencies and contacting the protective services hotline number or the local Area Agency on Aging. More information about APS and how to contact them can be found on the National Center on Elder Abuse Web site: http://www.elderabusecenter.org. Citizens or professionals who make reports only need to provide information on the victim's name, contact information, what the suspicions are, and why there is concern. Most state APS laws, regardless of whether the laws mandate reporting, protect the confidentiality of the reporting person, and also protect persons who make good faith reports from liability for reporting. Elder Abuse/APS workers will visit the home, investigate the allegations, determine the victim's risk and capacity to make informed decisions, make recommendations to increase the victim's safety, and arrange for supportive services.

Currently, the APS laws of 44 states and the District of Columbia make reporting elder abuse mandatory in some situations. In some states, everyone is a reporter, whereas in other states, specific professionals are named as reporters. For more information about state APS statutes related to mandatory reporting, visit the National Center on Elder Abuse Web site: http://www.elderabusecenter.org. The majority of state APS programs are administered either by a department of human or social services or the state office on aging. Anyone who may be a mandatory reporter should be familiar with his or her state's elder abuse reporting requirements.

Other agencies and remedies may be available to improve the situation. Consider contacting a local domestic violence program (National Domestic Violence Hotline: 800-799-SAFE) for the number of the nearest agency. Most domestic violence programs have 24-hour hotlines and can provide information and referrals about services and legal options available for the victim. Phone numbers for sexual assault programs can be found by calling the National Sexual Assault Hotline at 800-656-4673 or checking listings in a local phone book. Other services through the aging network, faith-based community, or other community organizations may have programs to help victims. Although faith-based leaders are in a unique position to encounter situations of elder abuse, they seldom make reports. But by providing services, such as pastoral visits and transportation to religious activities, the faith community can help to alleviate the isolation that leads to elder neglect and abuse.

ADDITIONAL CONSIDERATIONS FOR REPORTING/REFERRING ABUSE IN FACILITIES

Ombudsman offices or regulatory agencies sometimes receive reports of alleged abuse in facilities. The ombudsman acts as an advocate for residents, working to improve their safety and quality of life. Under the Older Americans Act, ombudsmen can report abuse only with the permission of the victim. For this reason, sometimes ombudsmen may be unable to report specific abuse situations to the regulatory agency, APS or law enforcement; however, ombudsmen are able to share generalized concerns about the quality of life in a specific facility. Contact information for the ombudsman can be found in the phone book or by contacting the local Area Agency on Aging.

State regulatory agencies are another place where allegations of abuse and neglect in long-term care can be referred. In every state, there are agencies responsible for the licensing and certification of long-term care facilities. In addition to making regular certification visits to facilities, these agencies are also charged with investigating incidents of dangerous or inadequate care. Also, state agencies regulate the licensure and board certification of certain professionals including physicians, nurses, and social workers. Situations of inappropriate or inadequate professional care should be referred to these licensing boards.

Reporting/Referring Self-Neglect

In most states, situations of self-neglect should be reported to APS. There are APS programs in every state and most communities. In situations of self-neglect, it is likely that the self-neglecting person will refuse the initial offer of services. It often takes repeated referrals and patient efforts on the part of APS before the worker is able to gain entry into the home. Keep in mind that self-neglectors, like everyone else, have the right to refuse to let strangers into their homes. And they may be even more reluctant to do so because they fear that outside intervention will result in the loss of their possessions, pets, and even their homes. Sometimes it is easier for a health care professional—either a physician or a nurse—to gain access to a self-neglecting elder. For that to occur, knowledge about the physical condition of the elder, such as known diseases and unhealed injuries, is important. Sometimes it is not possible to gain entrance into a self-neglector's home. Well-meaning attempts to do so may be unsuccessful and may result in increased withdrawal on the part of the elderly person. One study found that elder self-neglectors are more likely to feel intruded on by investigators than are elders who are abused by other people (Longress, 1994).

CONCLUSION

This chapter provided information on the types of elder abuse, signs and indicators of abuse, and the most likely persons to identify abuse and report it. In addition, it described the process of reporting elder abuse. The chapter emphasizes that because elders seldom self-report, it is essential for concerned family members, neighbors, friends, and professionals to be aware of the possibility of elder abuse and neglect, and to take responsibility for making reports to the appropriate authorities. The next chapter provides information on the systems and professionals who respond to elder abuse and neglect reports.

CHAPTER FIVE

Systemic Responses to Elder Abuse

Numerous systems and agencies investigate allegations of elder abuse and provide support and services for older victims. Like pieces of a puzzle, agencies can be scattered throughout the community and have little or no connection with one another. After an elder abuse, exploitation, or neglect report or referral is made, one or more agencies may work with an individual victim and/or perpetrator. This chapter describes the roles and responsibilities of the major systems that respond to elder abuse. Investigative systems include Adult Protective Services (APS) and the criminal justice system. Physical health needs are addressed by the medical system. Additional interventions and remedies are available from a variety of other agencies.

ADULT PROTECTIVE SERVICES

Core Duties

The purpose of APS is to reduce or eliminate the abuse, exploitation, and/or neglect of elderly and vulnerable adults. The primary responsibilities of APS staff are to take reports of elder abuse, exploitation, neglect, and self-neglect; make face-to-face contact with the victim to determine the immediate level of risk; assess the victim's capacity to give informed consent for any services to be provided; conduct a thorough investigation of the allegations; determine if there is a founded or actionable case; and, where appropriate, arrange for services to be provided to reduce the risk of further abuse. In most states, APS also serve vulnerable adults age 18 to 59 who are reported to be victims of abuse, exploitation, neglect, and self-neglect. In many states, APS workers investigate abuse that occurs in facilities, in addition to the investigations conducted by regulatory agencies.

If an allegation of abuse is founded, and the victim is capable of giving informed consent for the provision of services, APS can arrange for a wide variety of supportive services including, but not limited to, medical, social, economic, legal, housing, home health, law enforcement, or other protective, emergency, or supportive services. Victims who have the capacity to give informed consent may refuse any or all of these services. In fact, one of three abuse victims refuse the initial offer of services (Bozinovski, 1995). Victims who lack the capacity to give informed consent and are in imminent danger may have emergency services provided with the authorization of a court. Depending on state laws and regulations, APS may continue to monitor these services once they have been put in place, as well as provide therapeutic counseling or casework services until the victim's risk has been reduced or eliminated. In some states, the case may be passed on to a case management agency.

Legislative Authority

No federal statutes or standards govern the delivery of adult protective services, which is authorized by state statutes that vary in their definitions of abuse. However, every state elder/vulnerable adult protection statute or regulation includes physical abuse and financial exploitation. The majority of state statutes include sexual abuse and neglect. More than half the states also include self-neglect, and a handful include psychological abuse and abandonment. Currently, the APS laws in 44 states and the District of Columbia mandate the reporting of some situations of elder abuse to APS by selected professionals or, in some states, by anyone. Some state statutes also mandate that APS and law enforcement exchange information on the elder abuse reports that they receive.

Staffing

At least as many variations in the programs exist as there are states. Programs differ administratively, but the core values that provide direction to them are consistent. Staff of APS are usually human services workers whose primary responsibility is to receive and investigate allegations of abuse, neglect, and exploitation against older adults and/or vulnerable adults. In most states, administrative authority for elder and adult protective services is housed in either human services or aging services agencies. A few states have a bifurcated system in which one agency (usually aging services) investigates elder abuse and another responds to abuse of

TABLE 5.1   Primary Activities/Functions of APS/Elder Abuse Agencies

- Take reports of abuse, exploitation, and neglect
- Provide information and referral
- Make face-to-face contact with the victim within 24 to 72 hours
- Assess immediate risk to the victim
- Evaluate the victim's capacity to make informed decisions
- Investigate and substantiate abuse
- Develop a case plan
- Provide short-term case management and counseling
- Arrange for the provision of supportive services including, but not limited to:

  Referrals for physical and mental health assessments

  Cleaning services

  Financial management

  Transportation

  Home modification to meet the needs of persons with disabilities

  Temporary medications

  Assistive devices

  Food services, including Meals on Wheels or food stamps, when applicable

  Emergency housing

  Home repairs, including roofing, floor, and walls

  Pest and animal control

  Respite care or other provider services

  Residential placement

  Linkage to other service groups
- Assist with applications for health care and/or financial benefits
- Apply for temporary emergency guardianship court actions
- Testify in civil and criminal court actions

younger adults, ages 18 to 59, who have disabilities that prevent them from protecting themselves.

Educational requirements for APS workers and supervisors vary, ranging from a high school diploma to a master's degree, typically in the social sciences. A few states require professional certification or licensure.

Most states require an average of only 6.8 days of training for new APS staff, although many states allow new workers to do field work before completing basic training. Experienced APS workers receive an average of 3.4 days of ongoing training annually, and supervisors receive an average of 4.7 days. Only two states, Kansas and Utah, require that APS staff be licensed social workers (Teaster, 2002).

In general, APS hours are Monday through Friday during normal business hours. Reports can be made 24 hours a day, sometimes to the state elder abuse hotline or a local after-hours phone system. Investigations generally occur during business hours, although some communities do provide emergency APS services in crisis situations.

Ethical Principles

Although APS workers have no official professional guide such as the Hippocratic Oath, there are certain core values and principles that guide their practice. If they are a member of a particular profession (e.g., social work, nursing), that profession will have its own ethical code. The first principle is that every action taken by APS must balance the duty to protect the safety of the vulnerable adult with the adult's right to self-determination. Unlike children, adults retain their full array of civil rights unless those rights have been limited by the imposition of a court-ordered guardianship or conservatorship. This core value is the basis for all APS service delivery. It is also the most difficult value to adhere to when APS is trying to protect the adult's safety and support his or her right to make decisions, even if others deem these decisions as poor choices. In their practice, APS workers believe that:

- Adults have the right to be safe.
- Adults retain all their civil and constitutional rights unless some of these rights have been restricted by court action.
- Adults have the right to make decisions that do not conform with societal norms, as long as these decisions do not harm others.
- Adults are presumed to have decision-making capacity unless a court adjudicates otherwise.
- Adults have the right to accept or refuse services.

A second APS value is that older people and people with disabilities who are victims of abuse, exploitation, or neglect should be treated with honesty, caring, and respect (National Adult Protective Services Association, 2004).

CRIMINAL JUSTICE SYSTEM

Reports Made to Law Enforcement

The purpose of law enforcement involvement is to respond to calls from citizens. The primary focus of this response is to determine if there has been a violation of the law. In many cases, however, calls will involve simply providing assistance in resolving conflict or directing citizens to other public services. If the call is crime related, the primary focus will be on meeting the victim's immediate needs and establishing sufficient facts to hold the offender accountable.

As a rule, the focus of law enforcement is investigating crimes. However, in nonemergency situations in which someone has voiced concern about an older person who has not been seen for a period of time, law enforcement might be called to do a "wellness" or "welfare" check, which involves looking in on the older person to make sure that he or she is all right.

Individuals who are concerned about life-threatening situations or crimes usually call 911 or law enforcement. A dispatcher records the information and sends emergency medical technicians or paramedics to the scene to provide immediate medical treatment. Law enforcement also responds and may start an investigation immediately. If a crime is suspected, officers secure the scene, collect evidence, take photographs of the crime scene and parties, document the incident, and interview the victim, any witnesses and, if possible, the alleged perpetrator.

Core Duties

Law enforcement's primary responsibility is to protect the public and ensure that the laws are obeyed. Officers investigate violations of the law and make arrests when sufficient evidence is found. They also seek judicial approval for arrest and search warrants and serve them once issued.

The primary responsibility of a prosecutor is to enforce the laws in a fair manner. The head prosecutor is that jurisdiction's chief law enforcement official. Prosecutors review evidence; decide whether to file charges against individuals; represent the state, county, parish, or government in various court proceedings; may conduct plea negotiations or make sentencing recommendations; and may handle many different appellate matters. Some prosecutors also present cases to grand juries. Prosecutors may oversee investigations, provide legal guidance for law enforcement, and train a variety of criminal justice professionals.

Some law enforcement agencies, prosecutor's offices, or community-based organizations employ victim advocates (also called victim-witness coordinators or victim assistance providers). These advocates deal directly with crime victims. They assist the victim in understanding the court process, provide referrals and linkages to other agencies and programs, help the victim obtain transportation to the prosecutor's office or court, accompany the victim to court and provide emotional support, and help victims prepare victim impact statements. Victim advocates also help victims apply for funding from victim compensation, which can pay for things such as medical and mental health treatment, relocation when necessary, or replacement of damaged property, such as eyeglasses, door locks, and windows.

Probation officers supervise persons admitted to probation by various courts. Parole officers supervise persons who have completed periods of incarceration ordered by state and federal courts and who must also demonstrate their ability to live as law abiding persons in the community. Both parole and probation officers have powers to supervise and enforce conditions of probation as set by a court or parole authority, and to make arrests.

Staffing

The criminal justice system is generally thought to include law enforcement, prosecutors, probation and parole officers, judiciary, and corrections. Law enforcement includes a variety of peace officers, who are employed by local, state, or federal entities and who are given arrest powers. Educational requirements are set by employing agencies and vary from a high school diploma to advanced college degrees. Law enforcement officers ordinarily must complete a police training academy that teaches job-specific skills and knowledge, including relevant laws, search and seizure, control and arrest techniques, use of force, firearms and other weapons proficiency, and investigation of crimes. Most law enforcement officers work in the community. Law enforcement is available 24 hours a day, seven days a week.

Prosecutors are attorneys who typically possess an undergraduate degree and a postgraduate law degree. As attorneys, they have successfully passed a bar examination and have been admitted to practice in a state or federal court, or both. Prosecutors generally work with cases in their offices or in court during business hours Monday through Friday.

Employing agencies set the qualifications for parole and probation officers. These may include a degree in social work or mental health, general college degree, or specialized advanced degrees. Many states or agencies require initial training that focuses on relevant laws, arrest powers, report writing, family violence, substance abuse, counseling, mental health issues, and weapons use.

TABLE 5.2 Primary Activities/Functions of the Criminal Justice System

Discipline	Activities/Functions in Elder Abuse Cases
Law Enforcement	• Obtain medical care for injured victims
	• Investigate allegations
	• Identify criminal conduct
	• Collect relevant evidence
	• Apply for and execute arrest and search warrants
	• Conduct identification procedures
	• Process forensic evidence
	• Testify in court proceedings
	• Seek bail enhancements
	• Seize weapons, where permitted
	• Provide protection, when possible
	• Obtain court orders on behalf of victims, where permitted
	• Support protective service workers and other team members
	• Perform welfare checks
	• Perform civil process to retrieve property
Prosecution	• Answer criminal law questions
	• Provide information about the legal system
	• Identify criminal conduct
	• Provide assistance during investigation
	• Initiate charges
	• Conduct grand jury investigations
	• Prosecute cases on behalf of the state
	• Seek increased bail or remand
	• Obtain court orders
	• Issue subpoenas to secure witnesses and production of documents
	• Obtain conviction of perpetrators of elder abuse
	• Use information learned from team to craft sentencing recommendations

(continued)

TABLE 5.2 *(continued)*

Discipline	Activities/Functions in Elder Abuse Cases
	• Present victim impact information at sentencing
	• Seek conditions of probation to address underlying reasons for criminal conduct and separate victim and suspect
	• Seek orders of restitution
	• File motions seeking sanctions for violations of probation or failure to pay restitution
	• Appear at parole hearings to resist early release
Victim Advocates (Victim Witness) (may work in prosecutor's office, law enforcement agency, or community-based organization)	• Assist with preparation of a safety plan
	• Explain community-based resources
	• Inform about available legal options
	• Assist with obtaining court orders
	• Provide crisis intervention and direct to ongoing counseling
	• Assist with obtaining legal benefits
	• Arrange for emergency housing, including referral to appropriate shelters
	• Assist victims in enrolling in confidential address program, where available and eligible
	• Demystify the criminal justice system by providing information on the process, court procedures, participants and their role
	• Explain community resources, options
	• Make emergency housing referrals
	• Provide transportation to court
	• Provide court accompaniment for victims
	• Assist victims in preparation of impact statements
	• Advise of court dates
	• Provide limited emergency funds, when available. Note: Criminal justice-based advocates generally obtain information that can be used in court and do not have client confidentiality to the extent that community-based advocates do.

(continued)

TABLE 5.2   Primary Activities/Functions of the Criminal Justice System *(continued)*

Discipline	Activities/Functions in Elder Abuse Cases
Probation and Parole	• Supervise released persons
	• Require and monitor testing for substance abuse
	• Ensure that counseling and treatment programs are attended
	• Return to custody or court for suspected violations
	• Require perpetrators to report regularly
	• Supervise collection and regular payment of restitution
	• Monitor compliance with court orders

Ethical Principles

Criminal justice professionals share a common ethical principle of equitably enforcing the law and protecting the public. In general, each owes a primary duty to the community and public at large, rather than to an individual victim. Therefore, in carrying out their mandates, criminal justice professionals make decisions that protect the broader community, even if those decisions are at variance with the desires of a particular victim. Prosecutors are the attorneys for the entire community and their decisions focus on making the community safer, rather than acting to satisfy a particular person. Criminal conduct is viewed as an act against the entire community, not just as a private wrong against an individual.

Variations Within the System

There are local, state, and federal criminal justice systems, each with its own applicable laws and jurisdiction. Sometimes there is overlapping authority between agencies. For example, bank robberies may be investigated by local law enforcement in the community where the robbery occurred, as well as by the FBI. Prosecution may be by the local county prosecutor's office or the regional federal office of the U.S. attorney.

Crimes and actions in federally funded nursing homes may fall simultaneously within the jurisdiction of a local county, the state's Medicaid Fraud Control Unit, and the criminal division of the federal office of the U.S. attorney. These differences may result in multiple investigations and varied outcomes.

CIVIL JUSTICE SYSTEM

Core Duties

The primary responsibilities of civil lawyers are to counsel clients about their legal rights and obligations, advocate zealously on behalf of clients, and bring or defend civil lawsuits on behalf of their clients.

TABLE 5.3 Primary Activities/Functions of the Civil Justice System

Civil Justice	• Identify cases where guardianship or conservatorship is needed
	• Ask the court to declare that a person lacks decision-making capacity and needs to have a guardian or conservator appointed
	• Ask the court to appoint a different guardian or conservator if the existing individual is abusing, neglecting, or exploiting the incapacitated person
	• Defend an individual against a determination that he or she lacks decision-making capacity and the appointment of a guardian or conservator
	• Seek civil court orders to protect a victim of elder abuse
	• Bring lawsuits to preserve or regain a victim's assets or to seek monetary damages for harm caused by abuse or neglect (including such causes of action as theft, assault and battery, conversion, breach of contract, and negligence)
	• Counsel clients about ways of protecting themselves and their assets from abuse, neglect, and exploitation
	• Prepare legal documents that anticipate the possibility of decision-making incapacity, such as durable powers of attorney for finances, advanced health care directives, and trusts
	• Counsel clients on estate planning and prepare appropriate documents, including wills and trusts
	• Challenge the validity of a will or some other legal document because of undue influence
	• Seek or challenge the mental health commitment of an elder abuse victim
	• Counsel and represent clients in family matters such as separation and divorce

Staffing

Civil lawyers may work in a variety of settings. They may work in private law firms. Civil lawyers may work in legal services or legal aid offices, providing free legal services to older persons under certain circumstances. Civil lawyers also may work in government agencies, such as the local courts, the public guardianship program, the state attorney general's office, or the office of the U.S. attorney. Lawyers attend law school for three years (full time) after obtaining a bachelor's degree. They must take and pass a state bar examination to obtain a license to practice law.

A relatively new area of civil practice is called elder law. As the name suggests, elder law attorneys specialize in legal issues affecting older persons. A growing number of law schools offer courses on elder law that usually include some content on elder abuse, but most civil lawyers do not take those elder law classes.

Ethical Principles

Each state has its own ethical rules for lawyers licensed in that state. But the two highest ethical principles of the legal profession are consistent from state to state. The first principle is that lawyers should not represent clients unless they are competent in the areas of law relevant to the client's problem. The second principle is that competent legal services cannot be provided unless a client discloses all pertinent information. Toward that end, lawyers must maintain client confidentiality, protect privileged information, and ensure that other interests do not divide their loyalty to their client.

HEALTH CARE SYSTEM

Core Duties

Physicians must elicit patient histories, perform physical examinations, and make diagnoses. Once the diagnosis is known, an intervention is planned that might include medication, surgery, or another modality (i.e., therapy). Physician assistants and nurse practitioners perform these same basic functions, usually in conjunction with a practicing physician, although some, depending on a particular state's laws, may open their own practices. Nurses and social workers perform assessments and make recommendations concerning nursing or social interventions. Table 5.4 is a chart of health care professionals and their activities related to elder abuse.

TABLE 5.4   Primary Activities/Functions of the Health Care System

Health Care Professionals	Activities/Functions Related to Elder Abuse
Allied Health Care Professionals—Therapists, Dietitians, etc.	• Provide additional needed services or assessments • May have historical information on victim, family members, or caregiver
Coroner (may or may not be a physician)	• Responds to suspicious deaths, although may not perform autopsies • Investigates to determine cause of death
Dentists	• Report suspected abuse and neglect • Provide dental care and reconstructive procedures • Able to detect facial or dental injuries that may indicate physical abuse or neglect
Emergency Room Physicians	• Case identification • Treat victims • Referrals to other medical providers
Eye Specialists	• Detect injuries to face and eyes that may indicate abuse • Report suspected abuse and neglect • Provide eye care
Health Department	• Monitor public health thorough home visits, community clinics, house cleanup • Control of communicable diseases
Hospital Discharge Planners	• Work with APS and medical team to ensure that patient is going back to a safe environment
Hospital Social Workers (not Adult Protective Services)	• Provide detailed social history, counseling, case management services
Medical Examiner (is a Physician)	• Perform autopsies • Determine cause of death • Interpret medical findings • Obtain, test, and interpret toxicologic material

(continued)

TABLE 5.4   *(continued)*

Health Care Professionals	Activities/Functions Related to Elder Abuse
	• Provide forensic information and evidence
Nurses	• Provide nursing expertise, including case management
Paramedics/Firefighting Services	• Provide emergency medical care in the field
	• Transport victims to medical treatment facility
Physicians, Nurse Practitioners, and Physician Assistants	• Treat or cure disease states (e.g., vitamin deficiency, depression, heart disease, hypertension, diabetes)
	• Improve cognitive status by providing medication and mental retraining
	• Improve functional status by prescribing therapy and/or assistive devices
	• Prevent deterioration by monitoring health status
	• Prevent death by responding to acute changes in status
	• Treat behavioral disorders with appropriate medical and environmental modifications
	• Adjust/monitor complex medication regimens
	• Improve nutrition by intervening in disease states and prescribing dietary supplementation
	• Recommend appropriate modifications to living situation
	• Provide caregiver training
	• Educate the victim about their disease states and requirements for improved health
	• Provide palliative care at the end of life, by controlling pain and symptoms

(continued)

TABLE 5.4   Primary Activities/Functions of the Health Care System *(continued)*

Health Care Professionals	Activities/Functions Related to Elder Abuse
Sexual Assault Nurse-Examiners	• Document forensic evidence of sexual assault
	• Collect biological samples for testing from victims
	• Identify and evaluate cases of sexual assault in emergency departments
	• May be trained to recognize and intervene in other forms of abuse

Staffing

Health professionals work in a variety of settings, including hospitals, outpatient clinics, nursing homes, autopsy suites, and private residences through house calls. Some health care providers work in clinics or dental offices, which are open during regular business hours. Other health care settings, such as hospitals, are open 24 hours a day.

Nurses and social workers may have varying levels of educational preparation. Licensed vocational nurses have one year of courses; registered nurses have two years of college in some programs and a bachelor's degree in others. Social workers generally have an undergraduate degree in social work. Members of both disciplines can earn a master's degree or a doctorate in their respective fields. Nurse practitioners or physician assistants usually have a master's degree and have a period of apprenticeship that lasts from one to one-and-a-half years.

Geriatricians are physicians who have completed four years of medical school after earning an undergraduate degree, usually, but not exclusively, in a scientific discipline. After medical school, a would-be geriatrician generally undergoes a residency in internal medicine or family practice. Both of these residencies require a three-year period of apprenticeship under supervising physicians. To become a geriatrician, the physician must study for an additional one to two years in a geriatric fellowship program.

Ethical Principles

Everyone in the health care system is trained to be a patient advocate. Most physicians take the Hippocratic Oath when they graduate from medical school. Social workers and nurses have similar creeds. Nurses and physicians also adhere to the ethical principle to do what is best for the patient, without doing any harm. Unlike social work professionals, who pledge to maintain autonomy, other medical professionals are charged with the patient's safety and best interests. If these goals conflict, or in an emergency situation or when the patient is mentally incapacitated, the physician's duty to the patient's safety and best interests can override the patient's wishes.

Other Useful Information

Medical professionals may have varying degrees of knowledge concerning elder abuse or neglect. Most often these health providers are trained to minister to the individual and do not have a system perspective, especially concerning social issues. Almost no information about crimes and the criminal justice system are ever addressed in health professional training.

DOMESTIC VIOLENCE AND SEXUAL ASSAULT PROGRAMS

Core Duties

The primary responsibility of domestic violence and sexual assault advocates is to provide assistance in a crisis, as well as ongoing support and information to victims of domestic violence and/or sexual assault.

TABLE 5.5   Primary Activities/Functions of the Domestic Violence System

Discipline	Activities/Functions Related to Elder Abuse
Domestic Violence Programs	• Represent victim perspective
	• Provide information to the victim
	• Support victim through criminal justice system
	• Link victim to services
	• Provide services, including shelter
	• Assist with restitution
	• Operate crisis hotlines
	• Operate support groups
	• Operate shelter programs

(continued)

TABLE 5.5   *(continued)*

Discipline	Activities/Functions Related to Elder Abuse
	• Assist with preparation of a safety plan
	• Explain community-based resources
	• Inform about available legal options
	• Assist with obtaining court orders
	• Provide legal advocacy, including court accompaniment and support during legal proceedings
	• Provide crisis and ongoing counseling
	• Assist with obtaining legal benefits
	• Arrange for emergency housing, including appropriate shelters
	• Assist victims in enrolling in confidential address program, where available and eligible
	• Provide transitional housing, where available
	• Conduct batterers intervention programs, where available
	• Provide community education and professional training
Sexual Assault Programs	• Provide medical accompaniment during sexual assault examination
	• Provide legal advocacy
	• Operate 24-hour crisis line
	• Provide individual peer support and/or counseling
	• Conduct support groups
	• Provide information and referral
	• Provide self-defense programs
	• Provide community education and professional training

Staffing

Domestic violence and sexual assault advocates work with victims of abuse by providing them with information, referrals, and support during the period immediately following an abusive incident or as needed for years after. Advocates may have a variety of educational backgrounds, from high school diplomas to doctoral degrees, depending on the job specifications. The domestic violence movement encourages hiring of former victims of abuse, so many advocates work in the field because of their strong personal commitment to the issue. Domestic violence and sexual assault advocates generally work in nonprofit organizations. Some work in emergency shelters or staff 24-hour crisis lines. These services are available 24 hours a day, seven days a week. Other staff work with victims during business hours to assist them in other ways.

Ethical Principles

Safety is the highest priority for victims of domestic violence. Domestic violence and sexual assault programs operate from a grassroots perspective that originated from the concept of women helping other women with the violence in their lives. Programs use a self-help model, meaning that victims contact the program if they would like support or help. Staff members at the programs believe the victim's account of the abuse. No investigation is done to verify the victim's story. Interventions involve providing the victim with information and supporting whatever decisions the victim makes. Staff recognize that many victims feel powerless after a sexual assault or years of abuse. Restoring power over the victim's life is fundamental. Many shelter locations are at confidential locations so that the victim will have the opportunity to separate completely from the abuser. Confidentiality is paramount as a method to help enhance victim safety. Generally, domestic violence and sexual assault programs will not release any information about the victims and survivors who contact the programs without a signed release of information. Finally, advocates will stand by the victim, whatever decision she or he makes. Advocates may challenge policies, practices, or societal values that impede victim safety.

Variations

Domestic violence and sexual assault programs vary greatly throughout the United States. In some communities, domestic violence and sexual assault programs are separate. In many other communities, the programs are dual, meaning that one organization serves victims of both domestic violence and sexual assault. Some are small rural programs, with only a few staff. Other programs have more than 100 staff and run small campuses. Not all domestic violence programs offer emergency shelter. Most programs focus primarily on the needs of women, but many organizations throughout the country also provide services for men.

Although few programs offer direct services for older victims, more than 100 programs were identified that included support groups, elder advocates, and task forces (National Clearinghouse on Abuse in Later Life, 2003). Only 34 support groups specifically for older abused women were identified in a 2003 survey (Spangler & Brandl, 2003).

LONG TERM CARE OMBUDSMAN

Each state has a Long Term Care Ombudsman Program that is mandated by the federal government as a condition of receiving Older Americans Act funding. Long-term care ombudsmen act as advocates for residents of long-term care facilities (as defined by state law), regardless of the resident's age, and work to ensure that residents' rights are not violated. Ombudsmen respond to complaints from residents and, in most states, make regular visits to long-term care facilities. Some ombudsmen are paid staff, whereas others are volunteers. Their educational background and qualifications vary greatly.

ADDITIONAL AGENCIES THAT MAY OFFER USEFUL SERVICES FOR ELDER ABUSE VICTIMS

Table 5.7 is a list of agencies that may provide assistance to elder abuse victims. It is not comprehensive and serves only to illustrate the types of services and numerous agencies that may be involved in a senior victim's life. Specific services may vary according to the community.

TABLE 5.6   Primary Activities/Functions of Ombudsmen

- Advocate for residents' rights and quality care
- Educate consumers and providers
- Resolve residents' complaints
- Provide information to the public

TABLE 5.7   Primary Activities/Functions of Other Community-Based Agencies

Topic	Professionals Involved	Activities
Animals	Humane Society, Animal Control, Veterinarians	• Identify abuse • Protect and board pets • Provide medical treatment • Spay or neuter pets • Euthanize terminally ill animals
Attorney General's Office	Consumer Fraud	• Provide consumer education • Investigate allegations of consumer fraud • Litigate consumer fraud cases
Medicaid Fraud	Often in Attorney General's Office	• Investigate reports of abuse and neglect in long-term care facilities funded by Medicaid • Prosecute cases of abuse and neglect in long-term care facilities
Aging Network	Area Agencies on Aging	• Provide information about benefits • Meals on Wheels • Transportation • Tax preparation • In-home services
	Senior Centers	• Congregate meals • Socialization • Phone reassurance
Financial	Benefit Specialists	• Assist with getting benefits • Money management services • Bill-paying services that also balance checkbooks
	Social Security Representative Payees	• Payees receive a beneficiary's benefits payments and manage and spend those payments on the beneficiary's behalf

(continued)

TABLE 5.7 Primary Activities/Functions of Other Community-Based Agencies *(continued)*

Topic	Professionals Involved	Activities
	Representatives of Banking Institutions	• Identify suspicious transactions
		• Repository of documentary evidence
		• Analyze financial transactions
Mental Health	Psychiatrist and Psychologist	• Conduct mental health assessments
		• Treat mental illness
		• Initiate certification of patients for involuntary commitment and treatment
Substance Abuse		• Provide residential and out-patient treatment
		• Work with courts, probation, and parole to monitor compliance with program rules and regulations
		• Initiate certification of patients for involuntary substance abuse treatment
U.S. Citizenship and Immigration Services		• Hold and deport undocumented persons
		• Enable some victims to self-petition for the right to remain in the United States and seek citizenship
Social Workers (not APS)		• Provide individual and family counseling
Caregiver Advocates	Alzheimer's Association, etc.	• Education on disease
		• Support for caregivers

(continued)

TABLE 5.7   *(continued)*

Topic	Professionals Involved	Activities
Faith Community	Pastors, Priests, Rabbis, Church Groups, Parish Nurses, Lay Leaders	• Provide spiritual support for victims, families
		• Friendly visitors
		• Serve as guardians/representative payees
Disability Network		• Provide information on available resources and benefits
		• Advocate on behalf of persons with disabilities
		• Provide assistive devices and home modification
		• Offer retraining after disability onset
Community-/ Cultural-Specific Groups		• Social support
		• Translation services
		• Possible temporary emergency housing
Gay, Lesbian, Bisexual, Transsexual Services		• Social support
		• Possible temporary emergency housing
		• Provide crisis services and counseling
Housing		• Assisted living
		• Low-income housing
		• Home modification
		• Affordable housing resources

CONCLUSION

Victims of elder abuse, exploitation, and neglect may be served by any or all of the programs previously described. As a result, victims may encounter scores of people who ask them the same questions, provide them with confusing procedures or conflicting information, and leave them overwhelmed with options, yet still in danger. For victims to be better served, the agencies and professionals involved must understand their own and each others' roles, convey these roles clearly to the victim, maintain clear and frequent communication with each other and the victim, and coordinate their activities and services in a simple yet comprehensive manner that brings the maximum benefit to the victim as quickly and efficiently as possible.

One of the challenges of having victims involved with multiple professionals and systems is collaboration. As the previous chapters have indicated, elder abuse is a complex issue requiring a multidisciplinary response. The remainder of the book discusses the benefits and obstacles of collaboration and promising multidisciplinary practices in the field of elder abuse.

SECTION THREE

Collaboration

CHAPTER SIX

Collaborative Efforts: Benefits and Obstacles

OVERVIEW

The preceding chapters defined elder abuse and its forms. Characteristics of victims and perpetrators were explored, along with some of the many systems that may be involved in identifying and responding to elder abuse. In the ensuing chapters, the discussion includes intervention and the responses intended to improve the lives of elder abuse victims, both on the individual and societal levels. Because of the complexity of the problems faced by victims, as well as the diversity of responses required to help them, the authors believe that collaborative efforts can achieve better outcomes for seniors than individual or single-discipline responses.

Given the many professions that may be involved in identifying and intervening in incidents of abuse—whether physical or sexual abuse, financial exploitation, neglect, abandonment, emotional abuse, self-neglect, or any combination—development of comprehensive and effective responses is complex. Elder abuse is seldom a single act. More typically it is a series of actions or failures to act that cause harm to an elderly person. If responses are simply reactions to the presenting situation, the problem will not truly be addressed. If the physician simply treats a patient's dehydration without discovering that a care provider refuses to properly provide nourishment and medication to the elder, the problem will persist. If a banker stops payment on an elder's checks because of insufficient funds, but does not explore what has occurred or report what has happened, financial exploitation will continue. If law enforcement declines to arrest an elderly husband who has assaulted his wife because she is reluctant to press charges and he is her caregiver, then the abuse will continue.

HISTORICAL PERSPECTIVE

Historically, systems worked exclusively within their discipline or with a small group of related disciplines to perform their core functions. For example, law enforcement traditionally received calls for service, responded, interviewed parties, and, when appropriate, made arrests. They handed off their arrests to prosecutors, who decided whether to file a charge and, in cases where a charge was brought, managed and presented those cases in court. Although prosecutors relied on a variety of professionals from other disciplines, including physicians, bank employees, and law enforcement, to testify as witnesses, these relationships were case-specific. Similarly, physicians provided assessments and diagnoses to patients who came to them or worked with allied health care professionals and social workers to provide treatment, rehabilitative care, and discharge-planning services. Advocates assisted clients who sought out their services but, owing to the confidential nature of their relationship with their client and a prevailing philosophy of empowering clients through support and providing options that the client selected, did not seek out other disciplines to meet victims' needs.

Over time, professionals recognized that this "*silo*-like" approach had its limitations. Systemic flaws or gaps were hard to identify and repair when only one professional attempted to assess complex situations. Sometimes, systems' failures to coordinate resulted in wasted time and resources, duplication of effort, and victim/client frustration. For example, drawing on experiences in child abuse cases, young victims were forced to describe their experience to an initial responder, a follow-up investigator, a health care provider, a child protective services worker, one or more prosecutors, a judge, and finally a jury. These repetitive interviews traumatized the victim, created variations in accounts leading to questions about the child's veracity and reliability, and caused some children to be numb and flat when testifying (Bernet, 1997). In recognition of these realities, child abuse interview protocols were developed and special child interview centers were established (DeVoe & Faller, 2002). Instead of multiple interviews, a team composed of law enforcement, health care, prosecution, and child protective services conducts a single interview. One specially trained team member conducts the videotaped interview as other members watch through one-way glass and feed additional questions, if necessary. Also, child protective services staff work closely with law enforcement and may even respond jointly with them, so that case evidence can be developed while the child's living situation is assessed and decisions can be made if the child should be immediately removed to an emergency care setting. Following suit, domestic violence response teams began to partner law enforcement with a community-advocate when handling cases (Muellemen & Feighny, 1999). These collaborations were better able to meet the victim's needs for crisis intervention and law enforcement's need to collect evidence, interview witnesses, and identify criminal conduct.

In elder abuse, the recognition of the need to involve multiple disciplines has followed a similar course. Early responses tended to be undertaken by a single discipline. As it became evident that elder abuse's complexities could not be addressed comprehensively without working with others, collaborations were developed. Medical case review teams, fatality review teams, and fiduciary abuse specialist teams are examples of the some of the early collaborations that developed (Teaster & Nerenberg, 2000). Much of what developed into formal teams began as informal efforts between professionals from two or more disciplines. Each recognized the limits of their expertise and the benefits of involving others. For example, Adult Protective Services (APS) workers began to call law enforcement officers when they needed assistance gaining entry to a residence or needed protection from dangerous family members. Prosecutors worked with APS to obtain mental health assessments of victims to determine if they could give legal consent or testify. Victim witness advocates worked with community agencies to arrange emergency housing and benefits for elderly crime victims.

COLLABORATIVE AND NONCOLLABORATIVE APPROACHES TO ELDER ABUSE

Individual professionals and their systems can muster an array of interventions when working with victims and self-neglecters. These interventions are incorporated into a care or service plan. The processes or approaches to the application of interventions fall along a continuum from individual or *silo* responses to informal alliances to formal collaborations.

Unidisciplinary Silo Effect

The silo effect is seen when groups of individuals work in isolation, resulting in a single perspective on the subject and limited information about alternative approaches and resources. Working in isolation can lead to inconsistent, overlapping, and inappropriate responses and services for victims and interventions for perpetrators. If the victim and perpetrator are being seen by multiple systems working independently of each other, the participating agencies will be seen as lacking cooperation or competing, and this can result in a breakdown in communication

(Cote, 2002). For example, if a medical professional assists a daughter to become a representative payee for her mother's accounts but does not know that APS is investigating the daughter for financial exploitation of her mother, the physician's well-intentioned action may place the victim in further peril. Also, APS may conclude that the physician is uncooperative and acting in competition with them, and may hesitate to work with the physician or others at that facility. Similarly, if a domestic violence advocate is assisting an elderly client to obtain a protective order and leave an abusive relationship, and, unbeknownst to the advocate, a protective services worker has determined that the abuser is a stressed caregiver who needs respite care and assistance with his "difficult" spouse, not only will the victim be placed in harm's way, but the two workers and their systems may be acting at cross purposes. When a single discipline's response is ineffective, formal and informal collaborations afford more options and may avoid inconsistent and competing interventions.

Case Example: Margaret

Margaret, an 83-year-old woman with advanced-stage Alzheimer's disease, was brought by ambulance to a local hospital's emergency department. She was comatose and bruised all over her body from her head to the bottom of her feet. Medical staff suspected elder abuse and, in compliance with state law, reported the case to the local police department. Patrol officers interviewed some emergency department staff, took photographs of the injuries, and prepared an incident report that was forwarded to the detective unit for follow-up investigation. They were unaware of her medical history, social situation, and previous level of functioning.

The case was assigned to a detective who had little experience handling elder abuse cases. He determined that Margaret's dementia would prohibit her from ever being interviewed. He interviewed Margaret's son, Thomas, age 56, who was her caregiver, and learned that he had retired early from his job in the financial industry to care for his mother. Thomas said he loved his mother and did his best to care for her, but because of her condition and medication, she was prone to frequent falls. He believed that his mother did not receive proper care from anyone else and had removed her from a skilled nursing facility the day before her hospital admission. He said that in bringing his mother home, she fell repeatedly as he tried to assist her up a flight of stairs in their shared home. The detective believed that Thomas was sincere, cared deeply for his mother, and could not have intentionally harmed her. The detective was unaware of any additional evidence or sources of information and closed the case.

Margaret died in the hospital nearly two months later. She was never able to speak. An autopsy revealed the presence of widespread cancer and her cause of death was listed as "natural." The medical examiner was unable to link Margaret's death with her earlier beating.

A few weeks later, the local prosecutor's office was contacted by the coordinator of the elder abuse network, a group of local governmental and community-based organizations and agencies from the disciplines of health care, civil and criminal justice, protective services, domestic violence, and aging services. This network had been in existence for several years and met monthly to discuss complex cases, provide cross-training, and advocate for funding and service delivery with relevant bodies. The prosecutor's office and law enforcement agency participated on an as-needed basis.

The prosecutor was invited to the next network meeting. Also attending were representatives from Margaret's medical plan, home health care, visiting nurses program, the skilled nursing facility where Margaret stayed in the two months before her death, the public guardian's office, protective services, and others. They shared previously unknown information, including Margaret's medical condition; Thomas's involvement in her care; his suspicious behaviors as observed by visiting nurses, home health care, and skilled nursing facility staff; and their unsuccessful efforts to have him removed as her caregiver and guardian. Most important, the prosecutor learned that Thomas had removed Margaret from a skilled nursing facility against medical advice less than 24 hours before her admission to the emergency department. Because of their concerns, the skilled nursing facility had conducted a head-to-toe examination of Margaret, documenting an absence of any marks or bruises. They also provided the name of the taxi company that drove Margaret and Thomas home. Several agencies indicated that they had relevant information in their files that would be provided on receipt of subpoenas. With the additional information the criminal investigation was reactivated. With the information learned from the community agencies, critical witnesses and evidence were located. Thomas was arrested and, ultimately, a jury convicted him of elder abuse.

COLLABORATIVE APPROACHES

An elder abuse collaboration is a cooperative effort with other professionals and disciplines to best serve the needs of victims and society (Neufeldt, 1995). It consists of a small number of people with complementary skills who are committed to a common purpose, performance goals, and approach for which they hold themselves mutually accountable (Katzenbach & Smith, 1993). Their work is done by a group of people who possess individual expertise, are responsible for making individual decisions, share a common purpose, and meet together to communicate, share and consolidate knowledge, from which plans are made, future plans are influenced, and actions are determined (Brill, 1976).

In collaborations, participants commit to work together toward shared goals and agree to communicate, cooperate, and value the contributions of one another (Pfeiffer, 1998). Collaborative elder mistreatment alliances typically focus on one or more of the following: prevention, awareness, intervention, and systems review.

Collaborations take many different forms. They can be short term and formed on an ad hoc basis, or long-lasting permanent community fixtures. They can involve two, three, or more members from different disciplines. Collaborations may arise from acquaintances or friendships and may be driven by the various personalities of the members. Collaborations may come together as a result of geography or as a result of the responsibility of specific agencies to the community. Members of collaborations may meet periodically or regularly, and may operate using a structured or unstructured format.

The degree of formality of the collaboration occurs along a continuum. Some collaborations are formed on an ad hoc basis around a particular need of an agency or individual victim; there are no hard-and-fast rules or signed agreements. More formal collaborations may involve memoranda of understanding and have policies and procedures. These formal collaborations are often called teams.

Teams

Formal groups may be called teams, task forces, coordinating councils, or coalitions. There are differences between these terms, but in general all tend to operate with established procedures, guiding principles, and a common mission. For the purposes of clarity and simplicity, this book refers to all of these formal models as *teams*.

Teams addressing elder abuse typically function as either multidisciplinary or interdisciplinary units. Both types of teams pursue the same broad goals, but their differences lie in the way team members interact and how final decisions are made. In a true multidisciplinary team, each discipline provides information relevant to the team's decision; however, one person makes the ultimate decision. In contrast, in a true interdisciplinary team, each member not only provides information relevant to the decision to be made, but each participates in the decision-making process (Pfeiffer, 1998).

Multidisciplinary Team

A heart transplant team is an example of a multidisciplinary team. These teams are composed of nurses, social workers, hospital chaplains, ethicists, psychiatrists, cardiologists, and heart surgeons. Immunologists and other specialists are called in as needed to assess and intervene in one of the most medically complex lifesaving operations available today. Although the team has a variety of professionals, including multiple physicians and surgeons, all of whom provide information, there is one person, usually the transplant surgeon or the cardiologist, who has ultimate responsibility for the patient and makes the critical decisions.

Interdisciplinary Teams

A hospice or palliative care team is an example of an interdisciplinary team. In these teams, professionals from a variety of disciplines, including physicians, nurses, social workers, pharmacist, chaplains, and others gather to share information about patients and their families, including desires and needs. Decisions are made collectively, bearing in mind those needs and desires, and an intervention plan is designed. Professionals carry out the aspects of the plan according to his or her expertise and skill.

Although in the truest sense interdisciplinary teams and multidisciplinary teams are different models for decision making, these terms have often been used interchangeably, so that many interdisciplinary teams call themselves multidisciplinary teams. Many interdisciplinary teams even incorporate the term *multidisciplinary team* into their titles. Some statutes, such as those providing for information sharing, use the term *multidisciplinary teams* without reference to what kind of model best describes the team (California Welfare and Institutions Code §§ 15610.55, 15633). For purposes of clarity in this book, the term *multidisciplinary team* is used to describe both models, although the authors primarily are describing a team in which all members participate in the final decision-making process.

Informal versus Formal Collaboration

There are no precise criteria to determine how formal or informal a collaboration, including a team, may need to be. Collaborations choose to formalize procedures or to operate informally for such reasons as the preferences of participants and local or disciplinary conventions. The specific goal or goals may not require formal procedures. In some communities, disciplines may have informally worked together for years and see no reason to change successful approaches. In contrast, some collaborations must have structured policies and procedures to comply with statutes, such as information-sharing, or as requirements to receive grant funding. At minimum, collaborations with large numbers of members may require formal processes for participation. Some have chosen to formalize procedures to ensure the continuing participation of certain systems and disciplines (Teaster & Nerenberg, 2000).

TYPES OF COLLABORATIVE EFFORTS

Collaborations are formed for a variety of reasons. Some are formed to determine gaps in service. An example is a fatality review team. Others, such as coordinating councils or task forces, form to ensure that services are coordinated for community members. Some typically focus on facilities and their unique issues. These types of collaborations may focus on individuals, as well as the overall business operation of a facility or other enterprise. Some teams review and assess individual victims and, in some cases, their perpetrators to develop intervention plans, pursue legal remedies, and develop cases for court. These collaborations may be based in an institution such as a medical center, be a collaboration of experts such as a fiduciary abuse specialist team, or be a community network of aging services providers. All teams are concerned with and attempt to address victim safety, but some collaborative models specifically focus on methods to enhance victim safety, such as domestic violence response teams, including shelter workers and victims' advocates, and rapid response teams, including APS and law enforcement. Some fatality review teams may also help build cases (Teaster & Nerenberg, 2000).

ADVANTAGES OF ELDER ABUSE COLLABORATIONS

Although elder abuse cases are enormously complex and frequently force professionals to identify solutions or interventions that are least restrictive and promote victim autonomy, a multidisciplinary collaboration can muster a remarkable and unique array of resources. It is through collaboration that professionals can carry out their mandates and responsibilities to prevent gaps in services and ensure that the multiple needs of vulnerable victims are met. The advantages of a multidisciplinary approach over a single discipline's response are best understood by considering their benefits to the individual victim, the individual professional, the involved systems, and, finally, to society as a whole.

Victim Benefits

Multiple systems operating separately necessarily conduct multiple interviews and multiple investigations. With more agencies, professionals,

TABLE 6.1   Examples of the Collaboration Types

Systems Review	*Fatality Review Collaborations/Teams*

Systems Review — *Fatality Review Collaborations/Teams*
Their role is to review deaths of older persons that have resulted from or are related to elder abuse to determine what those systems might do differently to prevent similar deaths in the future. Some fatality review teams also assess deaths to recommend whether investigation and prosecution is warranted. This is the one type of team in which it is critical to have significant participation by the medical examiner or coroner. Fatality review teams generally develop and issue recommendations calling for such things as changes to agencies' policies and procedures, training of various disciplines about elder abuse, and legislative and regulatory reform. Facility review teams are a new phenomenon in the elder abuse field; there are currently eight known teams. They are located in Houston, Texas; Maine (statewide team); Orange County, California; Pima County, Arizona; Pulaski County, Arkansas; Sacramento, California; San Diego; and San Francisco. Several other states and communities are in the process of establishing teams.

Service Coordination — *Coordinated Community Response*
The Ohio Family Violence/Elder Abuse/Domestic Violence Roundtable is composed of leaders from Ohio APS, domestic violence programs, law enforcement, and the aging network. The purpose of this collaboration is to organize professionals and systems for collectively addressing elder abuse and domestic violence (Anetzberger, 2001). Family violence coordinating councils are composed of individuals or organizations with an interest in or that serve victims of family violence, with a goal of reviewing coordinating services to victims and ensuring that systems work effectively and train and educate a variety of professionals. These groups exist throughout the United States. Another example is the Oregon Elder Abuse Task Force, started in 1994 by the state attorney general.

Institutional and Facility Abuse — *Code Enforcement Team*
Its purpose is to inspect facilities where there are reported public nuisances or recurring reports of inadequate care. Representatives of regulatory and licensing agencies and protective services, such as local fire departments and law enforcement agencies, pest control authorities, building

(continued)

TABLE 6.1   Examples of the Collaboration Types *(continued)*

	inspectors, and investigators from offices of state attorneys general, city attorneys, and county counsel carry out inspections. Drawing on the expertise and authority of many officials, they conduct unannounced inspections of premises to identify dangerous, illegal, or unsanitary sites. They leverage their findings, pursue administrative and licensing actions, or may file civil or criminal lawsuits to obtain improvements, clean up problematic locations, seek changes in procedures or management, or even secure the closure of a facility. Teams may operate at the local or state level. Operation SpotCheck in Florida and Operation Guardian in California are examples.
Case-Based Teams	*Medical Case Management* The medical case management team cares for victims with complex medical needs and provides medical expertise to all team members. It usually operates within a health care system and draws on the expertise of medical specialists. Examples of medical case management teams are the collaboration between Baylor College of Medicine and Texas APS; the Vulnerable Adult Specialist Team, a collaboration of the University of California–Irvine with the Orange County APS; and the Violence Intervention Program, Adult Protection Team, collaboration of Los Angeles County and the University of Southern California Medical Center. Other medical schools around the United States have collaborated in a number of ways. These models address all forms of abuse and self-neglect (Heath et al., 2002). *Coordinated Community Agency Teams* In the coordinated community agency model, agencies have decided to collaborate on complex and confounding cases. These teams may have formed after realizing that many had previously attempted to serve the same family in multiple prior interventions. Agencies frustrated with these cases and often lacking resources bring these troubling matters to the team where a variety of community, health care, and legal services assess the situation and offer recommendations for a comprehensive response. Since community leaders from a variety of cultural groups are present, this model provides culturally competent assessments and interventions. To provide effective services while maintaining

(continued)

TABLE 6.1: *(continued)*

client confidentiality, these teams usually do not identify parties by name. Such practices are often necessitated if state laws do not authorize team members to share with the team information that is otherwise confidential. One example of a community-based model is the San Francisco, which provides case analysis and has over 50 individual agencies and organizations that participate. It is staffed and led by the Institute on Aging (formerly the Goldman Institute on Aging). Law enforcement may be part of the team, but their participation may be limited to matters with potential criminal conduct.

Fiduciary Abuse Specialist Teams
Fiduciary Abuse Specialist Teams focus primarily on developing financial exploitation cases. Teams are staffed by law enforcement, prosecutors, private and public interest attorneys, public and private conservators, bankers, securities and real estate brokers, APS workers, members of the Long-term Care Ombudsman Program, and experts in finances, insurance, care management, probate, gerontology, geriatrics, and psychiatry. The first Fiduciary Abuse Specialist Team was established in Los Angeles County in 1993 (Los Angeles County Area Agency on Aging, 2001). As the benefits of the model have been identified, other FASTs have been created so that there are teams now operating in Orange County, California; San Diego; parts of Oregon; and elsewhere. In the Oregon program, one element of the project is called "R2T2," in which analysts and retired employees of financial institutions have been recruited as volunteers to analyze evidence and assist law enforcement and prosecutors in building financial exploitation criminal cases.

Victim Safety

Domestic Violence Response Teams
These teams were formed to simultaneously investigate and build criminal cases, while at the same time meet the immediate social, safety, and psychological needs of victims in crisis, including elder domestic violence victims. The team typically has been composed of a law enforcement officer and a victim advocate from a community-based organization. The officer or deputy interviews potential witnesses, preserves and collects physical

(continued)

TABLE 6.1   Examples of the Collaboration Types *(continued)*

evidence, arranges for medical treatment for injured persons, and makes arrests when appropriate. The advocate meets privately with the victim to assure confidentiality, discusses short- and long-term needs and resources, assists with safety planning, and provides immediate support.

and organizations available to assist victims, the greater the likelihood that a member of the collaboration will be able to establish a relationship of trust. Many victims have been bounced from one agency to another or are seen by many agencies simultaneously (Heisler & Quinn, 2002). Collaboration among those agencies can reduce duplication of work and reduce the need for victims to retell what is often personal and uncomfortable information to recount. Coordinated multidisciplinary interview procedures and investigation protocols reduce the need for the repetition. From the victim's perspective, collaborative responses have access to more information than any individual, thereby increasing the likelihood of more effective decision making (Nerenberg, 2003).

With more systems able to recognize and respond to victims, earlier detection of problems is possible. For example, medical conditions may be identified sooner, leading to prompt treatment and improved quality and longevity of life. Other procedures also can be streamlined leading to more prompt interventions. Elder abuse collaborations, including teams, are better able to address victims' multiple needs, thereby developing a more comprehensive intervention plan. Victims may find it easier to arrive at an acceptable resolution when decisions are based on the varied resources available through multiple systems.

Member Benefits

Collaborative members benefit from increased knowledge of, and access to, available options, joint work effort, and streamlined tasks. Procedures may lead to earlier and quicker interventions, including those designed to preserve remaining assets and recover those no longer in the elder's possession but not yet dissipated. Professionals are better able to understand other disciplines, including their roles and limitations, and can support each other when difficult decisions must be made, such as the appropriateness of a conservatorship or guardianship or restrictive placement (Francis & Young, 1992). Individual members can enhance their own knowledge base, and inform and educate other participants about the principles and guidelines relevant to their own discipline. Collaborations can promote coordination between disciplines by clarifying each agency's policies, procedures, and roles, and educating one another about their "culture," strategies, resources, and approaches (Nerenberg, 1995, 2003). Teamwork itself can help reduce burnout, territorial disputes, and turnover and workload disparities, as the distribution of work on a case is coordinated (Heisler & Quinn, 2002; Nerenberg 1995).

System Benefits

With reductions in duplication of services, systems benefit from cost savings. Systems also gain when utilizing the informed opinions of collaborating partners during case evaluations and discussions. Expert opinion can lead to focused investigations and better conclusions, with less time and dollars spent on insignificant or unrelated issues. Because of established relationships and protocols, various organizational members will enjoy increased safety when law enforcement partners jointly participate in making house calls. In addition, the involvement of multiple agencies makes it more difficult for perpetrators to retaliate against any one organization (Quinn & Heisler, 2002).

Collaboration may lead to improved evidence collection. For example, in the criminal justice system, team participation with the historically difficult tasks of obtaining documentation, assessing evidence, identifying available witnesses, and locating critical expertise promotes successful prosecution. In the medical arena, physicians can make more accurate diagnoses and develop intervention plans with information from victims' advocates or protective service workers. Protective service workers can better craft service plans and address victim safety by drawing on the expertise of all team members, including aging services organizations, medical and mental health professionals, domestic violence, sexual assault and other advocates, law enforcement and prosecution officials, civil lawyers, and others.

Societal Benefits

Society benefits from reduced recidivism, more effective and appropriate interventions, and improved quality of life for victims. Collaborations that involve the criminal justice system can provide protection to the public through separation of victims from offenders, application of various sanctions including arrest, prosecution and punishment, and rehabilitation. The inclusion of medical professionals increases the health profile of victims and sometimes offenders, and can prevent repeated hospitalization and preserve health care resources. Involvement of civil law practitioners may better protect victims and their assets. Domestic violence, sexual assault, and other advocates can educate victims and their families, inform about or link them to resources and legal remedies and assistance, provide longer-term support, and assist with development of safety plans.

RECOGNIZING AND OVERCOMING OBSTACLES

This section identifies barriers and obstacles to collaboration faced by many collaborative efforts and suggests approaches to help avoid these problems.

> It is widely thought that effective teams are harmonious and unified. Not so. Excessive harmony can encourage intellectual dishonesty. Challenge, openness, and veracity among team members are essential characteristic[s] of successful teams. (Francis & Young, 1992, p. 10)

Sadly, experience has taught that obstacles are not unusual. And such challenges to cooperation and coordination can significantly reduce the effectiveness of the responding systems (Blakely & Dolon, 1991; Dolon & Hendricks, 1989). "Interagency coordination is like international diplomacy. It requires negotiation, personal communication, attention to the interests and constraints of participants, and procedures for resolving disputes" (Hofford & Harrell, 1995, p. 219). Challenges can include differing professional visions and philosophies; historical distrust and poor prior interactions; definitions and understanding about elder abuse; setting; the use of professional jargon; legal requirements and limitations; and roles, personality conflicts, and challenges to team processes, including conflicts of interest. Issues can be personal, systemic, or both.

PROFESSIONAL VISIONS AND PHILOSOPHIES

Interdisciplinary conflicts may arise from legitimate differences in professional philosophy, ethics, and perspective. Some conflicts relate to the historical development of a social movement. For example, early elder abuse theory focused on the demands of caregiving. The domestic violence movement identified abuse as grounded in societal views of patriarchy and the abuser's need to exercise power and control over the relationship. As the realization has grown that many acts of elder abuse are also acts domestic violence, the two movements that had operated quite separately have begun to attempt to collaborate. These efforts have not always succeeded or been without conflict. There have been disputes over development of age-appropriate services and the extent of the applicability of domestic violence dynamics to elder abuse (Nerenberg, 2000a). Domestic violence laws that may urge or even mandate arrest, minimum periods of custody, and temporary separation of the parties may not be acceptable to elder abuse professionals who are more used to picking and choosing remedies and responses on a more individualized basis (Nerenberg, 2000a).

Advocates and APS embrace principles of client autonomy and interventions that place the least limitation on the client while supporting the victim's desires and preferences. These values and core principles are in conflict with systems such as the criminal justice system that focuses less on the victim's desires and more on protecting the public and holding offenders accountable. Legislatures increasingly have criminalized acts of elder abuse, and states have enacted special statutes and mandated particular responses by law enforcement. Reporting laws in many states mandate that protective services workers and other professionals report certain acts of suspected elder abuse to law enforcement, even against client wishes. Laws and principles of protective services may well conflict. "The criminalizing of elder abuse may ... present conflicts for social service workers, who view their role as advocates charged with carrying out their clients' wishes.... (W)orkers may be faced with balancing their professional commitments against their civic responsibility" (Nerenberg, 2000a, p. 90). Because collaborative efforts are undertaken by practitioners from many professions, members' decisions and thought processes necessarily will be informed by their professional standards of practice, ethics, and guiding principles. As previously noted, these perspectives may well be antagonistic and inconsistent. For example, the physician may favor placement of the elderly patient in a nursing home because of her frail medical condition; the protective services worker may feel that remaining at home is more appropriate, as it is a less restrictive environment; the elder may articulate her desire to remain in home and be cared for by her son; and law enforcement may believe arrest and incarceration of the son are appropriate. If a team or other collaboration makes its decisions based on broadly based agreement, arriving at consensus on an acceptable intervention plan can be complicated by these conflicts. And if left unaddressed, these conflicts may well undermine the partners' confidence in the process and ultimately fail to protect the at-risk elder for whom the effort is undertaken. Addressing such professional differences requires acknowledging that differences exist; placing importance on drawing from various perspectives in problem solving; and ensuring equality of contributions among professionals in facilitating assessment and intervention. These solutions require a commitment to the group process and a willingness to communicate (Schimer & Anetzberger, 1999).

CHALLENGES RELATING TO HISTORICAL DISTRUST AND POOR PRIOR INTERACTIONS

As more systems came to respond to elder abuse matters, historical tensions between disciplines and their attitudes about the goals, motives, and validity of other approaches have made collaboration more difficult. Historically, law enforcement and protective services have not worked well together. Adult Protective Services typically lacked confidence in law enforcement, even when they knew of criminal conduct, and law enforcement seldom referred cases to protective services (Blakely & Dolon, 2000). Other studies showed that victim assistance programs did not make serving elderly victims an agency priority, and few agencies had experience actually assisting elderly crime victims. Many times these shortcomings were due to lack of training (Blakely & Dolon, 2000). Victim services rarely had provided APS with information about their services and, in turn, protective services had seldom provided training to advocates. In short, they each went "their own separate ways, rather than provide each other with mutual support" (Blakely & Dolon, 2000, p. 77). The picture was no better in terms of cooperation between protective services and prosecutors' offices. Criminal justice system professionals and protective services workers have differing perceptions about each other (Harshbarger, 1989).

> Historically, there has been a great deal of mistrust between the social service and criminal justice systems. While the social service system's approach is viewed as "helping" or "caring" to alleviate abuse, neglect, and exploitation, the criminal justice system's intervention is perceived as punitive and fault-finding. As a result, social workers have been reluctant to refer cases to the criminal justice system for fear that someone, usually the elder's caregiver, will be put in jail, the family will be destroyed, and the social worker's relationship with the family will be permanently damaged. Too often this reluctance translated into practice, and meant that the social service professional tried to patch together "families" that existed in name only, while the abusive behavior continued or escalated to the point where serious injury or even death was threatened. It was only at that crisis point that the criminal justice system was notified, after the damage had been done and the injury inflicted. Yet, even at this point, the criminal justice system's intervention was not always in the best interest of the victim. (Reulbach & Tewksbury, 1994, pp. 9–10)

Frustrating responses from systems have added to the difficulty of building collaborations. For example, in a study by Blakely and Dolon (2000), APS workers identified prosecution of perpetrators as one of the most important functions provided by the criminal justice system in elder abuse cases. At the same time, protective services workers named prosecution as the most difficult service to obtain from criminal justice professionals, citing "lack of interest or cooperation from prosecutors in bringing cases of elder abuse to court" (Blakely & Dolan, 2000, p. 87). Dolon and Hendricks (1989) found that police did not rank social service providers as useful, but social workers rated police as useful in addressing elder abuse cases. Similarly, a U.S. General Accounting Office national study, conducted in 1991, found that lack of positive relationships among agencies impeded successful implementation of the state's APS law (U.S. General Accounting Office, 1991). Balaswamy (2002) studied the relationship between APS and community services serving elder abuse clients. There was agreement that

> interagency coordination and collaboration are vital to the implementation of the APS law and creation of effective response systems. Specifically, the cooperation of various agency professionals and paraprofessionals who come into contact with the elderly play a critical role in the identification, assessment, and intervention in cases of elder maltreatment (Balaswamy, 2002, p. 2).

Nonetheless, these key participants had failed to develop collaborative and cooperative working agreements and relationships, resulting in scarcity of needed services to victims and their caregivers. Occupational groups from cooperating agencies lacked clarity regarding each other's roles and skills, leading to frustration among professionals who work together and, ultimately, noncooperation in the future.

Lack of agreement on intervention strategies by occupational groups was an additional barrier to cooperation, along with training deficiencies, lack of communication across disciplines, excessive workloads, ageism, monetary limitations, and disinterest. When agencies mandated to receive and act on information are perceived to disregard information from community agencies as a matter of course, there is reluctance to refer or report abuse to them.

A study of disagreements between APS and community agencies serving elder abuse victims found those differences related to the way they handled reported cases, appropriateness of certain interventions, and roles and functions of agencies processing cases. Many of these disagreements flowed from a lack of understanding of the APS law and its limits, including sharing of confidential information, and lack of clarity on roles and functions of agencies in processing cases. Adult Protective Services believed that because community agencies were unclear about their roles and governing principles, they pressured APS to investigate and intervene in inappropriate cases (Balaswamy, 2002).

These disputes also arise in institutional abuse matters. In a study of long term care ombudsmen, nursing home directors, and police chiefs, Payne (2001) found that ombudsmen have difficulty gaining respect and support from other professionals and that these difficulties are barriers to handling abuse cases. Payne urged that cooperation between disciplines be seen as the ideal response, not the occasional one. The failure to work cooperatively leads to the revictimization of the elder because the process failed to meet his or her needs. "These barriers can be confronted through multidisciplinary training, cooperation, and open communication" (Payne, 2001, p. 74).

CHALLENGES RELATING TO DEFINITION AND UNDERSTANDING OF ELDER ABUSE

Different disciplines define elder abuse according to what they have been taught, public perception, and their own experiences. These bases, whether accurate or not, form the framework for their work. Dolon and Hendricks (1989) surveyed social workers and police officers about their views of family conflict and their perceptions of each other. The study concluded that police officers believed that the issue of family conflict is more important than social workers did. In contrast, social workers viewed physical and financial dependency, mental health, and lack of resources as more important than law enforcement did. Also, there are great differences in how law enforcement and nursing home professionals define elder abuse. For example, nursing home professionals use an ethical-based definition, but law enforcement uses legalistic terms. That means that nursing home directors analyze abuse and neglect as a violation of an individual's rights, whereas law enforcement analyzes abuse in terms of a violation of the law (Payne, Berg, & Byars, 1999; Payne, 2001).

Payne (2001) found that when comparing nursing home directors, long term care ombudsmen, and police chiefs, nursing home directors were more likely to blame victims for the abuse than the other two groups. Males in all disciplines were more likely than their female counterparts to blame victims, and none agreed on the extent of elder abuse in nursing homes. In addition, they did not agree on the appropriate role of the criminal justice system in addressing abuse. These differences make collaboration difficult. If professionals are ill-informed about the extent of victimization and the underlying dynamics, appropriate interventions will be hard to develop. If a collaborating partner believes that abuse is caused by victim behavior, then interventions may focus on supporting the abuser, not making the actual victim safe. If parties are misinformed about the extent of abuse in facilities or any other setting, their analysis of the underlying problem and recommendation for an intervention may be erroneous.

Problems of misinformation and lack of information can be addressed successfully through training and education on the dynamics of abuse, current research on incidence and prevalence, and philosophical differences that can hinder cooperation and collaboration (Payne, 2001). Also, providing opportunities to work together, sharing joint efforts, and learning from successful collaborations in other communities will build trust and an awareness of the contribution other disciplines can offer.

CHALLENGES RELATING TO SETTING

Personal biases of professionals affect the selection of interventions. Biases arise from professional orientation and regional differences, including whether the professional works in an urban or rural setting. Schimer and Anetzberger (1999) studied how such differences affect decisions to pursue guardianship and civil commitment in marginal cases. They found substantial differences in how urban professionals relate to elderly clients, assess their needs, and use least restrictive alternatives. Urban professionals tend to use more formal and methodical assessment tools and interventions. They draw from service networks "rich" in resources and have a formal relationship with clients who are typically strangers. There is less tolerance for noncompliance, and restrictive legal interventions are used only when all less restrictive alternatives have been tried and failed. In contrast, rural professionals assess clients through interviews and clinical examination, relying to a lesser extent on formal assessments. Because of the relative lack of resources, they tend to cooperate more with other service providers to develop flexible and inventive interventions. They often know their clients personally and monitor them informally. There is considerable tolerance for noncompliance. They intervene formally only in crises and use legal interventions in those instances to "buy time" for service coordination. When professionals from urban and rural settings work together on behalf of a client, these differences can be barriers to arriving at consensus on deciding when to act and what interventions will be used.

Solutions to addressing such professional differences in an interdisciplinary context include acknowledging that differences exist; placing importance on drawing from various perspectives in problem solving; and ensuring equality of contributions among professionals in facilitating assessment and intervention. These solutions require a commitment to the group process and a willingness to communicate (Schimer & Anetzberger, 1999).

Use of Professional Jargon

Each discipline has a highly developed and specialized professional lexicon that conveys complex and comprehensive information in a quick and efficient way. Unfortunately, this special language is not likely to be understood by everyone on the team. Each member must be able to communicate information not only within his or her own discipline but to other members of the team for whom special terms will not be fully grasped. In fact, those terms may be confusing or divisive, and the efforts to treat all members as equally important will be undermined. The outcome can be resentment by those disciplines that are unfamiliar with that terminology. For example, the medical professionals on a hospital-based case management team were pleased to have APS workers in their group. With time together, and several case "successes," the medical professionals forgot that APS members were not familiar with their medical language, and they increased their use of technical terms without explaining their meaning. The medical team generated reports that were suitable for hospital charts, but too technical for some members to interpret. Team members who were not health care professionals became frustrated and resentful. The problem came to light during a later evaluation. It was resolved by having the medical team write its evaluations in layperson's terms so that all the members could receive and use the information.

The preceding example is not to suggest that some technical language or jargon is never appropriate. When such terminology is used, however, it must be defined so that the subtle meanings are fully conveyed. As an example, in the course of a case conference a physician stated, "fluid extravasated into the patient's lungs." Depending on the particular case, team members may simply need to know that the patient had fluid leaking into her lungs and that medical intervention was undertaken. If the issues are not just the patient's medical condition, but whether that condition was the result of criminal conduct and whether sufficient evidence exists to charge someone with starving the patient and, ultimately, causing her death, then the team needs additional information. In this latter situation, the team will need to know that "extravasation" is a leakage from the blood or lymph vessels and can be caused by severe malnutrition that, in the context of this review, supports a conclusion that criminal neglect, starvation, and, ultimately, homicide had been committed.

As another example, APS refers to the victim as a "client," a doctor uses the term "patient," and prosecutors and law enforcement use the term "victim," "alleged victim," or "complaining witness." The offender might be referred to as the "alleged perpetrator," "involved party," "suspect," "family member," "caregiver," "arrestee," or "criminal defendant." The same abusive act may be called an "allegation," "maltreatment," "mistreatment," "abuse," a "crime," "battery," "assault," or a "felony."

When communication must be precise and fully understood by everyone, professionals must know and use that other system's terminology or face the possibility of gross miscommunication. For example, when seeking help from law enforcement, social workers may need to use meaningful terminology such as "assault," "theft," or "rape" to get assistance, instead of the more familiar social work term "mistreatment." Law enforcement and prosecutors assess information in terms of crime elements and, unless presented with information that meets those elements, may be unable to take formal action. Medical professionals analyze presenting conditions in terms of diagnostic criteria supported by extensive literature.

If the purpose of the collaboration is to evaluate cases or situations, sufficient information presented in widely understood language must be used so that each involved discipline can assess and craft its role in developing an effective response (Thomas & Heisler, 1999). Collaborations are best served when language differences are anticipated and, to the extent possible, members agree to use accepted definitions. Early and ongoing cross-training may be critical to expanding understanding of terminology.

CHALLENGES RELATED TO LEGAL REQUIREMENTS AND LIMITATIONS

Because sharing of information is critical to effective collaboration, statutes limiting its sharing can pose enormous problems. A clear understanding of legal requirements addressing confidentiality and information-sharing may reduce frustration. For example, community-based advocates may be prohibited from sharing information without client consent. Family physicians may be prohibited from providing medical history or diagnosis without patient consent or court order. Law enforcement is often prohibited from sharing a suspect's prior criminal history or disclosing a particular victim's identity. Mental health and substance abuse providers are prohibited from discussing most information about an individual's participation and progress in a program. Adult Protective Services's records are also confidential and disclosure is severely restricted. The long-term care ombudsman representative is prohibited in most situations under federal law from reporting suspected elder abuse to authorities without client consent, a requirement that is especially difficult to comply with in situations in which the client lacks capacity to give consent. Even when exceptions apply, the identity of the reporting party usually remains confidential. Being mindful of what certain members may be prohibited from disclosing, care should be taken in deciding on the purpose of the collaboration and selecting multidisciplinary partners. If existing laws truly impede effectiveness, then professionals may need to consider pursuing legislative changes that enable greater information-sharing among professionals, and organizations may need to reconsider their membership or restrict how they conduct case review.

Also, agency policies, if not fully understood by every team member, can become obstacles when one member's refusal to act is viewed as lack of cooperation or refusal to do assigned duties. For example, patients being treated by a medical case management team that operated within a health care system were required to obtain an identification card before care was delivered. After an APS referral to the team, the medical social worker asked the APS worker to obtain a hospital identification card for his client. The APS worker resisted doing this, believing that the medical social worker easily could, and should, obtain the card. Each organization thought that the other was not doing its job, which led to resentment. Discussion revealed that the hospital viewed the issue as one of conflict of interest, and its policy prohibited the medical social worker from obtaining identification cards for APS clients. This discussion revealed another issue: team members did not know the difference between the role of the APS worker and the medical social worker. The team resolved this confusion by creating guidelines that clarified the roles.

Currently, these and other limitations have led some multidisciplinary collaborations to not discuss certain case specifics and refer to parties by initials or pseudonyms when conducting case reviews. Other groups have delayed initiation of case reviews until they helped change laws to permit information sharing. Some groups have limited their membership to municipal agencies that conduct case reviews under the umbrella of their shared representation by the city attorney or county counsel. Finally, when confidentiality laws prevented information sharing by certain groups in a community-wide multidisciplinary team, some courts have conducted fatality reviews of their own system's handling of a matter by convening a variety of professionals who were under the court's jurisdiction, such as court clerks, judicial officers, evaluators, mediators, and court investigators.

CHALLENGES RELATING TO ROLES

Because multidisciplinary efforts draw members from many professions, each participant's decisions and thought processes will be informed by his or her professional standards of practice, ethics, and guiding principles. These professional perspectives may well be antagonistic and inconsistent with those of other disciplines. Arriving at consensus can be complicated by these conflicts.

Some members may feel their roles are less valued than others. When professionals have advanced educational degrees and have status and authority within a large organization, less formally educated but highly and uniquely experienced professionals may feel marginalized. Some may have trained in or come from systems in which other disciplines are viewed with distrust or hostility. For example, not everyone working with elderly victims of abuse feels that the arrest of a family member perpetrator or involuntary placement of a victim or patient in a facility is appropriate. Not everyone agrees that self-determination and empowerment should prevail over a victim's safety and welfare. Variations in professional focus can be misunderstood as incompetence, disinterest, or unwillingness to be a "team player."

Some professionals focus exclusively on responding in the short-term or crisis situation; other disciplines provide both emergency and chronic care. The response of some professionals is designed to intervene around an event or situation. Other disciplines focus on enduring situations, prevention of future events, and meeting continuing care needs. Adult Protective Services and law enforcement are mandated to provide short-term responses, usually leaving chronic or ongoing service needs to others, such as victim advocates, case managers, and health care professionals. Some disciplines have independent authority to act with or without the victim's consent; others can act only in conformity with the wishes of a competent victim. If the victim has capacity, APS can only offer services, not impose them. A civil attorney acting on behalf of a competent client generally must follow the victim's directives. A physician, at least in certain circumstances, is obligated to act in the patient's best interests, even if it is against the patient's apparent wishes. For example, if a person's medical condition may be impairing his or her ability to think clearly and weigh information, and where no advance directive has been executed, generally the physician must act to preserve life. The prosecutor, the lawyer for the community or the state rather than for an individual victim, makes decisions based on the strength of the evidence, the ability to prove the case beyond a reasonable doubt, and the danger a defendant poses to the community. In weighing those considerations, the prosecutor may well prosecute over the victim's objection (Heisler & Quinn, 2002).

These differences can lead to significant barriers if not recognized by the collaborating partners. Professional mandates may require one or more members to act even if the rest of the partners disagree. Conversely, some members may feel their discipline is prohibited from acting in conformity with the recommendations of others, or may be concerned about potential liability if they participate in a particular course of action. For example, law enforcement may be required to advise a suspected perpetrator of his or her Miranda rights before conducting certain interviews. Notwithstanding confidentiality within a multidisciplinary team meeting, prosecutors may learn information during a case review that must be provided to the defense if a criminal case is filed.

These kinds of conflicts promote careful consideration of all options and the avoidance of formulaic decision making. The negotiation between professionals serves as a check-and-balance mechanism designed to develop an appropriate ethical case solution, one that ultimately best addresses the victim's needs and desires. It forces collaborative partners to be more innovative when crafting solutions. For example, in one case, the key component of the physician's recommendation that the patient be moved from her home was the need for supervised administration of life-sustaining medication. Adult Protective Services disagreed with the placement and instead urged that she be allowed to remain in her home because they believed it was the least restrictive environment and represented the victim's desires. The partners struggled to find a solution that was satisfactory to everyone and ultimately agreed to a case plan that allowed the woman to remain at home once APS identified a retired nurse in the neighborhood who was willing to administer the needed medications.

CHALLENGES RELATED TO PERSONALITY CONFLICTS

From time to time some professionals, whether working informally with other disciplines or within formalized teams, may appear difficult to work with or seem unable to collaborate. Some difficulties may flow from legitimate professional differences of approach, philosophy, and ethics. If professionals lack experience working across disciplines or within a team, reviewing the goals of collaboration may be helpful. Learning about other disciplines and the limits of their training, knowledge, resources, and the deliberative process also may improve cooperation. Working on hypothetical cases to develop trust, experience, and knowledge also can be valuable. Within formalized teams, facilitators and other members may need to work with individual members to identify and validate their particular expertise. In a few cases, none of these approaches will succeed. In such instances, that member's resignation or withdrawal from a team or collaborative effort may ultimately best serve the individual patient, victim, or client, as well as the other professionals' work.

ADDITIONAL CHALLENGES FOR FORMALIZED TEAMS

No matter how carefully a team is formed, or how thoughtfully developed and formalized its procedures are, there is little that can inoculate against all obstacles. The team's formative stage may run smoothly because members are often excited about the prospect of an improved response and collaboration with other disciplines. Sometimes conflict emerges when members begin to deliberate on cases. A clash of personalities or the addition of new members may lead to new problems. Obstacles may arise at any time and, if not addressed and resolved, may lead to the ultimate disintegration of the team.

All of the challenges identified previously can as easily arise within a formal team effort as within a more informal collaboration. In addition, some challenges arise because there is a team. These potential obstacles can be categorized as team membership issues, professional interdisciplinary differences, conflicts of interest, deviation from established processes, and maintenance and sustainability of the team. Some obstacles fit into multiple categories and some arise from sources external to the team.

TEAM MEMBER OBSTACLES

Examples of team membership obstacles include lack of participation from critical disciplines, lack of clarity as to the level of required participation, personality clashes within the team, and inadequate team staffing, as exemplified by a lack of team leadership, meeting facilitation skills, and administrative support. Members may face competing demands for their time or geographical barriers where there are considerable distances between offices and meeting sites. In metropolitan areas, there may be multiple law enforcement agencies serving the population. Deciding which one or ones should serve on the team can be difficult (Nerenberg, 2003). Possible solutions may include recruiting members from missing disciplines or agencies. If professionals currently working in the field are not available to serve, then recruiting retired professionals, such as law enforcement, financial planners and managers, stockbrokers, bankers, judges, and accountants, may provide the needed expertise. Community leaders may also be willing to assist the team in recruiting particular professionals, representatives of regulatory and licensing agencies, and services for persons with disabilities. Engaging the media and interesting them in writing and televising information about the team may also help in the recruitment of needed disciplines.

Team Member Roles

Clarifying roles and expectations can be accomplished by creating clear and comprehensive memoranda of understanding that delineate team expectations. Handbooks describing team roles, policies, and principles can be created and disseminated (Los Angeles County Area Agency on Aging, 2001). Administrative support can be obtained by identifying a provider or by agreement of existing members to share that responsibility on a rotating basis. Initial leadership may be provided by the organization making the effort to develop the team. Eventually the group should address the issue of who "leads" as part of the protocol. Smaller, less formal arrangements may not even need a formal leader. If a team leader lacks critical facilitation skills, another member with the needed skills can conduct case reviews. Alternatively, this expertise can be added to the team through training or the addition of a qualified person to act as the team's facilitator.

Competition for recognition and related "political" issues can be devastating to the team unless addressed. Everyone's personal and agency contributions should be recognized for their work toward improving the lives of elderly abuse and neglect victims. Authoring publications and press releases describing the work, accomplishments, and participants of the team will reduce competition. Also, selecting team leaders from a variety of disciplines will demonstrate the equal importance of each (Hofford & Harell, 1995).

Other obstacles include poor communication among team members and competition for recognition. Communication can be improved by recognizing the contribution of every member and providing clear case-presentation guidelines so that everyone understands the process.

Conflicts of Interest

Some teams have private professionals as members. Although self-employed persons can provide considerable expertise, it is important that teams have policies describing what members can and cannot do with the information they learn as part of the team. Nerenberg (2003) described some of the conflicts that have arisen when individuals have used the team mailing lists or case information to solicit clients or other employment. Also, team members, whether employed by agencies or private businesses, should not use the team as a means of forcing a member to accept a client who is ineligible for their services.

DEVIATION FROM ACCEPTED PROCEDURES

Teams will need to have the flexibility to deviate from prescribed processes, but changes that are contrary to basic goals and tested procedures may lead to roadblocks. For example, failure to follow the accepted methods for presenting cases may result in some members feeling excluded from the process. Failure to meet at regularly scheduled dates and times may result in excessive absenteeism. Failure to train and orient new team members may lead to role confusion and decreased team efficiency. Failure to continuously update and deliver training may result in use of improper procedures and create liability. For example, certain sharing of confidential victim medical records may now violate the Health Insurance Portability and Accountability Act, a federal law that was enacted to prevent disclosure of confidential patient information. Improper sharing of information or discussing privileged and confidential information outside the team may create civil or criminal liability. Adherence to existing procedures and policies helps avoid these types of problems.

LONG-TERM TEAM SUSTAINABILITY

It is easy to overlook long-term maintenance of the team. There is excitement and anticipation in the formation and work stages. There is enthusiasm for case conferencing and problem solving. But if the focus is exclusively on current issues, then longer term issues of sustainability may be overlooked to the detriment of the team. The effort will fail and the collaboration will falter. Obstacles to a team's organizational health include lack of funding, burnout, absenteeism, a shortage of cases, turnover of members, excessive caseloads, and loss of focus (Nerenberg, 2000c). In addition, a change in leadership or commitment to the team effort within the participating entities can also derail efforts.

Solutions to securing funding include convincing one of the participating agencies to provide staffing from within its ranks or to seek permanent funding within its own budget process. Alternatively, the team may need to employ fundraisers or grant writers to secure long-term funding from organizations or foundations. Excessive caseloads may require that the agency clarify its commitment to participating on the team. Burnout may be manifested by absenteeism and may be addressed by changing a particular member's assignment on the team, rotating participants off the team, or increasing the recognition of the individual's work. It may also result from that member's lack of authority or visibility within his or her agency. If the team needs a person with actual authority, the leadership may need to contact the agency head and educate him or her about the role and needs of the team and the accomplishments of the serving member. If only a change in that agency's membership will meet the team's needs, then it may be important to seek the designation and participation of a different person to serve.

A shortage of cases can be addressed by soliciting members to bring more cases to the team, expanding the team so that more agencies are able to present cases, or changing review criteria so that more cases are eligible for review.

CONCLUSION

This chapter described the advantages of collaborative responses as compared to traditional case management efforts by a single professional. Various types of collaborations and their benefits to society, victims, and participants have been highlighted. Potential obstacles and ways to overcome them have been identified. The focus now shifts to building a collaborative response and developing effective procedures. In the next several chapters the process for developing collaborations, including teams, and conducting their work are discussed.

CHAPTER SEVEN

Effective Interventions and Informal Collaborations

OVERVIEW

When an elder abuse case is reported, numerous professionals become involved in the lives of the victim and the perpetrator. Different systems respond, offering a variety of remedies to address the problem, including strategies to enhance victim safety and to hold the offender accountable. Because of the number of professionals involved, some form of collaboration is beneficial. In some communities, the response is an informal collaboration among key agencies working on the same case. In other communities, formalized teams have been developed. Chapters 9 and 10 discuss formalized teams. This chapter explores situations in which professionals respond to elder abuse cases and work together informally using a multidisciplinary approach. Composites of cases are presented to illustrate remedies from various systems and the need for collaboration, even when formalized teams have not been created. Key components of effective interventions and collaborations, as well as guiding principles, are discussed.

INFORMAL MULTIDISCIPLINARY RESPONSES

Informal collaborative efforts develop for a variety of reasons. Several professionals often begin talking about their frustration with the community's response to elder victims. These committed individuals look for opportunities to work together to improve their responses to older victims. For example, a law enforcement officer might accompany an Adult Protective Services (APS) worker to a home where the abuser is refusing to allow an interview with the victim. After working together on several cases, the law enforcement officer and the APS worker may begin to discuss or to co-investigate additional cases. The APS worker may use her social work skills to elicit information without a subpoena. The law enforcement officer may call APS on a more frequent basis about possible self-neglect and abuse cases.

Numerous examples of informal collaborations exist. APS and domestic violence advocates may co-facilitate support groups or conduct home visits together. Law enforcement can work with health care providers to obtain medical information necessary to make decisions about whether to bring a case to the prosecutors. Advocates, APS, or health care providers can serve as expert witnesses for prosecutors. Advocates and attorneys can work together with victims to provide remedies through the civil justice system. This collaborative work in the field is crucial to the success of elder abuse interventions. The following case illustrates intervention strategies from various disciplines and an informal collaborative working relationship.

CASE 1: EMOTIONAL AND PHYSICAL ABUSE AND FINANCIAL EXPLOITATION

Bertha Weeks, age 90, and her 68-year-old daughter Joan were being physically and emotionally abused by Sandy, Joan's 35-year-old daughter who lived with them. The two elderly women were afraid of Sandy. She was verbally abusive and had hit her mother several times. She had also threatened to hit Bertha, who was very frail. Sandy forged checks on her mother's account. She brought home strange men, with whom she had sex. Some of the men had stolen Bertha's and Joan's belongings.

When the police were called, Sandy was able to convince them that everything was fine. She claimed that Bertha was "senile" and that Joan was mentally ill, so neither could be believed.

Both Bertha and Joan were inarticulate when interviewed by the police. Bertha did not appear to understand the questions and Joan was silent.

After the police left, Sandy screamed at the two women. She threatened to "put them in a home" and to kill them. The two women discussed suicide because they believed that no one would protect them from Sandy.

Multidisciplinary Response

Law Enforcement

Frustrated with their inability to communicate with either Bertha or Joan, and suspecting that something was wrong, the law enforcement officers reported the situation to APS. Following their criminal investigation, Sandy was charged with assault, elder abuse, and theft. Joan's bruises were photographed and used at Sandy's trial.

Adult Protective Services

Two APS workers visited the home accompanied by law enforcement. While law enforcement officers took Sandy into another room to interview her, the workers separated Bertha and Joan and interviewed them individually. The worker interviewing Bertha noted that she was emaciated, very frail, and had a severe hearing impairment. The worker was able to communicate with Bertha to the extent that she agreed to go to the hospital for an evaluation. Meanwhile, the second worker encouraged Joan to tell her what was going on. Reluctantly, Joan admitted that she and her mother were afraid of Sandy. She said that Sandy had assaulted her on many occasions and that money was missing from her checking account. The APS worker immediately gave this information to the law enforcement officers, who then established sufficient probable cause to arrest Sandy. Bertha and Joan were taken to the hospital for evaluation.

Medical

The geriatrician found that Bertha suffered from mild dementia, malnourishment, severe hearing loss, osteoporosis, and arthritis. In addition, Bertha had suffered several strokes. Joan was also malnourished and had numerous bruises on her face, back, and arms that were in various stages of healing. Both women were very depressed.

Bertha and Joan were given food supplements. Bertha was provided with a hearing aid and medication. Both women were given antidepressants and mental health services.

Victim Advocate

While Sandy was out of prison on bail and awaiting trial, a victim advocate assisted Bertha and Joan in getting a restraining order to keep Sandy away from them and helped them through the court process. The advocate found an appropriate shelter for the two women, so that Sandy would not find them.

Prosecution

Sandy was found guilty of forgery, theft, and assault on an elderly person and sentenced to four years in jail. Law enforcement was not successful in identifying the men who had stolen Bertha and Joan's possessions, so no charges were filed against them.

After Sandy's sentencing, Bertha and Joan agreed to move together into an assisted living facility. Now that she was able to hear again, Bertha participated enthusiastically in social interaction. And Joan, who was no longer depressed, became active once again in her church community.

EFFECTIVE INTERVENTIONS THROUGH COLLABORATION

As illustrated in the previous case, numerous professionals encountered the victims and the offender. By working together, they enhanced victim safety and shared resources and knowledge. Effective collaboration requires a common understanding of the needs of victims and appropriate intervention strategies. A comprehensive intervention generally focuses on (1) safety, (2) health, (3) functional status including capacity, (4) legal status, (5) financial situation, and (6) social situation.

Figure 7.1 illustrates the relevant aspects or central life domains. Although many of these are pertinent to persons of any age, issues such as social situation, including support and functional status, come more sharply into focus with aging. The *social situation* domain refers to circumstances surrounding age, gender, living situation, as well as the extent of family, friends, neighbors, and faith-based and community affiliations. Educational level and cultural background, including spoken language, environment, and life experiences, are all significant. *Functional status* includes the ability to carry out activities of daily living and instrumental activities of daily living. The activities of daily living are ambulation, bathing, dressing, toileting, feeding, and continence (Katz et al., 1963). The instrumental activities of daily living describe higher order functioning such as driving or use of public transportation, management of medication and finances, housekeeping, shopping, cooking, and cleaning laundry (Lawton & Brody, 1969). Capacity is a critical aspect of this domain. *Health* is freedom from mental illness, organ-specific disease states, medication misuse, poor personal hygiene, and substance abuse. A senior's *financial situation* may consist of assets, debts, money-use patterns, and the presence of surrogate decision makers such as guardians, joint account holders, agents under a power

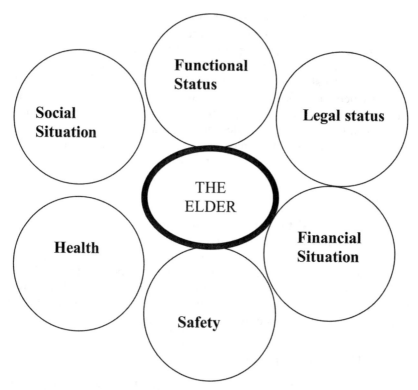

FIGURE 7.1   Dimensions of elder victims' lives.

of attorney, or representative payees. *Safety* considerations include the presence of firearms and other weapons, the ability to leave the residence in case of emergency, the capacity to obtain help if one becomes ill, and the presence of a safety plan should the victim be threatened by a perpetrator. *Legal status* includes authority to make decisions, controls on use of assets, immigration considerations, and ability and willingness to participate in legal proceedings.

Victim Safety

Victim safety should be the first step in any intervention strategy. In some elder abuse cases, the victim is at risk of serious harm or death if immediate action is not undertaken. Issues to consider when assessing victim safety are described in more detail in Chapter 11.

Remedies may come from a variety of systems. Law enforcement may arrest the perpetrator, who may then be prosecuted. Civil justice remedies can include restraining/protective orders, changing wills or guardianship documents, or legal separations or divorce to limit contact between the victim and perpetrator. Domestic violence advocates can develop safety plans with the victim. Emergency housing may be necessary, such as an elder shelter, battered women's program, or other place where the older person can stay temporarily while other interventions are taking place. To arrange for emergency housing, victims will need to have made arrangements for other dependents and pets. Many communities have safe havens for pets, which can be found by contacting the local domestic violence program or humane society.

Health

Often elder abuse victims are in regular contact with the health care system. Victims may need health care as a result of injuries caused by the abuse or other ongoing medical needs. Some victims are providing care and assistance for the abuser or other family members and will need to make arrangements for others while dealing with the immediate crisis. In other circumstances, the abuser is the primary caregiver for the victim and a new care arrangement will need to be made.

Victim Decisional Capacity

Although vulnerability is not synonymous with aging, degenerative processes can lead to physical frailty and cognitive impairment. Physical or mental decline can, in turn, lead to the loss of independence, which puts elders at risk for self-neglect and victimization. Old age makes some conditions inevitable, whereas others are the result of disease states.

Elders are perhaps the most vulnerable when they lose the ability to make decisions for themselves. Generally, disease states such as dementia or depression lead to loss of decision-making capacity. Elders without capacity make perfect victims, as they may not recognize when they are being exploited. They also may not be able to fend for themselves when abused or neglected.

Assessment of decision-making capacity is difficult. There are no screening tools available for nonmedical personnel. The gold standard for capacity assessment is the psychiatric interview, although in many cases a generalist or geriatrician can assess capacity. Some elders have preserved verbal abilities yet lack the insight and judgment required to make decisions for themselves. Assessments of these victims are particularly tricky. Determining decision-making capacity in unclear or contested cases requires either a forensic psychiatric interview or a full battery of tests performed by a neurophysiologist to examine cognitive skills and other brain functions. In jurisdictions where these specialists may not be available, environmental assessment, interview of collateral sources, and KELS (Kohlman Evaluation of Living Skills) testing—where patients are observed performing standardized tasks such as writing a check, reading a bill, making change, and identifying a dangerous condition depicted in a photograph—may be helpful (Kohlman-Thomson, 1972).

Legal

Victims often find themselves involved with the legal system. The perpetrator may have been arrested and charged with a crime. Victims may be interviewed about the abuse and asked to provide evidence and testimony. They may get restraining/protective orders or use other civil remedies. Some victims may find that the abuser is attempting to use the legal system against them. Abusers may try to manipulate victims into signing documents giving away money or property. Or an abuser may try to get the victim declared incompetent.

Physical Environment

Competent victims will need to decide where they want to live. Most elder abuse victims would prefer to remain in their own homes. Some may want to move to a smaller dwelling or into assisted living. Some residents of facilities may choose to move to a different facility.

Finances

For most elderly persons, talking openly about financial matters is difficult. This is the generation that survived the Great Depression, and many elders are reluctant to spend money on services, claiming that they need to "save it for a rainy day." Giving up control of personal funds is often perceived as the beginning of the end. For these reasons, discussions about financial matters should be conducted with tact and sensitivity. Acknowledging the elder's fears about running out of money and offering to find a way to make sure that does not happen can be reassuring.

In many communities aging services, American Association of Retired Persons (AARP) chapters, or other community-based organizations provide daily money-management and bill-payer services. These are most useful for older persons who still retain their capacity to make most of their decisions, but who have become confused and overwhelmed by unpaid bills. Another important service is a benefits specialist, who can analyze medical bills and make recommendations about benefits that the older person may be eligible for, as well as the most appropriate health insurance options.

For people who are in danger of having their monthly Social Security checks taken by others, the appointment of a representative payee can be helpful, provided that the appointed payee is trustworthy and will use all of the funds for the benefit of the elder. The local Social Security office should be contacted to set up a representative payee.

Powers of attorney for financial management can be useful, but only when the agent is someone trustworthy who will use the funds for the benefit of the elder. Unfortunately, powers of attorney often are seen by the agents as a "license to steal." If a power of attorney is the chosen option, the individual making the power of attorney should get legal advice about establishing procedures to prevent abuse.

In the event that an elder no longer has the capacity to make financial decisions, a court may also appoint a conservator or guardian of the estate. Finding trustworthy individuals to fulfill this role can be difficult. Sometimes an attorney, a banker, a trusted friend, or member of the elder's religious community is willing to provide this service. Courts do provide some oversight of conservators and guardians. Once again, however, selecting a person who will be mindful of his or her fiduciary duties and willing to be fully accountable is essential.

Social Support

Victims of abuse often lack social supports and ties to the community. Sometimes the abuser has isolated the victim. In other cases, the victim prefers being on his or her own, which may increase the risk for abuse. Improving the social support network of the victim can break the isolation and result in more "eyes and ears" monitoring for a recurrence of abuse. Some victims have lost touch with loved ones as a result of the abuser's behavior. In many cases, these relationships can be rekindled, especially if the victim has broken off contact with the abuser.

Another option to improve social contacts is to learn about the hobbies and interests of the victim. There may be clubs, social activities, or volunteer possibilities that will engage the victim. For persons of faith, religious or spiritual organizations offer numerous opportunities for education, as well as participation in community and social activities. Some older people may be interested in fitness, yoga, or meditation. Book clubs or sewing circles might be considered. Senior centers generally offer a wide array of programming for older persons.

Older battered women have benefited from support groups designed specifically to meet their needs. Some battered women's programs or aging network agencies run groups specifically for older women. These

groups give women a chance to talk about the abuse and to prob-
lem-solve with other women in a similar situation. For many women,
these groups have provided insight, comfort, and support (Spangler &
Brandl, 2003).

Pets may be another possible way to break isolation. Animals can
provide companionship to seniors who may enjoy providing care for
them. Keep in mind that pets may also be threatened or harmed by the
abuser as a way to get to the victim (The Humane Society of the United
States & Wisconsin Department of Health and Family Services, 2003).
Also recognize that some older people may not be able to afford the
expense of a pet or may not be able to provide the animal with the necessary exercise or a safe living environment. An elder who is not able to
keep his or her own pet might still be able to interact with animals by
volunteering at a local animal shelter.

Effective intervention plans involve learning about each of the areas
described previously and addressing the needs of the individual victim.
The next case illustrates responses by a variety of systems and model an
informal collaboration.

CASE 2: CAREGIVER NEGLECT

A doctor's office contacted APS to report that Rosa Costilla, age 92, had
been seen by the physician that day. She appeared to suffer from possible
neglect because of poor hygiene and malnutrition. She also had a lacera-
tion on her leg that continuously oozed blood and would not clot. One
day after the referral, Rosa's daughter, Juanita, brought her mother to the
emergency room because the leg was still oozing. At the time of admission, Rosa weighed only 58 pounds. Hospital staff became concerned
that Juanita was an adult with a cognitive disability, who appeared to
be unable to care for her mother and who refused to let Rosa speak for
herself. Hospital staff made a second report to APS.

Adult Protective Services made several attempts to see Rosa in her
home, but Juanita would not allow them entry. A tall, barbed-wire fence
with a gate surrounded the property. After multiple attempts, Juanita
finally said she would meet with APS. At the agreed-on time of the meeting, however, Juanita refused to come to the gate. When APS finally was
able to gain entry to the home, Rosa was found lying in a camp cot in the
living room. Juanita had to be separated from her mother so that Rosa
could be interviewed without interruption. Rosa appeared to have severe
dementia, so the interview was inconclusive.

Because of her poor physical condition, Rosa was hospitalized despite her daughter's objections. When Rosa was admitted to the hospital,

Juanita would not leave her mother's side. The daughter agreed to be admitted as well, and they shared a room. Rosa and her daughter appeared to have a lifelong pattern of interdependence that excluded other family members.

While in the hospital, when Rosa was given her food tray, Juanita would not allow her mother to feed herself and would take food away from her. Juanita claimed that her mother didn't like the food, even though her mother was clearly trying to eat it.

Rosa was found to have a vitamin B_{12} deficiency, malnutrition, and fecal impaction. Because of her advanced dementia, cognitive testing was not possible. Juanita was diagnosed with schizophrenia and mild mental retardation. She responded well to psychotropic drug therapy.

After Rosa's and Juanita's discharge from the hospital, Juanita initially improved her caregiving duties. Within a few weeks, however, she refused to continue the psychotropic drug therapy and reverted to her previous state. She was no longer compliant with doctors' orders regarding her mother's care. Juanita demanded to be left alone and her cooperation was intermittent.

Multidisciplinary Response

Because there had been two apparent severe elder neglect reports by health care professionals within 24 hours, this case was flagged for an immediate APS investigation. As Rosa Costilla was known to be 92 years old, it was likely that her daughter was over age 60. Thus, the presenting problem might have involved both caregiver neglect and self-neglect. The first time that APS was denied access to Rosa, an assessment team made up of law enforcement, a geriatrician, a home health aide, a mental health professional, a nutritionist, a developmental disabilities specialist, and a nurse was convened to assist APS in gaining immediate access to Rosa and to begin a comprehensive evaluation of both Rosa's and Juanita's conditions.

Adult Protective Services

After receiving two neglect reports of a very frail elder, APS made an immediate home visit. When denied access, they called law enforcement for assistance in gaining entry to the home. After the initial investigation that resulted in the hospitalization, APS gathered additional information from family members and the professionals involved, developed a case plan, and arranged for the provision of in-home services for Rosa and Juanita. Additional in-home services failed to improve Juanita's ability to care for her mother and Rosa's condition deteriorated. APS applied to the court for a guardianship appointment on behalf of Rosa. APS consulted with the long-term care ombudsman about the most appropriate placement for Rosa. After Rosa was placed in a long-term care facility, APS continued to monitor Juanita until her risk of self-neglect was reduced. APS also arranged for transportation for Juanita to visit her mother.

Law Enforcement

Law enforcement assisted APS in gaining access to Rosa. When in the home, law enforcement helped APS by separating Juanita from her mother so that Rosa could be interviewed separately. As the case progressed, law enforcement determined that there were grounds for a charge of criminal neglect against Juanita. As her mother's caregiver, Juanita was required to provide reasonable care that did not place her mother's life at risk.

Prosecutor

At this juncture, it was important that the facts were reviewed for possible criminal prosecution. Assuming that the elements of criminal neglect had been established through the law enforcement investigation, the prosecutor needed to assess whether the case could be proven beyond a reasonable doubt and whether the interests of justice were served by filing charges. Clear information about Juanita's mental illness and her ability to form intent was critical. If she lacked that ability, the case might not be provable. Further, even if the case were provable, the prosecutor might feel that a mental health response would be preferable to a prosecution. In that situation, the prosecutor might work with the mental health system and APS to obtain ongoing care for Juanita. Whatever approach was taken, the prosecutor would want to ensure that Rosa was safe, that she was getting the care she needed, that her dementia was being monitored, and that her changing needs were being met.

Health Care Professionals

Geriatrician

Prior medical information about Rosa's health status, weight, and presence of any illnesses that could result in wasting was critical. This information was obtained as quickly as possible by the team's geriatrician so that the patient's current condition could be accurately evaluated. Information about the danger to Rosa, given her current malnourished state, was very useful for APS in supporting the need for an immediate investigation. An evaluation of Rosa's level of dementia was also critical, as it could determine if she was capable of giving informed consent for her treatment.

A complete physical examination of Juanita revealed that she also was malnourished and had untreated medical conditions that were contributing to her inability to care for her mother.

Nurse

Once Rosa was discharged from the hospital, a visiting nurse assisted with her wound care and monitored her medications. The nurse also monitored Juanita's medications.

Home Health Aide

A home health aide assisted Juanita with meal preparation and supported Rosa's ability to feed herself. While she was in the hospital, Rosa was taught to feed herself again and she began to gain weight.

Nutritionist

A nutritionist developed a simple meal plan to ensure that both Rosa and Juanita were well nourished.

Mental Health and Developmental Disabilities Professionals

A mental health evaluation revealed that Juanita suffered from schizophrenia. She was given medication to which she responded favorably. Follow-up case management services from the developmental disabilities system ensured that Juanita continued to take her medication and trained and supported her in providing better care to her mother. Ongoing case management also helped to prepare Juanita for her mother's eventual placement in long-term care and assisted her in finding housing and support services, if she could no longer remain in the family home.

GUIDING PRINCIPLES: EMPOWERMENT AND SELF-DETERMINATION

An Empowerment Model

In addition to understanding the dimensions of an elder abuse victim's life, recognition of some key guiding principles will strengthen the response to the victim and improve collaborative efforts. One key principle promoted by social workers and advocates is an empowerment model.

> Empowerment is a process of helping people assure or reclaim control over their destinies, which entails maximizing their confidence, skills, and abilities [to] make informed decisions that are in their best interests, [and] having access to choices and available, accessible resources and options for the attainment of personal and collective goals (Nahmiash, 2002, p. 24).

In domestic violence and elder abuse cases, a framework using an empowerment model is often most effective. APS and advocates will often work with victims by assessing their situation and providing information and referrals. Services are offered rather than mandated. The victim is given the option to accept or reject any service, which restores decision-making power.

The empowerment model focuses on restoring power to victims to counteract the loss of control they often experience at the hands of their abuser. Perpetrators use the tactics described in Chapter 3 to isolate, intimidate, and coerce their victims. As a method to avoid harm, many victims relinquish decision making to the abuser. Therefore, mandating services, interventions, or health care is often counterproductive and based on a framework in which professionals believe they are entitled to use their authority to make decisions for the victim. Unfortunately, this dynamic is similar to the victim's current situation of being told what to do by the abuser. Mildred's case will illustrates the importance of an empowerment model.

CASE 3: DOMESTIC VIOLENCE

Mildred, age 81, called police at 1:00 A.M. She said that her husband Arthur, age 89, had just struck her several times on the upper arm, pulled her hair, kicked her in the hip to force her out of bed, and kicked her walker out of her reach. During the call the dispatcher heard Arthur curse at Mildred and say that he hated her.

Police found that there had been a history of domestic abuse throughout the marriage. Mildred had called police once many years ago after she was physically attacked and injured by her husband. At that time, Arthur claimed that his wife was faking her frailties. Mildred and Arthur had been married for 59 years. Mildred had arthritis, weighed 89 pounds, and was unable to shop or prepare meals. She never drove and relied on her husband to take her to appointments and activities.

She was prone to falls when she did not use her walker. She had had hip replacement surgery in the last eight months. Mildred was competent and fully capable of making her own decisions.

Mildred had a paid caregiver five days a week who cooked meals and cleaned. When the aide was not present, Arthur would not prepare meals for his wife and she lived on food supplements. She had fallen several times when she was trying to reach for food after Arthur refused to make her a meal.

Arthur was taken away by law enforcement. Mildred did not press charges. Upon Arthur's return, he said he would kill Mildred if she called police ever again.

Mildred did not call the police again, although there were many more serious incidents in which she suffered broken bones and a skull fracture. Her family wanted her to leave, but she felt she had married for life. She was afraid of Arthur and believed that he would kill her. Supportive family had moved hundreds of miles away to get away from the abuse. The adult son who had been physically abused by Arthur refused to expose his children to the violence.

Multidisciplinary Response

Law Enforcement

When patrol officers responded to the 911 call, they talked with Mildred who complained of pain to her arm, left hip, and head. Seeing visible bruising beginning to form on her arm, they interviewed Arthur and arrested him on suspicion of domestic violence. Because of his advanced age, he was booked at the county hospital jail ward. With Mildred's permission, law enforcement officers took her to the emergency room for a physical examination. Adult Protective Services was notified of Mildred's situation and her husband's arrest.

Domestic Violence Advocate

A domestic violence advocate interviewed Mildred and observed the bruising on her arm and head. The advocate noted her complaints of pain in these areas, as well as in her hip. Mildred was articulate, had a good memory, and was cooperative. After her relocation to the assisted living facility, the advocate provided safety planning information and follow-up trauma counseling, and supported her through the court procedures. Mildred appreciated being given options and support to make her own decisions.

Geriatrician

A geriatrician examined Mildred to determine and document the seriousness of her injuries, as well as to evaluate her overall health and review
her medications. Documentation of the injuries was used at the time of
Arthur's court arraignment.

Adult Protective Services

After she was discharged from the emergency room, APS arranged
for Mildred's placement in an assisted living facility that had been
designated for emergencies such as this one. APS described housing
options to Mildred and she chose to stay at the assisted living facility
on a permanent basis. She enjoyed the company and activities and the
fact that her meals were provided. After she moved away from Arthur,
her family quickly reunited with her. Her son assisted with payment
of her bills.

Prosecutor

The local prosecutor charged Arthur with felony domestic violence,
physical elder abuse, and neglect. He was arraigned, bail was set, and he
was remanded into custody where he remained. Mildred testified to the
charged criminal events before a judge. The judge believed her account
and found legal grounds to hold Arthur for trial on the charged felony
offenses. Shortly before his trial date, Arthur died of natural causes in the
hospital jail ward.

Like many older victims of domestic violence, Mildred felt
trapped and unable to reach out for help. Law enforcement and
prosecutors focused on holding her abusive husband accountable by
arresting and building a case to prosecute him. The justice system
does not operate using an empowerment model. Their role is to determine if a crime has been committed and to act accordingly. Mildred
was not given the choice about whether her abuser was arrested and
prosecuted.

The empowerment model was effective with Mildred as she worked
with advocates and APS. Workers in these systems offered Mildred information and discussed the services that were available to her. She was able
to make her own decision about her living arrangements and whether to
receive support and assistance from other agencies. Giving Mildred the
power to make her own decisions was crucial to her recovery and the
success of this case.

Self-Determination

In addition to an empowerment model, self-determination is another key concept when working with older victims to ensure that their rights are not violated. Adults with decision-making capacity have the right to make decisions about their lives and the services and interventions they will accept or reject. All adults are presumed to have decision-making capacity unless an assessment or court determines otherwise. Self-determination is a guiding principle for APS workers and advocates who will not tell victims what to do or force them to accept assistance. Self-determination means that everyone has the right to make his or her own decisions without interference from others. Empowerment means encouraging someone to exercise his or her right to self-determination. Both are critical to the APS worker. This often means that victims, like the rest of us, can make poor choices that sometimes leave them in precarious situations.

Adults with cognitive disabilities or dementia may not be able to make some decisions. A geriatric physician or a mental health professional can assess the elder's strengths and abilities. Seniors should be given the opportunity to make as many decisions about their own lives as possible, given their physical and mental health status. For example, an older person who cannot keep track of his finances may still be able to make his or her own medical decisions.

In contrast, the criminal justice system is not guided by the principle of self-determination. Law enforcement officers investigate crimes. Prosecutors represent the state, not the victim. This can be confusing to some elder abuse victims, who believe they must press charges for an action to be taken or who do not want a spouse or adult child arrested and are unable to stop the criminal justice process. It can also create tension between justice professionals and APS workers and advocates.

As with many self-neglect cases, Betty's case highlights the importance of self-determination.

CASE 4: BETTY: A CASE OF SELF-NEGLECT

A woman called APS complaining that her neighbor, Betty Stone, was living in a house full of trash and was "dangerous and half crazy." Betty was a 93-year-old widow who lived in a rundown house on the edge of the city. There were at least 75 bags of garbage rotting in the basement. Clothing, newspapers, and other items were piled almost to the ceiling throughout the house. Roaches and rodents rustled in the debris. There was a narrow pathway from room to room. When the weather permitted, Betty spent most of her time outdoors, as there was so little livable space inside her home.

Betty believed that intruders were entering her home, stealing her food and other belongings. Other than that, Betty insisted that she was fine, that she was "in the process of cleaning up the house," and that she did not need or want services from APS.

Because APS found no evidence of theft, and Betty refused additional services, the case was closed.

Multidisciplinary Response

Adult Protective Services

Many experienced APS workers had responded to earlier reports about Betty's situation with no success. After the fifth report, a new student intern accepted the case. It was the intern's first and only case at that time. She worked many hours each week on the case with a multidisciplinary team that she organized. She asked the interdisciplinary elder mistreatment team to evaluate Betty. The team included the following professionals.

Geriatrician

The initial visit was made at the house because Betty was reluctant to come to the clinic. Her previous medical history was unknown except for a bilateral mastectomy. Betty had normal vital signs. She was pleasant and cooperative. She was wearing a stained housecoat and walked under her own power. Chest assessment revealed bilateral mastectomy scars. Betty kept repeating the same phrases throughout the exam. Her Mini-Mental State score was 18/30, indicating moderate dementia. A full laboratory blood panel was drawn and was normal except that her vitamin B_{12} level was 198 (normal is 250 to 1,000). Betty was diagnosed with self-neglect, vitamin B_{12} deficiency, and Alzheimer's disease with psychosis. A vitamin B_{12} therapy was initiated, along with medication for Alzheimer's disease and psychosis. The medical team followed up with Betty during home visits.

Home Health Agency

An agency nurse provided a medication regimen for Betty's psychosis, as well as treatment for vitamin B_{12} deficiency.

Geriatric Mental Health Worker

The worker made home visits to monitor Betty's psychosis and made sure that she was receiving the correct medication regimen.

Law Enforcement

A senior community policing officer made several visits to Betty's home to reassure her that she was safe and that her belongings were not being stolen.

Betty's Family and Friends

Betty's only son was deceased; however, she had a daughter-in-law, Harriet, who was elderly and frail herself. Harriet wanted Betty to live close to her. Betty declined this offer because she did not want to move, but she was pleased that her daughter-in-law contacted her. Harriet agreed to make regular telephone calls to Betty to provide her with socialization. The APS intern worker and the case manager from the home health agency also stayed in close contact with the daughter-in-law. Betty's sister-in-law, Margaret, was instructed to call one of the team members if any problems arose. And a neighbor across the street was enlisted to drop in on Betty for additional socialization.

Aging Services

Meals on Wheels visited Betty five days a week. The Meals on Wheels delivery staff were in the unique position of seeing Betty in her home on a regular basis. Thus, they had the opportunity to notice changes in Betty's living situation and kept the rest of the team updated as to her day-to-day functioning. The staff enlisted the help of Betty's neighbor to sit with her and make sure that she ate her noon meal.

Health Department Code Enforcement

Given the condition of Betty's home, a safety inspection was requested. The inspector was unable to do an enforcement action because the violations existed only on the interior of the home.

Case Outcome

After many hours of working with Betty, the APS intern received a call from her one day. Betty told the intern that she was ready to sell her home and move. The intern had an assisted living situation lined up for Betty and enlisted a team of people to help her move and sell her items. Six months after Betty's move, she was content and enjoyed interacting with the other residents.

The APS intern used kindness, compassion, perseverance, patience, and teamwork to succeed. The investment of time she spent on the case would have been impossible for any other APS worker with a normal caseload, but with the multidisciplinary team and community response, it changed Betty's life for the better.

GUIDING PRINCIPLES IN FACILITIES

Promoting empowerment and self-determination continue to be important when working with victims living in facilities. These victims have the same rights as other competent adults. Those who no longer have the capacity to make their own decisions are particularly challenging cases. Informal collaboration may be crucial in these cases as is illustrated in the following case about Pearl.

CASE 5: SEXUAL ABUSE IN A LICENSED FACILITY

Helena, the head of nursing at a licensed residential care home, was surprised to see that Pearl had not come to the lobby in anticipation of her cousin's visit. She went to Pearl's room and found the door locked. She knocked but received no response. Thinking that Pearl had fallen asleep, she used her key to open the door. Helena observed George, the head of facility maintenance, in the room. He was zipping his trousers and buckling his belt, while Pearl quickly buttoned her blouse. Pearl looked embarrassed and tearful. When asked what happened, she said, "George loves me best. George loves me best."

Helena began an internal investigation. She found that George, a six-year employee, had keys for every room of the facility. He had befriended Pearl several months earlier, believing she was lonely and wanted his company. He did not deny the sexual contact, saying it had been consensual.

Pearl was 80 years old. She had significant cognitive impairment because of progressive dementia, most likely Alzheimer's disease. Otherwise she was in overall good health and socially intact, but unable to live independently because of her dementia. She had never married and was a retired elementary school teacher.

Helena believed that Pearl "just didn't know what she was doing." George was given a reprimand and warned to stay away from Pearl.

Helena did not report the incident to her administration or the local or state regulatory agencies, as she thought it was "no big deal."

George did stay away from Pearl, but subsequently sexually assault- ed several other residents of the facility. One of these residents, Molly, promptly reported the matter to a family member who immediately notified law enforcement. During the ensuing criminal investigation, officials learned about Pearl's victimization and Helen's failure to report the earlier incident.

Multidisciplinary Response

Abuse that occurs in long-tem care facilities is sometimes difficult to iden- tify. Not only are there many residents with varying degrees of cognitive ability, but there are many people, including staff, delivery people, family members, therapists, and the general public, who go in and out of the facility at all hours of the day and night. Although there are a number of systems identified as having responsibility to receive reports of abuse and to conduct investigations, it is easy for victims to fall through the cracks. Any situation involving the possible commission of a crime, in- cluding sexual assault, should always be reported immediately to law enforcement.

Law Enforcement

Molly's case was reported to law enforcement, which then began an investigation. The bedroom where the incident occurred was checked for additional evidence. The bedding and clothing worn by both par- ties were collected and examined for bodily fluids and hair. As part of that investigation, a court order was obtained that authorized the col- lection of body fluid samples from George. Additional investigative steps were taken to include interviews with other staff members and to obtain records that would place the suspect in the area with the victim and other information that would provide the basis of an effective criminal prosecution.

Forensic Nurse Examiner

Other prosecution concerns focus on whether the crime scene was pre- served and critical evidence collected. The victim, Molly, was examined (by medical professionals) for any injuries and bruises. A full sexual assault assessment was completed. A specially trained forensic nurse examiner collected swabs and combings. Biological samples were examined for sperm. A DNA collection kit was used to determine whether the suspect left any physical evidence of sexual contact.

Prosecution

The prosecution definitely wanted the other residents at the facility interviewed and George's movements checked. It is not unusual to find that there are multiple victims among vulnerable adult populations, such as in nursing homes. Some perpetrators seek such employment because of their access to victims who cannot resist, summon help, or be believed if they do report. In this case, the investigation identified Pearl as an additional victim.

Adult Protective Services

In many states, reports to APS are mandated when elder abuse occurs in long-term care facilities. Because the two cases involved possible sexual assault of an elder, law enforcement immediately notified APS, the state Medicaid Fraud Unit, and a victims' advocate so that a joint investigation could be conducted. A critical role for APS in facility investigations is to coordinate the activities of other professionals to ensure that efforts are not duplicated, information is shared appropriately, and the rights and wishes of the victim are protected.

Long-Term Care Ombudsman

The long-term care ombudsman acts as an advocate on behalf of residents in long-term care facilities. They are concerned about the quality of life of each individual resident, as well as all of the residents. As advocates, they can, with the residents' permission, share concerns and participate in activities designed to alleviate those concerns. Although it is quite possible that neither Pearl nor Molly had shared their sexual experiences with the ombudsman, once there was a sexual abuse investigation in the facility, the ombudsman became essential as someone in whom Pearl, Molly, and other victims could confide.

Local and State Regulatory Agencies

Under federal law, local and state regulatory agencies have responsibility for ensuring the quality and safety of care proved in long-term care facilities. Through periodic licensing inspections, as well as investigations of reports of abuse or poor care, they monitor the performance of the facilities and have the power to impose sanctions for poor or dangerous care. A report on George and Pearl's encounter was made to the regulatory agency; an incident report then generated a prompt investigation.

State Board of Nursing

Because Helena did not report the incident to her administration, the regulatory agency, law enforcement, or APS, she was reprimanded/sanctioned by the licensure board. She was also admonished that she could face criminal sanctions for her failure to report as required by law in her state.

CONCLUSION

As was illustrated in this chapter, numerous professionals become involved in elder abuse cases once they are reported. Different systems offer a variety of remedies to promote safety and hold abusers accountable. Intervention strategies for victims need to be comprehensive, and not focus simply on the abuse, but also address health, capacity, physical environment, legal issues, and social supports.

Interventions and collaborations sometimes fail because professionals do not agree or lose sight of guiding principles, such as empowerment and self-determination, when working together. Before working directly with victims, professionals are encouraged to discuss and develop basic core principles to ground their work. Examples of some effective guiding principles include the following:

- Focus on victim safety.
- Avoid siding with the abuser by agreeing with his or her excuses or blaming the victim for the abuse. Operate as if abuse could have occurred and gather information before dismissing a report, even if the allegations seem unlikely or the reporter does not seem credible. Any report from the potential victim deserves an investigation.
- Recognize and respect cultural and religious differences. Professionals should be aware that language barriers and value differences may create challenges.
- Treat older victims as adults, and with respect and kindness. Seniors should not be treated like children by doing too much for them, talking to others about them while they are present, or making decisions for them.

- Recognize that the victim may want to maintain the relationship and help the abuser. The victim may change his or her story, recant, or set up other roadblocks to help protect himself/herself or the abuser.
- Understand that abusers use isolation and misinformation as a tactic to keep victims off balance. Providing encouragement, support, and accurate information to victims can be extremely helpful.

Informal collaborations exist in many communities. These multidisciplinary approaches are often the most effective responses to elder abuse victims. Informal responses are most effective when professionals operate from similar guiding principles and maintain their roles and responsibilities. In some cases, informal collaborations evolve over time and become formalized teams. The next chapter describes the process for creating a team approach. Chapter 10 examines the mechanics of teams that focus on case review.

CHAPTER EIGHT

Team Processes

OVERVIEW

Previous chapters have discussed the importance of collaborative responses to elder abuse and have defined multidisciplinary teams as a way to build effective responses. They have described the relevant considerations when a community or individuals are developing their own response, whether formal or informal. After a decision is made to establish a formal team, there are steps that are most likely to lead to success. This chapter describes these important processes that include the following phases: planning, formation, working, evaluating, and sustaining.

STEPS OF TEAM PROCESSES

Planning:

- Vision.
- Needs assessment.
- Determine purpose.

Formation:

- Gather the critical persons/expertise.
- Define team goals.
- Develop collaborative agreements.
- Set policies and procedures.

Perform the work:

- Case review teams may conduct investigations/assessments, perform case reviews, and intervene.

- Systems review teams may audit systems and make policy recommendations.

Evaluate:

- Quantify workload.
- Assess client and participant satisfaction.
- Measure outcomes.

Sustain the effort:

- Act on the evaluation results.
- Do strategic planning.
- Publicize.

This chapter describes the steps of team formation through the eyes of a protective service worker, Ann. The chapter walks the reader through the processes that Ann and her colleagues follow as they assemble a team that addresses cases of financial exploitation.

A protective service worker, Ann, notes that many of her clients are victims of financial exploitation. She feels frustrated that few of her investigations result in arrest or prosecution. Ann attends a conference where she hears about a fiduciary/financial abuse specialist team, or FAST, and wonders if such a team could work in her community. What can Ann do to determine whether a FAST would meet the perceived need in her community?

PLANNING PHASE

The Vision

Collaborative efforts are formed for a variety of reasons, but essentially one or more practitioners believe that their traditional way of handling elder abuse cases is ineffective or could be improved and they become change agents. The desire for change may flow from a case failure, personal experience, frustration, or knowledge about an existing team. Also, recognition that elders are being seen by a system in increasing numbers, a grant opportunity, a change in laws or leadership, or new information may trigger a review of existing procedures, and a desire to handle matters differently. The idea may originate with an elected official, a practitioner, or a variety of professionals within a particular field.

On her return to the agency from the conference, what are the first steps Ann should take in the development of a FAST in her community?

Needs Assessment

After the idea is conceived, the next step is to gather documentation to support the need for change. This may include collecting data such as demographic trends, case examples, or pattern of service utilization. Some may conduct focus groups or survey older consumers and relevant professionals. A needs assessment is conducted and the data collated.

Ann analyzes her own cases and the cases of other workers in her agency. She documents that there was a 15% increase in the number of substantiated reports of financial exploitation. There was a commensurate increase in reports to law enforcement, but no increase in the number of cases filed and prosecuted. Ann contacts the community where the FAST had been established and learns that in the year after the team was formed, there was a 25% increase in prosecutions. With this information, what is Ann's next step?

Determine the Purpose of the Team

After the needs assessment, the next step is to convene a meeting of interested parties. That group determines whether the perceived need is legitimate and whether the parties are prepared to incorporate possible changes into their work to address the problem. If so, the group must then decide its purpose (Jay, 1999). That purpose may mean focusing on improved service delivery, such as starting a support group for older abused women or a rapid response team for a suspected elder abuse crime scene. The effort could also focus on public awareness education or professional training. Alternatively, the group could decide to focus on case review, meaning that a group of professionals, usually from several disciplines, convene to fact find, analyze, and intervene in a particular matter. Or, a group could decide to evaluate policies and systems to determine whether there are gaps in services or systemic breakdowns or to advocate for legislative change or different funding priorities.

In 2000, the National Center on Elder Abuse funded a study of multidisciplinary teams. Data derived from this study showed that 93.5% of teams provided expert consultation to service providers and identified system gaps and problems, and 80.6% planned and carried out investigation or care planning (Teaster & Nerenberg, 2000). This study indicated that of the 31 teams studied, most carried out multiple functions.

The interested parties will determine the general focus. What type of team will the group become—medical case management, fatality review, fiduciary abuse, code enforcement, or a coordinated community coalition? Will the approach be multidisciplinary or interdisciplinary? Once the focus and approach have been determined, the team is ready to move from the planning phase to formation.

Ann enlists the head of the APS agency, who invites members of law enforcement, prosecution, the banking industry, and health care—including a geriatrician, a forensics psychiatrist, and a psychologist—to a meeting.

Formation

The formation stage involves the selection of the participants from appropriate disciplines to be on the team. These participants determine the goals they intend to achieve and establish policies and procedures to guide the work. In this phase, team members also set the rules for case review and conflict resolution.

Select Core Team Members

Once the leaders determine the team's focus, members are selected based on the vision and the needs of the community (Francis & Young, 1992). The mission and purpose of the team will guide decisions about the expertise and composition needed to complete the group's tasks. For most teams, representatives from Adult Protective Services (APS), law enforcement, and health care are considered critical members. Many teams also include criminal prosecutors or civil or county counsel. If the team intends to focus on cases resulting in death, a medical examiner or coroner is crucial. If the team will address institutional abuse, representatives from the long-term care ombudsman program and regulatory or licensing agencies should be included. If the team will focus on financial exploitation matters, the group should be enhanced to include accountants and representatives from financial institutions. All teams should be flexible enough to permit the addition of other disciplines as needed (Nerenberg, 2003).

In the National Center of Elder Abuse study of multidisciplinary teams, law enforcement, APS, and geriatric medicine health services were the most common disciplines represented (Teaster & Nerenberg, 2000). Table 8.1 describes some of the disciplines that might participate on elder abuse teams. This is not an exhaustive list of every discipline that addresses elder abuse, nor does it include every possible profession that might be a member of a particular team. In addition, teams may vary in the particular skill set and expertise of individuals, even within the same discipline.

Being skilled or trained in a particular discipline does not always ensure that the professional is suited for participation in a multidisciplinary elder abuse team. Members should be knowledgeable about elder abuse issues or prepared to learn from those on the team who are. Members should have time in their work schedule that allows them to participate. Professionals selected must be committed to the multidisciplinary or interdisciplinary approach and be willing to give up some autonomy to achieve the goals of the team (Nerenberg, 2003).

TABLE 8.1 Types of Teams

Type of Team	Disciplines Involved
Coordinated Community Coalition	• Adult protective services
	• Aging services
	• Law—criminal, civil
	• Court
	• Faith community
	• Nursing
	• Long-term care ombudsmen
	• Social work
Code Enforcement	• Adult protective services
	• Animal control
	• Licensing and regulatory agencies
	• Law enforcement
	• Paramedics
	• Veterinary medicine
Fatality Review	• Adult protective services
	• Allied health—paramedics
	• Coroners
	• Dentistry
	• Health department
	• Law—criminal, civil

(continued)

TABLE 8.1   Types of Teams *(continued)*

Type of Team	Disciplines Involved
	• Law enforcement
	• Long-term care ombudsmen
	• Medicine—forensic pathology, geriatric medicine, general medicine
	• Victim advocacy
Fiduciary Abuse	• Adult protective services
	• Aging services
	• Banking
	• Faith community
	• Law—criminal, civil
	• Law enforcement
	• Medicine—geriatric medicine, psychiatry, forensic psychiatry
	• Victim advocacy
Medical Case Management	• Adult protective services
	• Allied health (paramedics, dietitians, therapists)
	• Dentistry
	• Ethics
	• Health department
	• Faith community
	• Law—criminal, civil
	• Law enforcement
	• Medicine—emergency medicine, geriatric medicine, psychiatry, forensic pathology, general medicine, forensic psychiatry, medical examiner
	• Nursing
	• Social work
	• Victim advocacy

Some teams may wish to have differing levels of agency participation. They may designate core, affiliate, or associate membership. Teams should develop processes for replacing members who move from the agency or whose terms have expired (Nerenberg, 2003).

Ad hoc Members

Some professionals may be core members of certain kinds of teams but play no role on others. Even when particular professionals are not team core member, these allies may still be pivotal to resolving individual cases (Francis & Young, 1992). For example, some teams include a criminal prosecutor and a civil attorney who works for and represents the jurisdiction in which the team is located. These professionals limit their participation to situations where legal matters are likely to be part of the case review or intervention plan. When they do participate, the prosecutor provides guidance on criminal matters, identifies criminal conduct, obtains court orders as part of charged cases, incorporates needed conditions in sentencing negotiations and recommendations, and responds to questions about criminal law. In some states, they also assist victims in seeking civil protective orders. The county civil attorney assists in identifying cases where guardianship or conservatorship is appropriate, seeks court orders to protect vulnerable elders, and initiates court proceedings to preserve assets. Domestic violence, sexual assault, and other victim advocates can also be important participants. Their knowledge of these specialized areas, community resources, and benefits can be invaluable in explaining victim behaviors, understanding service networks, and developing comprehensive intervention plans. Some advocates can fully participate on teams without breaching client confidentiality; others cannot because of their legal and confidential relationship with their client. Even when specific advocates cannot participate on the team, efforts should be made to include someone knowledgeable to represent the victim's perspective and desires.

The disciplinary leaders attended the organizational meeting. Each agreed to designate staff that would be their representative for the FAST. What additional policy and procedures were needed?

Set Goals

Once key participants have committed to joining the team and designated who will be their representative, the team must define members' roles, clarify goals, establish processes, and establish standards and methods to conduct and evaluate work. The participating members must decide on specific goals. This is an important step and allows buy-in of those who will actually be doing the work. Goals will vary depending on the type of team and the needs identified in the community assessment. These members must also decide whether the team will structure itself in an informal or formal manner. An informal group may address a specific task, meet as needed, achieve its task, and dissolve. A formal group will likely select leaders and members, establish operating rules, formalize procedures, and operate as a permanent body. The formal group often develops its overarching goals and will move from one task to another and may perform multiple functions.

Develop Collaborative Agreements

Collaborative agreements are needed to formally acknowledge the commitment of the various organizations. These agreements can take the form of memoranda of understanding, operating agreements, contracts, subcontracts, or interagency agreements. Formal agreements help ensure the continuation of the agency's commitment, memorialize the minimum level of its participation, and clarify the kinds of expertise that will be provided. Most important, formal agreements allow the team's work to continue when an organization's leadership changes. These formal agreements may or may not address budgetary concerns, depending on the will of and the funding available to the respective organizations.

In the study of multidisciplinary teams, more than 51% of members were required to sign memoranda of understanding or contracts. In this same study, 29% of the agencies were required to sign a written document that indicated their level of commitment to the effort (Teaster & Nerenberg, 2000).

Establish Policies and Procedures

The team must decide the roles of its members, establish the value of everyone's participation, and determine the ground rules for conflict resolution. Although this part of the formation stage is time-consuming, many mistakes that could undermine or sabotage the team can be avoided by paying careful attention at this time. This phase permits members to build relationships, develop trust, and understand the principles, ethical precepts, and resources of each discipline.

Determine Roles Within the Team

Within teams there are specific roles that must be filled, regardless of the type of team. These roles include leader, facilitator, recorder, time keeper, and administrative support staff. The leader ensures adherence to its vision. The leader is the moral voice of authority, the person in charge, or the ultimate decision maker. Selection of the team leader will vary according to the type of team and its focus. Team leaders should be chosen based on expertise and experience, as well as leadership skill. The leader may also act as facilitator, but this is not always the case. The facilitator's role is to ensure that all members are treated fairly and that procedures are followed (Francis & Young, 1992). More specifically, the facilitator ensures that team members explain professional jargon, follow time limits, and remain focused on understanding the facts. Note takers memorialize the information gathered by team members and the decisions that are made. The administrative support staff prepares schedules, sorts case intake forms, sends agendas, and maintains records of what occurs at meetings. The administrative staff also ensures that team members complete follow-up tasks and schedules periodic task updates for the team.

Adherence to the Principles of Effective Teams

The contributions of every team member are important and valued. Teams include members from diverse backgrounds; some have postgraduate degrees; others have less formal education but considerable field experience. All members' contributions are equally critical and valuable to the team's work and effectiveness (Dyer et al., 2003). Failure to equally value all members can create conflict and disenfranchise individual members. Early in the team's existence, time should be spent learning what each member and each discipline can contribute. The strength of the team will be determined by the individual member's expertise and the group's awareness of what each discipline can contribute. Policies and procedures should reflect the principle of equality of all members and their contributions.

Conflict Resolution

Given the diverse membership of elder abuse teams and the potential for clashes and disputes, members must agree to the methods for achieving shared goals. These goals may include stopping the conduct, protecting the victim, protecting the public (society at large), holding the offender accountable, restoring or improving the victim's quality of life, and attempting to rehabilitate the offender. Within different kinds of teams, some goals may be emphasized over others, or a team may use different approaches to achieving the agreed-upon goals. For example, some elder abuse fatality review teams only review deaths for the purposes of assessing systemic responses and identifying areas for public awareness and education and systemic change. Their primary goal is to improve interventions so that similar deaths do not occur in the future. A different fatality review team may also choose to focus on identifying cases for arrest and prosecution. Their goal is not only to improve systemic responses to victims, but to hold a particular offender accountable and stop the illegal conduct. When there are clashes, a review of these shared goals may be the only way to bring a team in conflict back to consensus.

The FAST forms, sets policies and procedures, designates the roles of the members, and completes a memorandum of understanding. The team begins its work that includes reviewing cases to identify criminal conduct and developing evidence sufficient to support criminal prosecution.

THE WORK

After the formation phases are completed, the work begins. Case review is discussed in more detail in the next chapter. Systems review teams focus on policy change and collaboration among various disciplines. Systemic change is discussed in Chapter 12.

The FAST has been in existence for three months and the members have begun to look at cases. The head of the protective service agency calls Ann and informs her that there is a budget crunch. The agency is reviewing its programs and needs to reduce its involvement in some programs. The agency head asks the worker to provide documentation that justifies their commitment of resources and continued involvement.

EVALUATION

Both elder abuse intervention itself and the benefits of team collaboration as a response are difficult to measure. When collaborative efforts are used, identifying and quantifying work and success are especially complicated. Where multiple members contribute to the work of the team, measuring the relative weight of each contribution may not be possible. There may be disagreement about what constitutes "success." For example, in a situation where a victim is separated from her caregiver-abuser, the team may feel that the outcome is successful because the victim is safe; the criminal justice professionals may be satisfied because a successful prosecution ensued, and social service professionals may be satisfied because the client was kept in her own home with appropriate social services. Nevertheless, the victim may be very dissatisfied, as she may feel she is no longer independent, may resent the involvement of strangers in her life, and may want to be with her abusive caregiver.

In light of these realities, every team must decide whose perspective will be evaluated: the victim-client, the team as a whole, or individual members and disciplines. Further, the team will have to decide what constitutes "success." Is it increased victim safety? Improved quality of life for the client? An arrest? A successful prosecution? Have the team processes worked? Has the team managed conflict effectively?

Teams may decide to evaluate different aspects of the work. Regardless of what a team evaluates, its effectiveness must be measured against the extent that the particular goals are met. It is critical to catalogue the work of the team, selected outcome measures, and participant satisfaction.

The Work of the Team

Teams can start the evaluation process by simply collecting baseline statistics on what they do. This information should be gathered whether or not the team contemporaneously begins a formal evaluation process. These data can be incorporated later into measurement strategies or analyzed retrospectively when unanticipated problems arise. Trends may emerge as the team matures and the early data will help guide the development of improved processes. Archived data may guide and inform future research and provide new information to the field.

Selected Outcome Measures

The appropriate outcome measures for interdisciplinary teams are not always easy to define. An appropriate team outcome could be the determination of the impact of the multidisciplinary approach on client recidivism. As new disciplines are added, the number of positive outcomes or the number of available options that are then incorporated into intervention plans could be measured. Other potential outcome measures include whether the team's procedures have reduced the number of overlapping services offered to a client, or the time between referral of the case and its case conference. The team can evaluate if it has handled more or fewer cases compared to another point in time and the number of systems that actually coordinated responses. The team may quantify important demographic information about their client base. For example, it is valuable to know how many of the situations that the team responded to involved clients who live with dementia and how many clients had multiple morbid events. Or, in how many of the abuse cases was depression an underlying problem? What are the trends based on gender, ethnic and racial background, and socioeconomic status? What are the referral patterns to the team?

Outcome measures could include evaluation of the team's success in addressing public health concerns such as quality of life. Issues such as limb salvage and appropriate use of public resources are all of pressing concern and are worthy measures of the team's work. In addition, reduction of morbidity from chronic diseases, such as diabetes, renal failure, and cardiovascular conditions, needs to be assessed. Functional status, including sensory changes, nutrition, and pressure ulcers in the context of elder abuse, is in critical need of study (U.S. Department of Health and Human Services, 2000). Any member of the team can provide ongoing measurement and evaluation or members can decide to rotate this task.

Example of Outcome Measurement

In a study conducted at Baylor College of Medicine, research assistants screened APS clients who had been deemed healthy to determine if there was undetected neuropsychiatric illness not captured by APS assessment instruments. The subjects underwent a series of medical and neuropsychiatric tests. The results showed that nearly half the APS clients had depression, dementia, and impaired executive function. This study indicated that there was a need for better screening tools to help APS specialists detect underlying medical disease in their clients to facilitate the appropriate referral for medical care (Poythress et al., 2001).

Ethical Aspects of Evaluation

In deciding which outcomes will be evaluated, the team must carefully assess whether the selected measures present ethical conflicts. For example, suppose a measurable outcome to be tested is whether, as a result of their participation on the team, law enforcement made more arrests, those arrests resulted in more prosecutions, and those prosecutions resulted in more people being sent to jail. This may appear to be valuable information, but it may actually present ethical conflicts for both law enforcement and prosecutors. Their role and ethical responsibilities must be considered.

> The U.S. attorney is the representative not of an ordinary party to a controversy, but of a sovereignty whose obligation to govern impartially is as compelling as its obligation to govern at all; and whose interest, therefore, in a criminal prosecution is not that it shall win a case but

that justice shall be done. As such, he is in a peculiar and definite sense the servant of the law, the twofold aim of which is that guilt shall not escape nor innocence suffer. He may prosecute with earnestness and vigor—*indeed, he should do so*. But, while he may strike hard blows, he is not at liberty to strike foul ones. It is as much his duty to refrain from improper methods calculated to produce a wrongful conviction as it is to use every legitimate means to bring about a just one. (*Berger v. United States,* 295 US 78, 88, (1935))

Prosecutors, however, are held to an elevated standard of conduct. A prosecutor is held to a standard higher than that imposed on other attorneys because of the unique function he or she performs in representing the interests of the community and government (*People v. Hill,* 17 Cal 4th 800, 72 Cal Rptr. 2d 656 (1998)).

Prosecutors must base charging decisions on objective facts and the available evidence. Recommendations for sentence must be based on the defendant's criminal history, danger to the public, likelihood of successful rehabilitation, and related factors, not passion, personal attitudes, or public pressure (California District Attorneys Association, 1985, 2001; National District Attorneys Association, 1977). When a measure of the team's success is whether more cases are being filed and if more people are sentenced to jail, a prosecutor's neutral application of legal and ethical requirements may conflict with the team's desire to improve its evaluative picture. Similarly, if an increase in arrests by law enforcement is a measure of team success, then law enforcement's neutral fact-finding authority and responsibility may be compromised by the team's need to show success. If avoidance of nursing home placements and maintaining patients/clients in their homes are considered measures of success, then team members who otherwise might recommend nursing home placement might well be reluctant to recommend the most appropriate care.

Satisfaction

Maintaining satisfaction of all parties affected by the team is crucial to sustaining the effort. It may be valuable to survey victims, their families, and team members (Francis & Young, 1992). Victims' satisfaction may be evaluated by assessing improved quality of life, reduction of isolation, increased feelings of safety, and whether the victims have made any changes in their life as a result of the team's intervention. In addition, questions about what services were most important to improving the victim's situation and what additional services were needed but were unavailable may guide the establishment of service priorities.

A team member survey could measure satisfaction within the team including:

- Was it worthwhile to serve on the team?
- Was their perspective valued?
- Was the process efficient?
- Did the process increase or decrease the time spent on individual cases?
- Was conflict within the team properly managed?
- Is there adequate administrative support of the team's effort?
- Are care plans adequately developed and implemented?
- Is adequate follow-up information provided to team members?
- Would a team member recommend that his or her agency continue to participate?

It would also be important to survey the involved agency leaders to ensure that the team is achieving the mission and goals of the agency and achieving the outlined vision. Satisfaction surveys may help identify breaks in service or the need for additional services, adding new disciplines to the team. They also may result in the creation of different procedures for the team's operation, leading to increased satisfaction, additional staffing, the solicitation of new members, and reduction in conflict, frustration, and burnout.

At a meeting of the FAST, the members of the team acknowledge a successful year. The leader poses a question about how they can maintain the effort over time. What are the strategies for sustaining a team effort?

SUSTAINING TEAM EFFORT

Initially, participants are excited by the potential to improve services, streamline work, and conserve resources. Teambuilding is laborious, but then the work begins and teams become reenergized. In many ways, the planning and formation phases are the easiest. The work of case review, which is focused on the victim, is stimulating and rewarding. The sustaining phase is tedious and time consuming, and may be the most difficult.

Over time, processes slip, teams lose focus, and participating members move on. As we have seen, evaluation is one way to catalogue a team's accomplishments, measure the effectiveness of processes, and determine whether the overarching goals are being achieved and remain relevant. See Chapter 7 for a more complete discussion on obstacles to the collaborative process.

IMPLEMENTING CHANGE BASED ON THE EVALUATION RESULTS

If done early and frequently, evaluation will lead to prompt responses to problems and keep participants and their agencies involved. Ultimately, evaluation coupled with change and refinement in processes will lead to the improved delivery of services or care. These processes include updating membership, dealing with turnover, maintaining professional excellence, providing ongoing training within the team, and ensuring consistent funding.

As the nature of cases evolves, or as indicated in the results of the evaluation process, members from new disciplines may need to be added to the team. Sustaining processes should involve orientation of new members, which includes training on the roles and expertise of the other team members. In turn, new team members should educate existing members about the scope and processes of their discipline.

CONDUCTING STRATEGIC PLANNING

Many teams engage in a strategic planning process, either during the formation stage or later if they are running into problems. Strategic planning can be extremely useful in setting a common vision and goals for the working group. Participants of teams often come with different agendas about the primary purpose or the methods for achieving the mission of the team. A strategic planning process provides individuals with a structure to work within as a team to come to a common understanding of the goal of the group.

It can be helpful to hire or find a volunteer who is skilled at group facilitation and strategic planning to run the process. Although it is not impossible, it can be difficult for a group member to remain objective and not try to direct the group in a certain direction. Recordkeeping also is important to maintain a historical document highlighting the process and noting the decisions that the group made so they do not need to be revisited.

Numerous methods and exercises exist for strategic planning. A frequently used process involves seven steps. Before the seven-step process, groups do an exercise to select partners. One method for determining who to invite to the team is to list every type of person and profession that might have something to add and to note their potential contribution. Including older people on any team is extremely valuable. Representation from different groups of ethnicity and religion is also crucial.

The seven-step process includes the following:

Step 1:   Setting the ground rules
Step 2:   Seeing the vision
Step 3:   Stating the mission
Step 4:   Surveying the community
Step 5:   Identifying strengths, weaknesses, obstacles, and threats
Step 6:   Setting goals
Step 7:   Planning action

A series of small and large group exercises can be done to help the team with each of these steps. A description of this process can be found in "Building Coalitions to Combat Domestic Violence" (Albright, Brandl, Rozwadowski, & Wall, 2003).

UTILIZING DATA TO DIRECT RESEARCH

Where a team designs an evaluation that studies its interventions and case plans in light of improved health for patients and clients, it provides invaluable baseline research data for other teams and elder abuse researchers. It also may guide the development of future public policy. For example, little is known about the forensics markers in community and institutional abuse. Unlike child abuse, where considerable research has been done on relevant indicators, the effects of aging coupled with the lack of forensic research make the determination of elder abuse problematic (Dyer, Connolly, & McFeely, 2003). Data derived from elder abuse teams could greatly inform and guide future research. Obtaining institutional review board approval of forms and processes can be difficult, considering the fact that the population in question is made up of vulnerable individuals. Obtaining institutional review board approvals from multiple institutions could be so cumbersome that any project could come to a halt. It is recommended that one institution undertake the task of publishing, with input and authorship from others.

The members of the team could draw on the expertise of others to review and interpret their data. Tapping into a research program in a nearby medical, social work, law, or public health training [facility] may lead to interesting work for the schools and valuable information for the team. Team members may want to select an advisory committee made up of local or national experts to provide an oversight function and add new perspective to the work. In the National Center of Elder Abuse study, one-third of the teams surveyed relied on state agencies, such as state units on aging, state protective service programs, or the state attorney general's office, for guidance and technical assistance (Teaster & Nerenberg, 2000).

DISSEMINATION OF INFORMATION ABOUT THE TEAM

Team members may want to develop a Web site or a newsletter to keep members of their own or other organizations informed about their progress (Nerenberg, 2003). Publication and dissemination of educational materials inform others about the team's progress and are helpful when recruiting new members. The information may assist others forming similar teams, allowing them to benefit from effective practices and avoiding pitfalls by sharing lessons learned. In addition, granting agencies and the public at large may become more educated about emerging issues and responses and be more willing to support them. Writing about an effective team also may lead to legislative reform, or modify standards of professional practice. The spread of information to other professionals may ultimately affect victims of elder abuse well beyond those reviewed within the geographic confines of the individual team.

As Ann reflected on the team's progress, she was pleased that the team had an active, ongoing membership. Law enforcement regularly referred cases to the team and attended meetings. They also persuaded the local prosecutor to attend. Over the last year, the team conducted cross-training of members, identified back-ups for each partner, and saw an increase in referrals of 20%. Law enforcement received the cases earlier in the process and was able to identify those that previously were never treated as crimes. Banks were now reporting suspicious conduct, something they had not previously done. As a result of these improvements, law enforcement was able to increase the number of arrests it made by 15% over the previous year. The prosecutor was able to charge nearly all of the cases, and several already had resulted in convictions. The team had been able to lock down and recover victim assets in the amount of $60,000 as a result of their work

In addition, the team produced an annual report, conducted informational seminars, produced a public service announcement, and created and distributed a brochure on financial exploitation. As a result, the county commissioner appropriated funds to staff the team. The team also witnessed an increase in the number of referrals in response to the educational programs and public awareness activities. After hearing a pubic service announcement about the team, a retired banker volunteered to assist the team in assessing suspicious financial transactions.

Accomplishing the Work

CHAPTER NINE

The Work of a Case Management Team

OVERVIEW

Once the planning and formation stages are completed, teams are ready to get to work. Some teams focus on system change such as fatality review teams or coordinating councils. Systemic collaborations are discussed in Chapter 12.

Case management teams review specific elder abuse cases and create intervention plans using a multidisciplinary approach. This is accomplished in several phases. Phase I is the referral, Phase II addresses the investigation or assessment, Phase III focuses on case review and the development of an intervention plan, and Phase IV consists of implementing the intervention plan.

The flow diagram in Figure 9.1 illustrates these processes.

The work of the case management team may be undertaken primarily by a single agency with input and direction from other organizations (single-agency model), or multiple groups may participate in all phases of the work (multiagency model). In either model, the work is carried out in the same four-phase sequence.

PHASE I: CASE REFERRAL

The team's focus has shifted from the development of the collaboration to consideration of the individuals to be served. The team should have set boundaries and limits on the cases to be reviewed. The case eligibility criteria, methods for case presentation and communication, and determinations of how to make, record, and monitor decisions should have been adopted before any cases are presented.

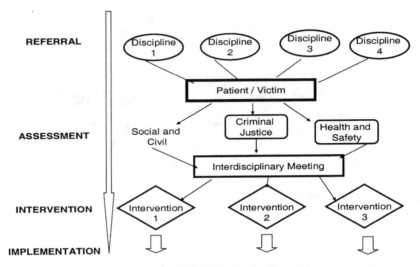

FIGURE 9.1   Flow Diagram of the Work of a Case Management Team.

Establishing Criteria for Casework

One of the first decisions is to determine who the team will serve. For instance, a fiduciary (financial) abuse specialist team (FAST) may decide to address only cases of financial exploitation or may expand its inquiry to address financial abuse accompanied by other forms of elder abuse. One team may address abuse against vulnerable or dependent adults; another might address cases involving elders with or without accompanying disabilities. The case criteria must address what kind of cases will be managed, the types of abuse and interventions, the setting in which the abuse occurred, and logistics concerning the meeting itself. Examples of significant decisions to be resolved include these:

- Will the team review cases exclusively involving elders or all vulnerable and dependent at-risk adults?
- Will the team serve clients with or without existing medical coverage?
- Will the team serve clients where the elder does not currently require medical treatment?
- Will the team consider all forms of abuse, neglect, and exploitation, or only abuse and neglect?
- Will the team consider cases of self-neglect?
- Will the team review cases occurring in institutional settings and board and care facilities, or only those within private residences?

- Will the team review cases that have resulted in death?
- Will the team review cases that did not involve team members and their agencies?
- Will the team revisit cases that were previously handled?
- Will the team review every case referred to it?
- Will the team review cases referred by members of the public?
- At what stage in a case will the team review it?

Application of Policies and Procedures

Ideally, members should have established regular times, locations, and length of meetings before sitting down to perform the casework. Unless time is spent discussing and agreeing on a method for handling case conferences and resolving differences of opinions, conflict may result. Before beginning case review, members should discuss professional differences of approach and legal limitations, such as the fact that law enforcement cannot share criminal histories, advocates may be unable to share client-provided information, physicians may be required to treat all parties, while other participants may be prohibited from serving anyone except the client or the perceived victim. In certain kinds of cases, including domestic violence, a law enforcement team member may be mandated to investigate reported conduct, prepare a formal report, and arrest a suspected perpetrator, even against the wishes of the elder or other team members. Similarly, if there are allegations of child abuse, many members may be legally required to report them to authorities, irrespective of the views of others.

Communication of Information

Communication and case presentation issues include deciding how cases will be referred for discussion, when and where to meet, how and who will create the agenda, how and to whom materials will be exchanged, and how members will communicate during meetings. For example, many teams have found it helpful to have the initial case presentation made by the referring discipline. Some groups have developed intake forms to ensure that critical information is collected and conveyed to other members. Team members should discuss issues concerning transmission of these forms. Certain methods of transmitting information, particularly electronic communications, including Web sites, e-mails, and faxes, may not provide the appropriate level of confidentiality required for sensitive matters, such as abuse type and medical history. Interdisciplinary communication can be complicated as a result of the exchange of information, decision making, and conflicting professional views. All members should understand the impact of confidentiality on the exchange of information. (A broader discussion of confidentiality is found in Chapter 7.)

Given the involvement of many different disciplines, presenting information so as to be understood and valued by everyone on the team can be complicated. Each discipline applies its own "worldview." For instance, classic social work training teaches that the best practice is to broaden the scope of assessment to include all immediate and extended relationships, and a detailed life history. This may be thought of as the "rule in" worldview, that is, to incorporate the broadest scope in each evaluation. Physicians, in contrast, are trained to use data to quickly narrow the possibilities and arrive at the most likely diagnosis. This is the "rule out" view, which narrows and limits the information to that which is absolutely critical to a decision (Qualls & Czirr, 1988). Similarly, law enforcement is trained to gather facts relevant to criminal conduct and focus on the current incident, rather than a broad historical perspective or the relevant social factors in the offender's situation.

These differences in worldview may clash at the case conference where the extent of detail and the words chosen require care. Although some members may feel more comfortable presenting detailed accounts of their investigation to their peers, in a team setting it is crucial that material be synthesized, so only what the team *needs* to know is presented. This process of paring down information may conflict with certain disciplines' training and daily practice. But the failure to do so may alienate and frustrate other professionals, who feel their time is being wasted with trivial and extraneous details. For example, the team does not need to know all the facts leading to a physician's selection of one drug over another, or each of the diagnoses considered but rejected, unless that information is relevant to the team's decision making. Law enforcement does not need to recite each investigative step taken, the questions asked, the number of pictures placed in a photo spread, or the particular rights read to a suspect. Instead the team needs to know if a crime has been committed, if there are remaining forensic issues, and whether a charge has been filed. Similarly, Adult Protective Services (APS) specialists need to focus on the critical facts rather than each step undertaken to arrive at them, as well as on providing relevant but limited details. In cases where greater detail is needed, it can be provided as a follow-up to members' questions and during the team's discussion.

Decision Making

A clear understanding of the undertaking and expectations of each member and their organization is necessary. Most formal teams have found it essential to formalize their relationship and their expectations through memoranda of understanding, operating agreements, contracts, sub-contracts, or interagency agreements. The group should determine how decisions would be made: Will the team vote or try to arrive at a consensus? If a vote is taken, must there be unanimity or something less? Every member must be respected for the expertise he or she brings to the work. In a collaborative model, all contribute to the discussion and the decision making. The specifics of individual cases may dictate that a critical decision be made by one or two members; in the multidisciplinary team model, the role of decision maker is not owned by any one discipline and is often determined by consensus.

Conflict Management

Differences of opinion are to be expected; the success of the team depends on having a process to manage conflict and arrive at a case resolution. A more complete discussion of potential sources of conflict is found in Chapter 7. Ideally the process for conflict management is determined in the formative stage of team development.

Having established criteria for case selection, communication, decision making, and handling conflict, team members can begin to refer cases to the group. A member from any participating discipline, including from agencies not represented on the team, may refer cases. Generally, the referring discipline or organization has performed an assessment, formed an opinion about the suitability of the case for review, and communicated the need for review to the other team members.

PHASE II: ASSESSMENT OR INVESTIGATION

Team priorities should guide the scheduling of case assessment. For example, if a team's purpose is rapid response to emergency reports of suspected abuse, then the team necessarily will respond more quickly than a case review team addressing routine situations. A medical-based team may schedule according to preset criteria or use nurse case managers to triage cases. Cases where a person or their assets are in immediate danger must be addressed expeditiously.

Once a case has been triaged or assigned to the team, the members usually proceed with assessment or investigation according to the standard operating procedures of their disciplines and organizations. The work of some of the involved disciplines is described in Chapter 5. Using a team should streamline the work of other members. For example, the medical team may not need to make a house call but can see the client in an outpatient setting if they know that the APS caseworker will do a thorough environmental assessment. If it is critical for multiple team members to make a home visit, they may jointly visit a client in the home, thereby avoiding multiple visits, as well as increasing the safety of the client/patient and each participating professional.

Table 9.1 outlines the types of information that the various disciplines derive from their investigations or assessments.

After each participating team member has completed his or her evaluation of the patient or victim, a meeting is called or, if there is a standing meeting time, the information is brought to the group at the scheduled time. Members are expected to have completed their work before the meeting, so that the case can be competently and comprehensively discussed and an appropriate plan can be crafted.

TABLE 9.1   Data Obtained in Phase II of Case Work

Discipline	Data Derived Through Assessment or Investigation
Adult Protective Services	• Field assessment of the client
	• Assessment of living environment
	• Collateral history from family members, involved parties, neighbors
	• Assessment of financial situation
	• History of prior abuse or allegations
	• Potential perpetrators
	• Awareness of community services
	• Functional assessments
	• Services already involved or needed
Civil Law	• Understanding of guardianship/conservatorship
	• Understanding of court orders
	• Understanding of actions for lawsuits
Law Enforcement	• Suspicious behavior and criminal conduct
	• Information about neighborhood, e.g., "drug infested"
	• Photos of victim/patient/client

(continued)

TABLE 9.1   *(continued)*

Discipline	Data Derived Through Assessment or Investigation
	• Suspect information
	• Evidence
	• Interviews of victim, perpetrator, witnesses
	• Documentation of all observations and actions
	• Relevant diagnoses
Medicine	• Information distinguishing abuse and neglect from medical conditions
	• Prognoses
	• Mental capacity assessment
	• Effect of medications on the mental and functional state of the patient
	• Interpretation of medical records
	• Mechanism of injury
	• Cause of death
Prosecution	• Type of criminal conduct
	• Elements of crime
	• Burden of proof
	• Information on legal requirements
Victim Advocacy (both in criminal justice system and in the community)	• Advocacy for the victim
	• Expert information on family violence and sexual assault
	• Expert information on the impact of events on the victim
	• Obstacles and threats to victim safety
	• Knowledge of community services and compensation programs

PHASE III: CRAFTING AN INTERVENTION PLAN

The goal of case review is to develop a comprehensive case plan—a roadmap for the course of action to address and resolve the presenting issues, whether they are medical, psychological, legal, social, or a combination. Social workers may call this part of the process *case reading*; medical professionals use the terms *case conference* or *case presentations*. Throughout this chapter the term *case review* is used.

Case review in elder abuse seeks to develop optimum and individualized outcomes. The case review process includes recitation of the known facts, social history, medical history and/or conditions, mental status, perpetrator information, and previous interventions and actions. Case reviews generally include any evaluations previously performed by team members or disciplines. After relevant information is presented, the ensuing discussion leads to the identification of possible interventions and resolutions, and the follow-up steps to be undertaken. These are prioritized and the sequence of responses established. In some teams many members will participate in carrying out the intervention steps. In others, the team offers suggestions and helps craft the intervention but only the presenting member carries out the plan.

Reviewing the Allegation(s)

Case reviews of situations with living victims (patients/clients) usually begin with a review of the allegations to try to understand what occurred and the contributing factors. This process leads to the development of an intervention plan that addresses the victim's (patient's/client's) social, functional, health, and financial circumstances. These are discussed not in isolation, but as interrelated domains that bear on the individual as a whole. This is a markedly different focus from that associated with traditional systems. For instance, medical professionals focus only on disease states and organ systems. Such an approach has significant limitations in that medical status is only one aspect of the elder's situation. Focusing only on that one aspect fails to consider the related and interconnected problems that also must be resolved. In the elder abuse multidisciplinary team, the medical professional, in conjunction with other team members, examines disease states and assesses their relationships to social and financial states and functional ability (Poythress, Harrell, Booker, & Dyer, 2001). For example, if the senior is living in squalor, this situation may be due to underlying neurocognitive disease, severe arthritis limiting function, insufficient funds to make repairs or clean, or any combination thereof.

The traditional approach to elder abuse victims (patients/clients) requires members to focus on that aspect of the case that they are most suited to address. To effectively deal with the complex issue of elder abuse, however, teams must collectively address the multiple domains central to the senior's life (see Figure 7.1, Chapter 7). Consideration of the central life domains of the victim/patient/client will inform the team about the multiple causes and degree of the dangerousness of the situation, all of which are highly relevant to the creation of an effective intervention. No single team member will have complete information on each domain. Each member collects relevant pieces while performing their traditional duties and reports their findings during the case review.

In addition to the central life domains, each elder's cultural, ethnic, and religious background should be considered and culturally appropriate interventions selected whenever possible. If the assembled team members do not have the particular expertise to deal with a culturally based issue, it is appropriate to add community members of the group to serve on an ad hoc basis. Longer term, the team should consider if it should add permanent members from particular cultures, religions, and other populations to best serve their communities.

Case Review Process

There is some variation in how teams present cases. In the single agency model, only one member or agency will have worked with a client and that person will have all the available information to present to the team. In multiple agency teams, many members will have worked on a case, and each has relevant information to present.

Single Agency Model Case Presentation

During the team meeting, the agency working with the client presents the case. [Clients] are referred to by their initials or by a pseudonym. The agency representative presents the known facts, and [client] social, financial, and other information. If medical information is known, it is provided. The presenting agency may have worked with the client before and attempted a number of interventions. Each is described, as is the degree of success. Agencies may become frustrated by their inability to fashion a comprehensive and effective resolution and ask other team members for their suggestions. Members ask questions and suggest possible interventions. The group then assesses the ideas suggested by the team and develops a list of potential intervention steps. Sometimes, the suggestion is to bring the matter to another team member's agency or discipline. For example, the legal services team members may suggest that the client consider pursuing a court order to evict an abusive family member and that their agency can assist. The medical professionals may suggest that the client be medically assessed and offer to conduct the assessment. Law enforcement may suggest that the victim make a crime report so that their agency can conduct an investigation. After recommendations are made, it is up to the referring agency to implement those steps. The agency provides updates as the case develops.

Multiple Agency Model Case Presentation

During the team meeting, information is provided by each of the members who have conducted an investigation or assessment. Generally, the person who referred the case to the group will begin the presentation. Typically, this presentation is the most comprehensive and provides baseline historical information that includes the elder's central life domains. Thereafter, other involved agencies or professionals supply additional information. Team members may ask clarifying questions during or after individual presentation.

At the conclusion of all presentations, a broader discussion ensues. The critical features of the case are distilled, leading to the development of a more complete understanding of the situation and broad agreement on the factual context. As the team reaches consensus on the facts, the contours of a case plan begin to emerge and possible interventions are identified. It is at this juncture that philosophical conflicts may surface. By this point, each of the participating members feels an ownership of the work and a responsibility to "their" client. Particularly difficult problems arise when the team contemplates an action that some members feel is too restrictive (Dyer, Silverman, Nguyen, & McCullough, 2002).

An Ethical Conflict: Autonomy versus Safety

A recurring and problematic ethical conflict for multidisciplinary elder abuse teams is the balancing of victim (patient/client) autonomy with safety. Broadly speaking, members of disciplines trained in the social work approach consider the preservation of autonomy a key component of their professional and ethical responsibilities. Other professionals, such as law enforcement, prosecutors, and physicians, are charged with preserving the safety of citizens. It is relatively easy to achieve consensus when reviewing cases where seniors either clearly have or clearly lack decision-making capacity. Resolving cases involving seniors with questionable ability to make their own decisions may be highly contentious. Honoring the wishes of an elder with capacity demonstrates respect, while honoring the wishes of an elder without capacity who requests to stay in an unsafe situation may be tantamount to abandonment.

This situation is not easily solved. Resolution requires careful assessment and fact finding, open communication, and team members' willingness and ability to look beyond their own professional framework to achieve consensus. The team members and the persons they serve will benefit from the struggle associated with this and other ethical issues. These types of conflicts tend to hone the interdisciplinary and intervention skills of the team members and help them broaden their perspectives and identify new and different solutions that better address the elder's desires, while offering adequate safety protections.

Intervention Plan

The outcome of the case review process is the development of a mutually agreed on case plan, often called an intervention plan. Just as the case review process draws on expertise from a variety of disciplines, the case plan considers the various remedies and resources available through each discipline and selects those most appropriate. The development of an intervention case plan incorporates the team's overarching goals of stopping the abuse, protecting the victim and the public, restoring the victim's losses, holding the offender accountable, and, when possible, offering the abuser the opportunity to be rehabilitated. Interventions should be designed to accomplish these goals and, at the same time and to the extent possible, promote autonomy. The intervention case plan is a dynamic document and, as such, must be reviewed periodically to ensure that it remains relevant to the elder's health, safety, and social situation. Care plans also must be flexible so as to meet the person's short- and long-term needs and to accommodate changes in circumstances. For example, an abusive daughter providing care to her mother was removed and a new caregiver was put in her place. All was well until the new caregiver became acutely ill and a suitable temporary replacement had to be found.

In Table 9.2, the wide array of possible interventions by various disciplines is catalogued. In developing intervention plans, teams will select among these many alternatives in crafting a plan that best serves a particular situation and client.

PHASE IV: IMPLEMENTATION OF THE INTERVENTION PLAN

Once the team has devised a plan of action, it must proceed with the implementation. Many team members work for public and private service organizations and carry heavy caseloads. Those caseloads can make

TABLE 9.2   Intervention Strategies by Discipline

Discipline	Intervention Strategies
Adult Protective Services	• Cleaning services
	• Home modification to meet the needs of persons with disabilities
	• Obtain temporary medications
	• Referral to health care for physical and mental assessments
	• Obtain food services, including Meals on Wheels or food stamps, when applicable
	• Arrange for emergency housing
	• Arrange for home repairs, including roofing, floors, and walls
	• Provide short-term case management
	• Arrange for pest and animal control
	• Secure caretaker or other provider services
	• Provide linkage to all other service groups
	• Assist client to apply for financial and health care benefits
	• Advocate for clients in court
Civil Law	• Seek protective court orders on behalf of client
	• Initiate law suits on behalf of clients for such causes of action as assault and battery, conversion, breach of contract, negligence, divorce, eviction, or revocation of a contract or deed
	• Prepare advanced directives, including powers of attorney
	• Seek or defend against guardianships/conservatorships
	• Establish or change documents such as trusts and wills
Law Enforcement	• Identify criminal conduct
	• Collect evidence of a crime
	• Arrange for and conduct forensic evidence examinations
	• Conduct identification procedures, including photos and lineups

(continued)

TABLE 9.2   *(continued)*

Discipline	Intervention Strategies
	• Apply for and execute arrest and search warrants
	• Where permitted, obtain court orders on behalf of victims
	• Seek bail enhancements
	• Where permitted, seize weapons and remove firearms
	• Obtain medical care for injured victims [patients/clients]
	• Obtain psychiatric care for mentally disturbed persons
	• Perform welfare checks
	• Accompany team members on house calls/home visits
Medical	• Treat or cure disease states (e.g., vitamin deficiency, depression, heart disease, hypertension, diabetes)
	• Improve cognitive status by providing medication and mental retraining
	• Improve functional status by prescribing therapy and/or assistive devices
	• Prevent deterioration by monitoring health status
	• Prevent death by responding to acute changes in status
	• Treat behavioral disorders with appropriate medical and environmental modifications
	• Adjust/monitor complex medication regimens
	• Improve nutrition by intervening in disease states and prescribing dietary supplementation
	• Recommend appropriate modifications to living situation
	• Provide caregiver training
	• Educate the patient about their disease states and requirements for improved health

(continued)

TABLE 9.2   Intervention Strategies by Discipline *(continued)*

Discipline	Intervention Strategies
	• Provide palliative care at the end of life by controlling pain and symptoms
Prosecution	• Provide information about the legal system
	• Provide assistance during investigation
	• Initiate charges
	• Prosecute cases on behalf of the state
	• Conduct grand jury investigations
	• Obtain court orders
	• Seek increased bail or remand
	• Issue subpoenas to secure witnesses and production of documents
	• Obtain conviction of perpetrators of elder abuse
	• Seek conditions of probation to address underlying reasons for criminal conduct and separate victim and suspect
	• Seek orders of restitution
	• File motions seeking sanctions for violations of probation or failure to pay restitution
	• Present victim impact information at sentencing
	• Appear at parole hearings to resist early release
Victim Advocacy (Community-based)	• Operate support groups
	• Operate shelter programs
	• Assist with preparation of a safety plan
	• Explain community-based resources
Note: Information obtained from a victim is legally protected and confidential	• Inform about available legal options
	• Assist with obtaining court orders
	• Provide crisis and ongoing counseling
	• Assist with obtaining legal benefits
	• Arrange for emergency housing including appropriate shelters
	• Assist victims in enrolling in confidential address programs (where available and with eligibility)

(continued)

TABLE 9.2   *(continued)*

Discipline	Intervention Strategies
Victim Advocacy (Victim Witness Assistance Programs)	• Assist with preparation of a safety plan
	• Explain community-based resources
	• Inform about available legal options
	• Assist with obtaining court orders
Note: Criminal justice-based advocates generally obtain information that can be used in court and do not have client confidentiality to the extent that community-based advocates do.	• Provide crisis intervention and direct to ongoing counseling
	• Assist with obtaining legal benefits
	• Arrange for emergency housing, including referral to appropriate shelters
	• Assist victims in enrolling in confidential address programs (where available and with eligibility)
	• Demystify the criminal justice system by providing information on the process, court procedures, participants and their role
	• Explain community resources, options
	• Make emergency housing referrals
	• Arrange respite care so that a victim who is a caregiver can attend court proceedings
	• Provide transportation to court
	• Provide court accompaniment for victims
	• Assist victims in preparation of impact statements
	• Advise of court dates
	• Provide limited emergency funds (when available)
	• Pay to change locks and repair broken windows and doors
	• Provide a stipend for permanent relocation (where available)

it difficult to track the work of the team as it is performed and completed. Many teams maintain files and collect data to track cases and the success of recommended interventions. Generally, administrative support is needed to maintain accurate files of use to all team members.

Victims with chronic problems benefit from a professional who establishes a long-term relationship with them. Continuing long-term relations between service provider and client may be preferable, but it is not always possible. Where multiple members participate in the implementation stage, some team members are required to complete their part of the plan and close their agency's case as a result of statutory time limitations or caseload.

Teams should continuously evaluate their effort. This includes a review of the casework process and its impact on the participating disciplines. Self-evaluation should also focus on the successful implementation of the plan and the eventual impact on the elder. In Houston, Texas, the Texas Elder Abuse and Mistreatment Institute performs six-month evaluations of all patients to assess their scores on a functional and cognitive battery of tests, and to monitor success in addressing the initial allegation. This information is collected, analyzed, and reported back to the team members in aggregate form (Poythress et al., 2001). When possible, team members should track outcomes and update team members on case developments and progress.

Generally speaking, the work performed by elder abuse case management teams proceeds according to the four phases of referral, assessment, crafting an intervention plan, and implementation. In the single agency model, a member of the referring agency actually carries out the last phase. In the multiagency model, however, the implementation plan that was jointly-developed may be carried out by various members of the team. The cases that follow demonstrate the work of both a multiagency and single-agency case management team. In all instances the names are fictitious.

MULTI-AGENCY CASE: DORIS

Phase I: Referral

Doris was an 83-year-old female who was residing in her home. The APS hotline received an intake call stating that Doris's son, Ralph, was verbally and emotionally abusive to her. During the initial face-to-face visit with Doris, Ralph was present and very upset about the involvement of APS. He did not allow the APS worker to interview Doris privately. He followed Doris and the APS specialist throughout the house demanding to know what was said. Eventually the APS worker and client had to talk in the worker's car to prevent Ralph from listening and interfering. Doris denied that her son mistreated her. She did say, however, that it bothered her that he lived in her home, was employed, and refused to contribute to household expenses. Doris was not interested in APS intervention. During the course of the interview, it became very clear that Doris was suffering from a cognitive impairment and was also continuing to drive.

After speaking with Doris, the APS worker attempted to interview Ralph. He was verbally aggressive and accused the APS worker of "brainwashing" his mother against him. Ralph would not sit down to provide a statement. When asked if he had been verbally or emotionally abusive to his mother, he responded, "I might have called her a name or two." As his anger escalated, his mother tried to calm him down and he yelled at her. He refused to participate further in the interview and demanded that the APS worker leave immediately.

Ralph called the APS worker shortly after her return to the office. He accused her of not doing her job and meddling. He was verbally aggressive and irrational. The APS worker terminated the threatening conversation. Thereafter, Ralph contacted the APS hotline and accused Doris's granddaughter, Jackie, of financial exploitation. Ralph also threatened to harm the APS worker. He indicated he had a gun and was prepared to use it if Jackie tried to start anything with him.

The APS worker contacted Jackie for collateral information. Jackie confirmed that Ralph called Doris a "bitch" and "fool," and that the entire family feared him. Family members would not visit Doris if they knew that Ralph would be there. Jackie also revealed that Ralph had served several jail terms for assault with a gun. She believed that he was financially exploiting her grandmother and had access to her funds. One of Doris's accounts had been closed two years earlier because of his previous financial exploitation.

Doris's case met the criteria for referral to the local elder abuse case management team and the APS worker made a referral.

Phase II: Assessment/Investigation

APS

The protective service worker learned that Doris was a widow, owned her own home, and had a savings account with unknown contents. Her monthly income consisted of $800, which came from a widow's pension and a Social Security retirement benefit. The worker also learned, through further investigation, that the Social Security Administration had suspended Doris's checks when the account where her check was directly deposited was closed. No one had changed the information with Social Security, so she was without income and also had lost her Medicare Part

B coverage. Several months later the situation was corrected and Doris received a lump sum payment of $12,000. It was deposited into her savings account and later disappeared. Attempts to determine what had happened to the money were stymied when the bank refused to provide any information regarding the account by telephone.

Law Enforcement

The law enforcement liaison officer confirmed that Ralph had been in jail for assault and drug charges. He recommended that community agency and medical staff not attempt to enter the residence without a police escort. The officer agreed to accompany the medical team members on the house call.

Medical Team

The health care team performed a complete geriatric assessment and concluded that Doris had Alzheimer's disease. She was diabetic and took her medication only occasionally. She was not being given a diabetic diet, nor was her blood sugar level monitored. They requested that a geriatric psychiatrist also evaluate Doris for decision-making capacity. The psychiatrist determined that Doris lacked decision-making capacity.

Phase III: Development of an Intervention Plan

The team members gathered to discuss Doris's case. Members were unanimously concerned about Doris's safety, so the timing of Phase III was expedited. All agreed that Doris did not understand the consequences of her decision to continue to live with her son. Doris's daughters expressed a wish to become more involved with their mother's care but hesitated out of fear of Ralph, who had repeatedly impeded efforts by APS and the family to intervene. Ralph was a convicted felon, had told the call taker at the APS hotline that he had a gun and was prepared to use it, and was known to be a violent person. The team members were concerned about the potential harm to Doris or her guardian should a guardianship be established. There was also concern that once Ralph became aware that his source of support was being threatened, he would harm Doris or her estate. In view of these concerns, the team requested that a temporary guardian be put in place to protect Doris and her estate until permanent orders could be made.

The team recommended that Doris and her son be separated. Several methods were discussed, including a legal eviction, a court order excluding Ralph from the residence, or a criminal prosecution if sufficient evidence existed. The team recognized that each of these steps took time, during which Ralph remained in the home, increasing concerns for Doris's safety.

Phase IV: Implementation of the Intervention Plan

APS

The APS worker, in consultation with the medical professionals, arranged temporary placement for Doris in a secure and confidential location equipped to handle persons with dementia. Ralph was unable to locate her during this time.

Law Enforcement

Ralph was subsequently arrested on a parole violation and a new charge for threatening the APS worker.

Prosecution

The prosecutor filed a criminal charge and requested a criminal court protection order to prohibit Ralph's contact with Doris and the APS worker. The prosecutor also sought denial of Ralph's release on his promise to return to court whenever ordered. Ralph was convicted of the charge. At sentencing the prosecutor recommended that Ralph be incarcerated. In the same proceeding, the court issued a restraining order prohibiting Ralph from contacting his mother.

APS

After Ralph was arrested, incarcerated, and a criminal court order obtained, APS assisted Doris in returning to her home. Security improvements, such as changed locks, a new unlisted phone number, an alarm system, and other safety devices, were made. APS located a suitable family member who moved into Doris's home and agreed to serve as guardian.

Medical Team

Members of the health care team arranged for a daily care provider to meet Doris's health needs at her home. The medical house call team continued to monitor her medical situation. Doris's Alzheimer's disease was stabilized through medication and her cognitive symptoms did not worsen. Her blood sugar levels were under control and her overall situation was improved.

SINGLE AGENCY CASE: ESTELLE

Phase I: Referral and Phase II: Assessment Intervention

Estelle was 80 years old and lived with her son in subsidized housing when the case began. She had multiple medical problems, some cognitive impairment, and walked with a cane. She received Social Security benefits and belonged to a managed health care plan. Social work assistance was provided on an as-needed basis through this plan. Six months earlier, Estelle's telephone service was disconnected owing to nonpayment of the bill. She enlisted the services of a social worker, Mary, who helped Estelle obtain telephone service again and enlisted the assistance of a money manager to help with bill paying.

Two months earlier, Estelle received an eviction notice and was told she was $2,500 in arrears on her rent. Estelle was alarmed and confused, as she had given her son, Charles, age 57, the rent checks to deliver. He had failed to deliver the checks. Mary checked with Estelle's bank and learned that other money had disappeared from her account. Estelle had not received bank statements and several checks were missing from the back of her checkbook. Estelle insisted Charles was not stealing from her.

Mary contacted Legal Aid and, with their help, worked out an agreement with the housing agency to repay the back rent. Charles agreed to assist in paying back half the back rent by working part-time at his old job. The housing agency agreed to drop the eviction action. The possible check fraud was not reported to police at Estelle's insistence.

Phase III: Development of an Intervention Plan

Two weeks earlier, Estelle received a call from an employee at her day center who said he had helped Charles remove money and checks from her purse. Estelle told Mary about the call. The worker called APS and the police. Estelle refused to talk to the police who came to interview her. Mary then presented the case to the team because of concern that Charles, a drug user with a criminal history that included check fraud, would financially exploit his mother again. In addition, the son now refused to help his mother repay the back rent and there were concerns that she would be evicted.

The team members discussed the case and suggested the following interventions: that Charles be evicted from the home unless he agreed to pay his share of the rent; that an attempt be made to renegotiate the back rent agreement so that Estelle had more time to pay, as she must pay the entire back rent herself; that a more protective financial management be developed for Estelle, such as execution of a durable power of attorney with a responsible person, identification of a representative payee, or even a guardianship for finances, if other approaches failed; and that follow-up be made on the missing checks to see if a criminal case against the son could be developed.

Phase IV: Implementation of the Intervention Plan

Mary undertook the recommended interventions. She contacted law enforcement who, in turn, contacted the bank to see if they had the suspicious checks. She assisted them in identifying suspicious transactions and, in turn, police were able to identify Charles as having passed four checks through several ATMs. The total loss in these transactions was $1,500. Officers obtained an arrest warrant against Charles and arrested him. He eventually pled guilty and was sentenced to a period in jail and ordered to undergo drug treatment. He also was ordered to stay away from Estelle and her residence and to repay the stolen money. Mary convinced Estelle to sign affidavits of forgery for the four checks and the bank restored the money to Estelle's account. Estelle agreed to accept the services of a representative payee. Now the payee makes her payments, bypassing Charles. Her checking account now requires that there be two signatures on checks for more than $50.

The team members are also concerned that once Charles is released from custody, Estelle will let her son back into her home and he will continue to exploit her. Mary is helping Estelle practice what to do if Charles comes to the house and asks to stay with her. The housing facility has alerted security staff to watch for Charles and to notify police if he appears as he would be in violation of the court order.

CHAPTER TEN

Enhancing Victim Safety Through Collaboration

"Elkmore Man Indicted in Wife's Slaying"

Police found 72-year-old Jane Hoffman lying on her bed, dead from a gunshot to the head. Her husband, who had planned to kill himself, lay asleep next to her. Hoffman told police he and his wife were in "severe financial difficulty" and that "he could not have his wife learn about the financial situation because it would be unbearable for her."

Cecil Whig, June 8, 2004

"No Prison in Death of Woman"

Alexandra, age 37, shut her Alzheimer's stricken grandmother, age 86, in a basement room. Four days later when she called the police, her grandmother was dead. "Prosecutor Paul Parker said it appeared the victim had crawled out of bed in an attempt to reach the door. He said the woman weighed 59 pounds, was emaciated, and had been lying in a bed stained with feces and urine." The judge rejected jail time saying, Alexandra "had done the best she could under the circumstances."

Salt Lake Tribune, June 29, 2004

"Deaths Prompt Two Families to Sue Local Nursing Homes"

The family of John Zajch Sr. is seeking $2 million in damages in a suit against Kindred Nursing Centers. The suit alleges that Zajch was admitted to the facility without bedsores. When he was moved from the nursing home to the hospital, bedsores extended through skin and muscle tissue to the bone. He died from blood poisoning caused by multiple pressure sores. The wife in another family is suing the facility claiming that an employee improperly placed a feeding tube in her husband's stomach, leading to his death.

Virginian-Pilot, June 19, 2004

"Reno Man Admits to Killing His Parents"

Huntoon, age 55, admitted that he killed his 86-year-old father and 84-year-old stepmother. He claimed that he had beaten them both with a hammer, and that he may also have attempted to choke or strangle one or both of his victims. Several people interviewed suggested that there had been abuse at the home and that his parents may have been trying to kick him out.

KRNV.com, June 29, 2004

Seniors are killed or seriously harmed by abuse and neglect every day. Victim safety must be the primary goal of intervention in elder abuse cases. Previous chapters have described the benefits and challenges of collaboration and have discussed informal "practice-based" approaches and the use of formalized teams. This chapter ties these concepts together by illustrating a multidisciplinary approach to promote safety of elder abuse victims. Lethality assessments and safety planning tools are described. Worker safety, especially during home visits, is discussed. A case illustration demonstrates the concepts presented in this chapter.

ELDER ABUSE CAN LEAD TO SERIOUS HARM OR DEATH

As the newspaper articles at the beginning of this chapter indicate, some cases of elder abuse led to the death of the victim. In facilities, the death may be caused by neglect, poor care, inadequate medical treatment, or malpractice. In some cases, a staff person may be a serial killer who performs "mercy killings."

Homicides also occur in the community. A spouse or partner who has been abusive and controlling for years commits homicide. New partners may have married for money or possessions and may kill the elder to get the estate of the older person. Adult children or grandchildren may also use lethal violence to get possessions. Some abusers have mental illness and inadvertently kill an older person. In single female victim/single male offender homicides reported for 2001, 8% (158 victims) were age 65 or older (Brock, 2003).

In many cases resulting in death, there are no external injuries (Hawley, McClane, & Strack, 2001). This creates special problems for those responding to death calls. Screening for a history of domestic violence or elder abuse and carefully investigating the scene are important. Where the death is suspicious and an autopsy is conducted, blunt trauma injuries, fingernail marks, petechial hemorrhages in the eyes, skin, internal organs, and undersurface of the scalp may well be found (Hawley et al., 2001). An illustration of the difficulty of determining whether a death—or even just an injury—resulted from physical abuse is provided in the following discussion about the challenges of identifying strangulation.

Professionals may fail to identify strangulation and suffocation, serious forms of physical abuse that can lead to death. Strangulation is a form of asphyxia characterized by closure of the blood vessels and air passages of the neck as a result of external pressure on the neck (Iserson, 1984; Line, Stanley, & Choi, 1985). Suffocation is the cutting off of the airways by covering the mouth or nose or by sitting on the victim's chest. Nationally about 10% of violent deaths are due to strangulation. Women are strangled six times as often as men, although a small woman can strangle a much larger man. Unconsciousness can occur in seconds and death within minutes (Strack et al., 2001). Most strangulation is manual, that is, committed using one or both hands; however, ligature strangulation, in which the perpetrator uses a cord or other binding around the victim's neck, is not uncommon.

Strangulation is closely associated with domestic violence, especially in younger victims. No studies examine its incidence in older couples, so these data are drawn from studies of younger adults. A San Diego study of 300 strangulation cases found a history of domestic violence in 89% of cases. Overwhelmingly (99%), perpetrators were male (Strack et al., 2001).

Seniors are not only at risk of homicide, they also experience higher rates of homicide/suicide than younger people. In cases of homicide/suicide, the perpetrator takes the life of the victim and then kills himself. One study indicates that most (83%) homicides/suicides are of the spouse/partner type. The balance of cases involve other familial relationships such as adult children, siblings, or parents (Cohen, 2000).

Cohen's research suggests that there are at least three subtypes of homicide-suicide among older adults. Approximately 30% involve previous domestic violence; 50% are dependent/protective long-term relationships, where the man is dominant and one or both parties have been ill; and 20% are symbiotic relationships, characterized by extreme interdependence (Cohen, 2000).

Characteristics noted from Cohen's research suggest that men are always the perpetrator and guns are the method of choice in 90% of cases. These are not acts of love and compassion, but rather desperation and depression. They are not suicide pacts. The wife often was not a willing participant, even though the perpetrator had planned the event for months or years (Cohen, 2000).

Predisposing risk factors of homicide/suicide include:

- Advanced age
- A long-lived marriage
- Depression and other psychiatric problems in perpetrator
- Perpetrator is a caregiver
- Perpetrator has a controlling personality
- Multiple health problems in perpetrator
- Marital discord
- Family discord
- Social isolation
- Perpetrator giving things away (Cohen, 2000)

Lethality Assessment

Research on lethal elder abuse and potential risk factors is scarce. Drawing on data from domestic violence literature may provide information that is useful when working with older victims. No tool can decisively predict which victims are at risk of being killed. In a few situations, friends, family, or professionals appeared not to have any indication that abuse was occurring or that homicide was imminent (Websdale, 1999). However, professionals can look for some common risk factors that may assist in assessing lethality as a method to help victims ascertain their own level of risk. Any lethality assessment tool should not be used as a checklist that is handed out to victims. Rather, it should be used as a tool to discuss with a victim the circumstances of the abuse and to begin safety planning (Websdale, 1999).

Several lethality assessment tools created by experts in the domestic violence field may provide information that is also applicable to many elder abuse victims. According to Campbell (1995), experts in the field have identified the following key risk factors associated with perpetrators:

- Access to/ownership of guns
- Use of weapon in prior abusive incidents
- Threats with weapons
- Serious injury in prior abusive incidents
- Threats of suicide
- Drug or alcohol abuse
- Forced sex
- Obsessiveness/extreme jealousy/extreme dominance

More recent research by Campbell, Webster, Kozoil-McLain, and Block (2003) on high-risk factors for intimate partner homicide found that (1) women threatened or assaulted with a gun were 20 times more likely than other women to be murdered, (2) women threatened with murder were 15 times more likely than other women to be killed, and (3) when a gun is in the house, an abused woman is 6 times more likely to be killed than other abused women. Drug and alcohol abuse increase risk, but other factors such as threats to kill, extreme jealousy, attempts to "choke," and forced sex represent greater risk. Threatened or attempted suicide was not found in this study to be a predictor of intimate partner homicide (Campbell et al., 2003). Other researchers and experts in the domestic violence field have similar findings. Hart (1988) identified attempts, threats, or fantasies of homicide or suicide as key indicators of a risk of possible serious or lethal assaults. Other factors include "availability/access to willingness to use or history of using weapons; obsessiveness; isolation of the batterer and his degree of dependence on the battered woman; rage; depression; drug and alcohol consumption; and access to the victim" (Websdale, 1999). Block (2003) found that risk factors for lethal domestic violence where there has been a history of abuse are: (1) the type of past violence, such as prior incidents resulting in permanent injury, a severe beating, strangulation, burning, internal or head injuries, and the threat of or actual use of a weapon; (2) the number of days since the last incident; the closer the time between the new incident and the previous one, the greater the danger (lethal homicide typically occurs in the 30 days after an incident, though some occur within 1 to 2 days); and (3) the frequency or increasing frequency of past violence. Finally, Websdale (1999) found the most prominent factors in both multiple and single killings, in order of importance, are:

- A prior history of domestic violence.
- An estrangement, separation, or an attempt at separation nearly always by the female party.
- A display of obsessive-possessiveness or morbid jealousy on the part of the eventual perpetrator often accompanied by suicidal ideation, plans, or attempts; depression; sleep disturbances; and stalking of the victim.
- Prior police contact with the parties, more so in cases of single killings, often accompanied by perpetrators failing to be deterred by police intervention or other criminal justice initiatives.
- Perpetrator making threats to kill victim, often providing details of intended modus operandi and communicating those details in some form or other, however subtle, to the victim, family members, friends, colleagues at work, or others.

- Perpetrator is a family member who has used violence before and sometimes has prior criminal history of violence. Included in this group is a small but significant number of killers who have both access to and a morbid fascination with firearms.
- Perpetrator consumes large amounts of alcohol or drugs immediately preceding the fatality, especially in cases of single killings.
- Victim has restraining order or order of protection against perpetrator at time of killing (Websdale, 1999).

Seeking help or separating from an abusive relationship is a significant risk factor for serious injury or death. Abused women who were killed or killed their abuser were more likely to have sought outside help than women who were severely beaten but not killed. Approximately 75% of homicide victims and 85% of victims of severe but nonfatal violence had left or tried to leave in the prior year. In 45% of lethal domestic violence cases, a woman's attempt to leave the abuser was the precipitating factor for the killing (Block, 2003).

Another factor worth exploring is substance abuse by the perpetrator. Risk of lethal or nearly lethal domestic homicide is increased when associated with alcohol and drug use by the offender. A violent intimate relationship, in which the abuser is described as a problem or binge drinker or drug abuser, is extremely dangerous. In a review of lethal homicide cases, researchers found that in the year before the homicide, female victims used alcohol and other drugs less frequently and in smaller amounts than their abusive male partners. Two-thirds of female homicide victims tested negative for the presence of alcohol. In this study, more than 75% of homicide and attempted-homicide female victims and 90% of abused victims did not consume alcohol either before the homicide or the more recent violent incident. More than 80% of abusers who killed or seriously abused female partners were problem drinkers and tended to binge drink. More than two-thirds of homicide and attempted homicide perpetrators used alcohol, drugs, or both during the incident; less than 25% of victims did so (Sharps, Campbell, Gary, & Webster, 2003).

The availability of weapons was identified as a significant risk factor in all studies. The picture that emerges from the article "When Men Murder Women" is that "women face the greatest threat from someone they know, most often a spouse or intimate acquaintance, who is armed with a gun. For women in America, guns are not used to save lives, but to take them" (Brock, 2003).

Stalking

In addition to the risk of being killed, perpetrators may stalk older victims. Stalking has rarely been thought of as an issue in elder abuse. National studies have focused on the general population, and, in particular, younger persons. These studies showed that nearly 5% of women and 0.6% of men are stalked by a current or former intimate partner during their lifetime. This translates into approximately 503,485 women and 185,496 men who are stalked annually in the United States by current and former intimate partners (U.S. Department of Justice, National Institute of Justice & The Centers for Disease Control and Prevention, 2000).

Most victims are women (78%). Women are significantly more likely than men (60% vs. 30%, respectively) to be stalked by an intimate partner; 80% of women stalked by former husbands are also physically assaulted, and more than 30% are sexually assaulted (Tjaden & Thoennes, 1998; U.S. Department of Justice, National Institute of Justice & Center for Policy Research, 1997). Where stalking victims obtained restraining orders, 69% of women and 81% of men said their stalker violated the order (Tjaden & Thoennes, 1998).

Current or former husbands are perpetrators 38% of the time; current and former cohabitating partners are the perpetrators 10% of the time; and current and former boyfriends are the perpetrators 14% of the time. Intimate partners who stalk are four times more likely to physically assault their victims and six times more likely to sexually assault their victims (U.S. Department of Justice, Office of Justice Programs, 1998).

Until recently, little was known about elder stalking. Jasinski and Dietz (2003) studied elder domestic violence and stalking rates among persons 55 and older. Using a study group of 3,622 older adults drawn from the National Violence Against Women Survey, they found that domestic violence and elder stalking share many similarities to similar conduct involving younger persons. Rates of domestic violence and stalking were consistent with those in the younger population. In both age groups, significantly more women are victimized than men. In stalking, women are victimized more than three times as often as men. Income was not a factor in either category in elderly adults.

The average age of elder victims was 66.4 years. More than two-thirds were unemployed and one-third had a disabling chronic disease or condition. Being a female, married, and with a partner in poor health were associated with greater risk of domestic violence.

Stalking is a pattern of conduct that produces fear. Statutory definitions vary, but elements typically include willful and repeated following or harassing of a particular person, accompanied by a threat or behavior that is threatening and would be so perceived by a "reasonable person." Many states require that the target be placed in actual fear and that the perpetrator have the apparent ability to carry out the threats, even if there is no actual intent to carry it out. Harassment is understood to mean a course of conduct, that is a series of acts over a period of time, however short, that evidence a continuity of purpose (U.S. Department of Justice, National Institute of Justice, 1993). It is conduct, often criminal in nature, involving acts of pursuit and "behavioral intrusion" that are threatening and may be dangerous. Every state and the District of Columbia have enacted criminal laws prohibiting it. It is also prohibited under federal law (Meloy, 1998).

Contrary to public impression, most stalking does not involve celebrities. Rather, most stalking is between persons who know one another, including current and former intimate partners (Meloy, 1998; Zona, Palarea, & Lane, 1998). It is often associated with the souring of a relationship (U.S. Department of Justice, National Institute of Justice, 1996) and is an effort to win the victim back or exact revenge for the perceived slight of leaving (Hall, 1998). About 60% of stalking began before the relationship ended (Tjaden, 1997). In the context of domestic violence, it begins when the batterer believes he is losing or has lost power and control over the intimate partner. The batterer, unable to accept rejection and her leaving, will harass, threaten, and assault her (U.S. Department of Justice, National Institute of Justice, 1996). Tjaden (1997) found that about half of female victims had been stalked by a current or former marital or cohabiting partner. Eighty percent had been physically abused and 31% were sexually abused by their intimate partner. "Stalking is how some men raise the stakes when women do not play along. It is a crime of power, control, and intimidation very similar to date rape (De-Becker, 1997). It occurs across the life span (Jasinski & Dietz, 2003).

In an attempt to instill fear, perpetrators may send unwanted letters, cards, and gifts; make telephone calls at all hours; survey victims; break into the victim's home to steal personal items, rearrange furnishings, or vandalize property; wiretap the victim's telephone; read or steal mail; send the victim magazines; file false police reports and lawsuits against the victim; spread rumors and gossip; harass victim's family, friends, and neighbors; send e-mail transmissions; and post Internet messages about the victim. Some stalkers will make overt threats; about three-fourths will spy on or follow the target; about a third vandalize the victim's property; and about 10% threaten to or kill the victim's pets (Tjaden, 1997). This campaign of conduct is profound and life changing for the victim, as it typically persists for months or even years (Meloy, 1998). "The ominous threats, constant surveillance, and intrusion into the victims' lives have long-term, damaging psychological effects. Living in fear takes a toll on the quality of life" (Hall, 1998).

Victim-Centered Safety Planning

Given that some older victims are in danger of being stalked, seriously injured, or killed, safety planning is a crucial component of any intervention. The term *safety* may have different meanings for various professionals. Too often, safety involving older persons focuses on ensuring that rugs and cords are placed so that no one trips and falls. Although strategies that focus on the physical health and well-being of older persons are important, safety planning for victims of elder abuse involves additional components.

A safety plan considers issues necessary to enhance the security of current victims of abuse. Safety planning is a proactive process that addresses how to respond to abuse in day-to-day living, as well as in a crisis situation. Anyone can talk with a victim about how to enhance safety (e.g., get weapons out of the house, have a plan of who to call in a dangerous situation, get a cell phone or life-line alarm pendant). However, domestic violence advocates are trained to do comprehensive safety planning with victims. Many victims benefit from talking with an advocate and developing a safety plan. Victims' plans respond to the range of batterer-generated and life-generated risks. The process of planning may include evaluating whether remaining in or ending a relationship will reduce or increase risks, and how their abuser will react (Davies & Lyon, 1998).

Safety planning is a process where a helper and a victim jointly create a plan. The safety plan is victim-driven and -centered. It is based on the victim's goals, not the professional's opinions.

Abusers often isolate victims and do not allow them to make their own decisions. Safety planning is a process that restores power and control to victims as they make decisions about how to enhance their own safety. A good safety planning process provides the victim with information and an array of options to choose from. Then the victim decides whether to stay with the abuser or to leave, and how to remain as safe as possible under the existing circumstances.

Safety plans include:

- Prevention Strategies: Preventing future incidents of abuse (e.g., going to shelter or moving to another residence, obtaining a restraining/protective order, hiding/disarming weapons, changing schedules and routes to avoid being found).
- Protection Strategies: Discussing methods victims can use to protect themselves during an abusive or violent incident (e.g.,

having an escape route, or having victim seek shelter in a room where a door can be locked, with a working phone available or where weapons are not present).

- Notification Strategies: Developing methods for seeking help in a crisis situation (e.g., cell phones, emergency numbers readily available, alarm pendants, security systems, a towel in the window or other coded method to notify a nearby neighbor to call the police, code words that can be used during phone conversations with friends/family/neighbors to alert them that the victim needs help (for example, if the victim says "apple pie" in the phone conversation it is a coded message to call the police).
- Referral/Services: Recognizing and using services that can offer assistance (e.g., domestic violence, sexual assault, adult protective services, criminal justice, aging and disability network, faith and community organizations).
- Emotional Support: Considering methods of emotional support and ways to become less isolated (e.g., music, exercise, yoga, reading positive or spiritual materials, hobbies, art, friends, support groups, and other community activities).

Recognize that the victim may want to stay with the abuser, may be in the process of leaving or returning to the abuser, or may have left and ended the relationship. In each of these situations, the five components of safety planning listed here are crucial.

For Victims Who Have Left or Are Leaving

For victims who are leaving or who have left, additional issues need to be considered.

Where will the victim live?

- Can the person remain safely in his or her home?
- Is there an emergency shelter in the community?
- Are friends or family an option?
- Are church groups or other organizations an option?
- Where does the person want to live after the immediate crisis?

Money

- Can the person get money for the short term?
- Are there financial programs available to assist the person? APS may be helpful in assessing eligibility for benefits.

Health

- What health-related items (e.g., medications, glasses, walker, hearing aids) will the victim need to live without the abuser?
- Who is the victim's primary health care provider? Has the victim considered talking with a health care provider about the abuse to get help with health issues and documentation? In most states, health care providers are mandatory reporters, so discuss with the victim whether he or she is comfortable with reporting.
- Is respite care available through social services?

Who else is affected by the abuse?

- Who can help with children, grandchildren, or other persons living with the victim?
- Can a friend or family member care for pets or livestock if the person can't take them along? (If not, local domestic violence programs may have information about "safe haven for pets" programs.)

Legal

- Has the abuser been arrested? If yes, what support does the victim need?
- Does the victim want a protective or restraining order? Local domestic abuse programs or APS may be able to assist with obtaining restraining/protective orders.
- Are there immigration issues? Contact a local domestic abuse program or a legal aid program or lawyer specializing in immigration.

Safety planning steps

Quality safety planning involves the following steps:

- Building rapport and listening to the victim.
- Learning about what the victim fears, both from the abuser and the consequences of any action that might be taken.
- Asking what the victim wants to do and why. Learning why or the motivation behind the victim's decisions can help a worker understand the victim's goals. The worker may be able to suggest other options or methods of reaching the same goal. For example, the victim may state she does not want to leave the abuser. If the worker asks why, she may find that the victim is

afraid to leave her three cats behind. The worker can let the victim know about "safe haven" programs for pets.
- Thinking creatively, together, about a variety of options and ideas.
- Building a safety plan that is victim centered.

Safety planning involves problem solving in advance of what a victim can do during and after a crisis. Simply making referrals to other agencies is not safety planning. In addition, safety planning is a fluid process. Life circumstances change for the victim and the abuser. Safety plans need regular updating to remain current (National Clearinghouse on Abuse in Later Life & Wisconsin Coalition Against Domestic Violence, 2003).

Safety planning with persons with cognitive disabilities creates unique challenges. In some cases, the victim will remember only one or two steps of the plan, such as "Call Alice" or "Call 911." Posting 911 stickers on telephones may be helpful in some situations. In many cases, the safety planning process will need to be done with a caring individual who will work with the victim with cognitive disabilities. A sample safety planning tool for persons working with someone with a cognitive disability is available from the National Clearinghouse on Abuse in Later Life, a project of the Wisconsin Coalition Against Domestic Violence, on the Web at http://www.ncall.us.

Traditional safety plans are available from local domestic violence programs or statewide coalitions. Sometimes these tools are not in large print or appear to be written for younger women, so they may need to be modified to meet the needs of older victims. Sample safety planning tools for older people and for victims with physical or cognitive disabilities also are available from the National Clearinghouse on Abuse in Later Life, on the Web at http://www.ncall.us.

Collaborative Response to Enhance Victim Safety

In addition to safety planning with victims, using a collaborative approach with the tools from multiple systems can be the most effective method to enhance the security and well-being of the victim. Table 10.1 illustrates some of the tools available from a variety of systems to enhance safety.

Worker Safety

In addition to the need to focus on victim safety, workers who enter homes where abuse is occurring need to be mindful of potential danger. Workers conducting home visits have been threatened, hit, and held hostage

TABLE 10.1   A Multidisciplinary Approach to Victim Safety

Discipline	Tools to Enhance Victim Safety
Domestic Violence and Sexual Assault Programs	• Victim-centered safety planning
	• Emergency shelter
	• 24-hour crisis line
	• Legal advocacy, including assistance with restraining orders and orders of protection and court accompaniment
	• Confidential address programs, where available
	• Free cell phones set to 911
	• Information about how technology can be used to locate victims
	• Assistance with emergency housing for pets
	• Support groups for elderly victims to discuss strategies for maintaining safety with other victims
Victim-Witness Advocates	• Safety planning
	• Confidential address programs, where available
	• Court accompaniment for elderly victims
	• Support for elderly crime victims
	• Safe waiting-room area
	• Pay to replace locks and broken windows and doors
	• Pay to install security systems
	• Free cell phones set to 911
	• Provide funds and assist with relocation
	• Enroll victims in victim notification programs
	• Provide updated information on case status and offender's release dates
	• Notify if failure to attend warrants are issued
Adult Protective Services	• Emergency and longer-term housing in a confidential location
	• Maintain a perpetrator registry
	• Do background checks on potential caregivers

(continued)

TABLE 10.1   A Multidisciplinary Approach to Victim Safety *(continued)*

Discipline	Tools to Enhance Victim Safety
	• Free cell phones preset to 911
	• Provide life-line pendants
	• Arrange self-sheltering for pets
	• Obtain emergency removal orders
	• Obtain in-home services for victims to break isolation and have other persons visiting the home
Law Enforcement	• Arrest offender
	• Incarcerate offenders
	• Seek bail enhancements
	• Where available, obtain court orders for victims
	• Emergency involuntary mental health commitments
	• Remove firearms and other deadly weapons where permissible
	• Provide civil standbys for removal of property
	• Assist with legal evictions
	• Operate victim notification system
	• Arrest offenders for failures to appear and probation or parole violations
Prosecution	• Obtain court orders for victims
	• Seek bail increases
	• Request conditions of bail or other release such as electronic monitoring of suspects
	• Oppose release without bond
	• Seek incarceration of offenders
	• Notify victims of changes in case status and the offender's custodial status
Civil Attorneys	• Obtain court orders to protect victims
	• Seek appointment of surrogate decision makers

(continued)

TABLE 10.1   *(continued)*

Discipline	Tools to Enhance Victim Safety
	• Seek termination of legal relationship between victim and perpetrator (e.g., divorce, separation, annulment)
	• Lawfully remove perpetrator from household
Health Care	• Admit to hospital under a false name
	• Restrict public access to patient
	• Place in less public area of hospital or very public area so that staff can keep an eye on the victim
	• Place in a secure part of hospital
	• Check identification of visitors
	• Screen in-coming phone calls

at knifepoint or gunpoint while completing an investigation. Professionals should also be aware that they may become targets if a perpetrator believes they have the power to decide what will happen to the client or if the perpetrator blames them for the situation and seeks revenge. Therefore throughout the investigation, assessment, and execution of the intervention plan, the focus must be on whether the perpetrator poses a risk to the victim and others. Even when a plan is developed that addresses safety, ongoing evaluation of risk mandates that if the danger level rises, the case plan may need alteration (Heisler & Brandl, 2002a, 2002b).

Professionals who conduct home visits should prepare beforehand by gathering information. Questions about prior calls for service, number of occupants, weapons, substance abuse, any known mental health history, and presence of dangerous animals should be asked. Workers should also take steps to enhance their personal safety before leaving the office. They should notify other office staff of where they are going and update that information upon arrival at the location and again as they leave. In the field, service providers should carry appropriate safety devices, such as flashlights and a fully charged cell phone. The cell phone should have a button set for the local law enforcement agency's emergency number. Workers should know how to contact law enforcement for a rapid response and what to say to ensure a high priority response. Workers should take safety precautions once they arrive at the home. Considering where to safely park and assessing the situation before entering the home for dangerous animals and other potential problems is a best practice. When in doubt, workers should not conduct visits alone and should bring law enforcement if deemed necessary (Heisler & Brandl, 2002a).

Some victims of elder abuse have communicable diseases and professionals must protect themselves, as well as other clients/patients with whom they may have contact. Professionals must be mindful of the potential for personal harm and take universal precautions to avoid spreading infections and other diseases. Avoid contact with any bodily fluids, including blood, saliva, urine, feces, vomitus, seminal fluid, sputum, and open wounds. Every professional should receive training in universal precautions, and team members should carry appropriate protective gear when in the field (gloves, masks).

CASE ILLUSTRATION

The case of Leroy is used to demonstrate a multidisciplinary approach to enhance victim safety.

Presenting Issues

Leroy, age 64, worked as a janitor at the local brewery. He stayed to himself and did not socialize with other employees. His co-workers noticed that he showered at work every day. They occasionally saw welts and bruises on his back and chest.

A gas meter reader took monthly readings in Leroy's neighborhood. Several months in a row, the meter reader watched Leroy go through a cellar door and not come back out. She wondered if something was wrong and called APS.

Initial Investigation

The APS worker started the investigation by going to Leroy's home. Before conducting the home visit, the APS worker gathered as much safety information as possible. The worker learned that no previous APS or police reports had been filed from this residence. Without talking directly to the family, the worker was unable to ascertain whether large dogs or guns were on the property.

Before leaving the office, the worker told other staff the address where she would be conducting the home visit and when she expected to return. She made sure she was wearing comfortable flat shoes in case she needed to leave quickly. She turned on both her cell phone and pager.

The worker approached Leroy's home cautiously. She parked on the street, not in the driveway where she could be blocked in. She noted that the neighborhood appeared to be a safe, quiet residential setting with older homes fairly close together. As she approached the home, she looked for evidence of large dogs and found none.

After being admitted to the residence by Leroy's wife, the worker introduced herself and asked to speak to Leroy. He arrived in the living room about 15 minutes later, looking disheveled and confused. The worker attempted to talk with Leroy alone, but his wife was clearly within earshot throughout their initial conversation. Leroy told the worker that everything was fine and that he chose to sleep in the cellar because his wife snored. He said he was tired from a long day at work and asked to go rest. The worker used the interview to attempt to build rapport with Leroy without pushing for answers, as she was concerned about Leroy's safety if he disclosed too much information while his wife was listening.

The worker was glad to learn about Leroy's job at the brewery and attempted a second interview after work the next day. During this interview, which was conducted in a private meeting room, Leroy told the APS worker that his wife, Gloria, and their adult son lived in the house. Leroy was forced to live in the cellar and sleep on a lawn chair. He used the toilet and purchased food at a nearby gas station. Leroy showed the worker his ribs, which appeared to be badly bruised. He told the APS worker that Gloria had hit him with a frying pan.

Victim Safety

The worker was concerned about Leroy's safety and health, especially given his bruised ribs. They talked about whether it was safe for him to return home that night. Leroy did not feel in immediate danger. He simply wanted to be allowed to live in his house with his family.

The worker asked Leroy if there were guns in the home and how he would escape if another violent incident occurred. They discussed which rooms might be more dangerous if Leroy were trying to escape from abuse, such as the kitchen where knives were present. Leroy said that if he were in danger he could call 911 if he could get to a phone. The worker agreed to try to get Leroy a free cell phone programmed to 911 from the local domestic abuse program. Leroy also said he would be able to go to his neighbors for help if necessary. Together the worker and Leroy developed a safety plan in case of a crisis.

In addition to planning for a crisis situation, Leroy and the worker discussed what he might need to have with him if he needed to leave quickly. Leroy realized he would need his security pass for work and some money. The worker also suggested some clean clothes and documents such as his Social Security card and health plan paperwork. Leroy also needed to be sure to pack his glasses and medications. He agreed to pack a small bag with the things he would need and want to have with him if he left quickly. Leroy also had a cat that he dearly loved and was worried his wife would not care for the cat if he left. The worker looked into temporary housing options for the cat if Leroy needed to stay somewhere overnight.

Other Key Components of an Effective Intervention

In addition to focusing on immediate safety planning, the worker and Leroy needed to address other key components, covered in Chapter 10, to create an effective intervention plan.

Health

Leroy did not want to go to the hospital immediately to have his ribs checked but agreed to call his doctor. He made an appointment for the next day and the doctor found several broken ribs. Leroy also appeared depressed. He was thin and not taking care of himself. He also was incontinent, which was the reason given by his wife that he could not live upstairs. According to Leroy's wife, he was "destroying her carpeting." Leroy's doctor remembered a conversation during their last visit that indicated that Leroy drank daily at the brewery before coming home.

The challenge the doctor faced was determining how to assess the cause of the medical circumstances Leroy presented. On the one hand, the doctor asked questions about substance abuse and noted that Leroy was still drinking every day. Multiple rib fractures are seen commonly in persons who abuse alcohol. His urinary incontinence could be the result of an enlarged prostate or alcohol abuse. Leroy's thin appearance may indicate malnutrition, possibly due to or exacerbated by his drinking. Depression is another consequence of drinking and could also be contributing to his malnutrition.

The doctor also asked questions about Leroy's home life and learned about the abuse. Now the physician could attribute Leroy's malnutrition to the withholding of food. His depression could be the result of abuse, and perhaps the reason he began drinking. His rib fractures could have been caused by blunt trauma, such as the result of being pushed down the stairs. Additional blood work could help clarify the extent of his drinking and the reason for his weight loss. Unfortunately, there are no forensic markers to guide physicians in determining the cause of fractures due to abuse (Dyer et al., 2002). Thus, one of the dilemmas for Leroy's doctor was differentiating which medical finding was caused by elder abuse, alcohol abuse, or both.

With collateral history from APS, more history from Leroy, and some lab studies, the physician could establish the possibility that the rib fractures and other findings were the result of abuse. Accurate documentation of the physical examination, history and lab tests, pictures of his injuries, and a clear statement about the presence of signs of abuse could greatly assist the prosecutors and others collaborating on Leroy's case. As Leroy's ribs began to heal, he felt stronger and was able to follow through with his safety plan and make decisions about how to improve his life.

Victim Capacity

While various professionals had begun working directly with Leroy, his case was brought for review to an interdisciplinary team consisting of law enforcement, APS, health care providers, and a domestic violence advocate. Initially, law enforcement suggested charging the wife with abuse of a vulnerable adult because "no man in his right mind would put up with that behavior." The APS worker and domestic advocate argued that Leroy did not fit the state definition of a vulnerable adult because he was capable of holding down a job at the brewery for a number of years. Instead, they suggested that this was a case of domestic violence.

A geriatric physician agreed to evaluate Leroy. He found Leroy competent. This information was important to the APS worker, who recognized that providing Leroy with information so that he could make his own decisions about his life would be the most effective strategy. Safety planning strategies were discussed at a level appropriate to match Leroy's functioning.

Legal

Several legal interventions improved Leroy's safety. In Leroy's community, APS provided reports of any investigations that might be criminal to local law enforcement. The police reviewed the report and decided to interview Leroy, who told the same story he told to APS. Leroy asked that his wife not be arrested or hurt. Because law enforcement did not get this case immediately, there was little physical evidence at the scene to collect or document. Law enforcement used a subpoena to obtain the hospital records and learned that there was medical evidence to support that Leroy has been physically abused and neglected. Leroy's wife was charged with domestic violence under mandatory arrest laws. Law enforcement gathered evidence of domestic violence and presented it to the prosecutor. The prosecutor pressed charges against Leroy's wife. She pled guilty in exchange for agreeing to participate in an abuser's treatment program and pay a fine.

Leroy worked with a domestic violence advocate to obtain a restraining order when his wife started harassing and threatening him because she wanted the charges dropped. He was also able to obtain financial help from the Victim Compensation Fund by working with a victim advocate/witness staff person located in the prosecutor's office.

The APS worker also suggested that Leroy talk with an attorney to learn more about his options and civil remedies. Leroy learned that he could get a divorce or legal separation if he chose. He could also establish financial and health care powers of attorney to name someone other than his wife as the decision maker if he became incompetent.

Physical Environment

Initially Leroy was admitted to the hospital after his doctor's appointment for a complete examination, which gave him a few days away from home to think about his options. Because of limited insurance, however, he was forced to make a decision within a day about where he wanted to live.

Like most victims, Leroy wanted to remain in his own home, but his wife was very angry about being arrested for domestic violence. She changed the locks and screamed at Leroy whenever she saw him.

Leroy lived in a community without an elder shelter. The local battered women's program did not house men, but did have vouchers allowing abused men to stay at a local hotel at no cost. Leroy stayed at the hotel for several weeks while APS and the domestic violence advocates worked with the local housing experts to find an affordable apartment in a senior apartment complex.

Finances

Finances became an immediate issue for Leroy as he moved into his new apartment. He was able to return to his job, but he did not make much money. He was fortunate to have health insurance. Leroy was going to need financial assistance to keep the apartment. Leroy's story got the attention of the local media. Members of the community wanted to help and donated money, furniture, and appliances to help Leroy move into his new apartment. Leroy worked with a benefits specialist to apply for Social Security. He worked with a financial advisor through the Area Agency on Aging, who helped with a budget and balancing his checkbook.

Social Supports

Leroy had always been described as a loner, even in grade school. He had made few friends at the brewery and had no activities outside of work. The APS worker tried a number of alternatives to increase Leroy's social network and support system. Finally, on learning that he was a veteran, she found a program for World War II veterans that he joined and where he made a few friends.

Outcome

Leroy was able to move into his own apartment and keep his job at the brewery. A domestic violence advocate helped him get a restraining order and accompanied him to court when his wife was charged and sentenced. He spoke to an attorney about changing his will and medical power of attorney. He met with a lawyer about getting a divorce but decided not to pursue one.

The case review team continued to meet every month. Leroy's case stayed on their agenda for about nine months. The APS worker lived in Leroy's neighborhood and occasionally saw him. Even after the case was closed, she provided periodic updates to the team about how Leroy was doing, based on her chance meetings on the street.

Like most victims, once the abuse was identified many professionals came into Leroy's life. Their ability to work informally in the field and to use the case review team significantly improved communication, resulting in enhanced victim safety and benefits to the professionals in saved time and resources.

Unfortunately, safety planning and intervention strategies alone may not end some abusive behavior. Some perpetrators continue to harm their victims regardless of the interventions offered by professionals. Other offenders move on to new victims. These perpetrators need to be held accountable using a collaborative approach discussed in the next chapter.

CHAPTER ELEVEN

A Collaborative Model for Holding Abusers Accountable

The preceding chapters have provided a foundation for a discussion of offender accountability and its relationship to system collaboration and victim safety. This chapter focuses on how professionals in those disciplines bring their expertise to the issue of accountability. Understanding how accountability supports safety and an improved quality of life is important. One of the goals of a collaborative system is to hold the offender accountable for his actions. This affords greater protection to the victim and sends a message to the public that this behavior is unacceptable. Effective offender accountability and victim safety require strong collaboration supported by quality case building that leads to successful prosecution.

Historically, the criminal justice system was ill-prepared to assist in addressing the issues of elder abuse. Research conducted in the 1970s disclosed that law enforcement perceived elders as an "unpleasant nuisance," and that elderly victims experienced difficulty with the prosecutors and the court. It also found that most older people lacked an understanding of the nature and scope of the role of the police (Blakely & Dolon, 2000). Subsequent research revealed that the older people often had negative relationships with social services and that law enforcement and social services seldom joined in cooperative action. There was very little contact initiated by social services when criminal acts were found, owing to social service professionals' lack of confidence in the criminal justice system (Blakely & Dolon, 2000).

More recent responses to elder abuse are the results of lessons learned from the domestic violence field. The criminal justice system has become more engaged. It now addresses the accountability of the offender in a substantive way. This approach recognizes that elder abuse is more than simply problems resulting from the stress of caregiving and an issue best left to social services. It begins to reflect a shift in focus from the victim to the perpetrator (Brownell, Berman, & Slamone, 1999). The criminalization of elder abuse is a result of the recognition that it is a form of family violence. This association makes it easier to "mobilize the assistance of law enforcement and the criminal justice system" (Wolf, 1999b).

Wolf explains that, historically, crimes against elders and perpetrated by strangers were handled by the criminal justice system; and crimes of elder abuse, neglect, and exploitation by family members in the home setting were handled by the public welfare system.

> It became apparent in the last decade that, although elder abuse was a public welfare matter and later taken over as an aging issue, it could also be viewed as a crime. Today, police officers, prosecutors, and health and social service providers realize that they all have an important role to play in preventing victimization of elders, whether perpetrated by strangers or family members. (Wolf, 2000b, p. 20)

Some may feel that criminalization of elder abuse may have underlying problems, but it does focus on the need to hold the offender accountable for behavior that is in violation of criminal statutes designed to protect the public. There is a subtle tension in balancing the wishes of the victim, such as to remain in the abusive environment or be unwilling to prosecute the offender, and the desire of the criminal justice system to punish, deter, or incapacitate the offender. As this chapter illustrates, other systems also have the capability to hold offenders accountable. Protective services, victim advocates, attorneys, and others who can provide the necessary support systems that enhance victim's safety and possibly restore the victim to a previously nonvictimized state, all have a critical role to play.

Systems other than criminal justice have both the desire and the mechanisms to hold offenders accountable for their actions while providing a broader array of choices and services when collaborating with others. Some of these mechanisms deal directly with the perpetrator, others with the victim, and in some instances, both. With that in mind, the response systems addressing offender accountability are examined.

LAW ENFORCEMENT

The gatekeeper for the involvement of the criminal justice system is most often law enforcement. The ability of law enforcement to recognize, respond to, and investigate cases of suspected elder abuse is the basis for successful prosecution and subsequent actions that protect the victim and the public from further harm by a specific offender. Thus law enforcement's role is that of a first-responder and often the primary investigator. In the majority of local law enforcement agencies, both functions may be the responsibility of a single person. If cases are accepted by other law enforcement agencies at the state or federal level, then they will most often be handled as purely investigative matters, as these agencies are rarely first responders. It is critical for social services or other disciplines that work with elder abuse victims to contact law enforcement as soon as they suspect a crime. This will contribute significantly to evidence preservation and efforts to promote victim safety.

Collaboration between law enforcement and social services does not always meet expectations. A lack of training for law enforcement, a lack of understanding on the part of victim advocates, and an absence of a legacy of teamwork and effective alliances all contribute to preventing effective collaboration (Blakely & Dolan, 2000). One of the major challenges in collaboration is determining when to involve law enforcement and the criminal justice system. Blakely and Dolan surveyed protective service workers concerning their views of the role of law enforcement in elder abuse cases. When asked about their expectations of law enforcement, social service professionals responded that "accompany workers on visits to the victim's home" was first and "arrest the perpetrator" was sixth; however, "stop the abuse" was second. When asked what service was most difficult to obtain from the criminal justice system, the first was prosecution and the second was arrest (Blakely & Dolan, 2000). This would lead to the conclusion that holding the offender accountable is a desired outcome for both protective services and criminal justice professionals. This research reflects the different professional perspectives and priorities and presents a significant challenge in promoting improved collaboration. Law enforcement has, historically, not been involved in elder abuse incidents and often lacks the knowledge necessary to craft an effective response to the victim and work collaboratively with other systems. To improve this response, it is critical to understand the basic roles and responsibilities of law enforcement and, subsequently, the other functions within the criminal justice system. Some of the specific functions of law enforcement are:

- Accompany team members on calls/home visits.
- Seize weapons, particularly firearms.
- Establish that the conduct is criminal in nature and that sufficient facts are gathered to support a criminal prosecution.

- Arrest the offender.
- Provide initial contact with a victim advocate.
- Assist in obtaining emergency orders.
- Gather evidence.

Law enforcement is often the only public agency that has a 24-hour, 7-day-a-week response system and that actually deploys personnel on that basis. They are easily accessed through the 911 call system and will respond to almost any type of request. Most calls for service to law enforcement do not involve crimes, but are "order maintenance" or "conflict resolution" matters. Response to such service calls fit well within a community policing approach, in which the role of law enforcement has expanded from controlling crime to supporting community building. Law enforcement has traditionally focused only on those events involving suspected criminal behavior. That approach limited them to assessing a situation, determining if a criminal act had occurred, and initiating an action based on the officer's findings. The determination of whether or not a criminal act has taken place is dependent on the particular criminal code of each individual state. One complication is that many states have difficult, even confusing, definitions of criminal conduct involving elders or other vulnerable adults. It is within this statutory framework, however, that law enforcement must operate. How this process works is often confusing to those who have only a passing knowledge of law enforcement procedures or who gain most of what they know from popular television shows.

How then does law enforcement define its role and go about the business of investigating crime? Many of these techniques are used by other systems. This process begins most often with a call from what could be a number of sources: social services, concerned family members or caregivers, neighbors, and persons or service providers who may have a direct contact with the potential victim. The first responder (law enforcement) does an initial assessment to determine whether there is a possibility that criminal conduct has taken place. This is done within the definitional framework of each state's existing criminal code. If the state does not have specific statutes addressing abuse, neglect, and exploitation of elders or other vulnerable adults, the first responder must take the fact pattern presented at that moment and attempt to place it within the context of an existing criminal statute. For instance, the commonly used term *physical abuse* must often be fitted to such criminal terms as *assault, battery, aggravated assault, attempted murder, domestic violence, sexual battery, kidnapping*, or *sexual assault*. All crimes have unique elements that must be present to classify an event as criminal. These elements also provide the investigative framework for the officers. It determines what facts are necessary to establish that the event is criminal in nature and what has to be proven in court "beyond a reasonable doubt." This legal standard exceeds that required in a civil proceeding.

Every preliminary criminal investigation should initially focus on two primary questions: what happened and how did it happen? All too often, individuals will attempt to begin with "why did this happen?" This can lead to making the observations and facts fit the preconceived answer to "why?" Every criminal case is composed of three factors: physical evidence, witnesses, and suspects. To have the best chance of a successful prosecution, at least two of the three must be present. Physical evidence may be the most crucial and is most time-sensitive. Delay in reporting often leads to the loss or destruction of physical evidence. Also, witness statements may be suspect if there is a lengthy delay in reporting. Assuming that the initial investigation goes well, the next step for law enforcement, and for many social service agencies, is the follow-up investigation.

Elder abuse investigations are complex. If assigned to law enforcement officers who have little or no background or training in this area, there is the potential for missing key facts or being unable to anticipate case difficulties leading to poor outcomes. Investigators become discouraged and fail to follow through. Fortunately, most law enforcement investigators have the skills necessary to conduct complex investigations and the willingness to seek out experts to assist in the areas where they lack training or expertise to manage. For the most part, elder abuse investigations require the same skills as any other crimes against persons. Skilled investigators have the necessary background to gather facts, interview people, and organize material. The application of a multidisciplinary approach to these cases provides the expertise not available within the law enforcement community. Access to such experts as physicians, social workers, victim advocates, elder law specialists, and others whose skills match the facts in the case supports quality case building.

The initial stages of an investigation may not always provide clear indication of criminal activity. Most cases will involve more than a single form of elder abuse and may have a victim who is a less than an accurate "historian" as to what happened and how it happened. As in other forms of family violence, it is important that the investigator develop a case with multiple sources of evidence so that the victim's role is minimized. Victims are often ambivalent toward prosecution and feel protective toward the abuser, particularly if the abusers are their children. Because of advanced age or frailty, the victim may not survive until the prosecution begins. Prosecution of an abuser without the testimony of the victim is possible and should be the goal of any investigation. The focus should be on evidence-based prosecution in which the case is built on the physical evidence, witness statements, and any suspect admissions and confessions.

The Case of Marilyn and William Spencer

Marilyn Spencer is 73 years old, divorced, and financially comfortable. Her son, William, is in his mid-40s, unemployed, and lives with his mother in her home. He has a minimal work history and has not held a job for several years. He drinks frequently and his mother's attempts to get him to stop drinking, get a job, and become self-sufficient have failed. Marilyn would not evict him as he has nowhere to go and no income. In fact, he obtained access to his mother's bank accounts and credit cards. On New Year's Day, during the late afternoon, Marilyn asked William to join her at the dinner she had just prepared. William became angry, struck her several times in the face, pushed her to the floor, and kicked her. She called police.

On arrival, police interviewed Marilyn, saw swelling on her face, and spoke with William. They obtained a statement from the victim and photographed visible injuries. Their initial assessment of Marilyn provided some indication of diminished capacity. The victim was advised to contact police the next day for a follow-up investigation, to include more photographs. An initial determination was made that there was sufficient probable cause and William was arrested for felonious assault and elder abuse. Marilyn was linked to a victim advocate who had responded to the scene. She was advised of her legal rights, available civil and criminal court orders, and services she could use during the court case. The local APS was also advised of the possible need to conduct an assessment for services. The victim advocate provided additional information regarding services available from the domestic violence program in the area.

The Spencer case presents many of the collaborative and accountability issues faced by those responsible for elder abuse and neglect investigations. What are the other functions of the criminal justice system that can be brought to bear in a case such as Spencer's?

Prosecution

Prosecutors, also known as district attorneys or states' attorneys, are charged with the following responsibilities:

- Providing guidance to law enforcement on effective case building in order to have a successful prosecution.
- Filing charge(s) against perpetrators.

- Assisting in obtaining court orders, subpoenas, and search warrants.
- Requesting conditions of bond that promote victim safety.
- Obtaining convictions.

Judiciary (Criminal)

- Issuing search and arrest warrants.
- Setting conditions of bond that promotes victim safety.
- Issuing restraining orders.
- Ordering restitution.
- Crafting dispositions that enhance victim safety, such as offender treatment programs, compliance orders, offender registration, and, when appropriate, incarceration.

Corrections

- Monitoring compliance with court orders.
- Providing appropriate treatment programs.
- Monitoring registration, if appropriate.
- Monitoring probation or parole conditions.
- Recommending revocation of probation or parole if there are violations of conditions.

Cases should include other professionals if there is to be an effective response to both victims' needs and offender accountability. Adult protective services can assist in determining whether the victim requires in-home services. They can also provide information if prior abuse reports have been received regarding this family. Expert medical opinion may be needed if the records disclose possible prior abuse or neglect. Basic evidence collection techniques, such as photography, body charts, victim and suspect statements, and other documentation, contribute to case building.

Case building can often be subjected to decision making by nonparticipants. A recent U.S. Supreme Court decision has made the act of victim interviewing by those investigating abuse, such as law enforcement or Adult Protective Services (APS), a more complicated process. This decision has significantly changed the rules in a criminal case for receiving witness statements in a court case when the witness is not present to testify in person, a not uncommon circumstance in elder abuse cases. In *Crawford v. Washington,* 124 S. Ct. 1354 (2004), the Supreme Court ruled that prior testimony and witness statements that are testimonial in nature are inadmissible unless the witness is currently unavailable and, on a prior occasion, the defendant (abuser) had the opportunity to cross-examine the witness. "Testimonial" includes formal statements made to law enforcement and other governmental officials for the purpose of proving or establishing facts in a court proceeding. Statements made to an elderly witness's friend or acquaintance and to nongovernmental persons are not effected by *Crawford*. Although courts continue to interpret this ruling and clarify its application, it is evident that more recently developed and approved methods of proving cases by taking videotaped statements or grand jury testimony from victims are no longer permissible. Statements made to family members, friends, neighbors, doctors and other health care professionals, financial advisors, and others must now be located and documented. Increasingly, competent elder victims of abuse will be required to testify in court and undergo cross-examination by their abuser's counsel. Finally, any conduct by an abuser to threaten, intimidate, or harm a victim must be documented as the abuser forfeits the right to cross-examination when a victim's unavailability is caused by the abuser's misconduct. *Crawford* provides an example of the need to tailor investigative techniques and the case-building process to anticipate future court challenges to the methods used by the investigators. The ability to remain flexible and promote effective collaborative processes can develop an effective response to decisions such as this.

Collaborating to Hold the Offender Accountable

What are the critical factors in a case that contribute to the need for effective collaboration? Law enforcement is actively engaged in the case-building process, that is, collecting forensic evidence, conducting interviews, gathering background information on the victim and perpetrator, and processing the crime scene, but other professionals may be needed to provide direct assistance to the victim. Early involvement of other professionals also can contribute to the fact-gathering process and implementation of those actions can help hold the offender accountable. The first consideration must be the immediate protection of the victim from further harm. This may involve informing the prosecutor that special conditions need to be attached to the bond preventing further contact, obtaining a protection order, or assisting other family members in providing support and protection. Arresting the abusive caregiver creates additional demands on protective services to provide a level of support that will maintain the victim's independence and dignity. There may be practical issues, such as changing locks, arranging for transportation, or obtaining needed medical services, that can be met by local agencies. These are but a few of the areas that can best be addressed by collaboration between systems.

There is an assumption that law enforcement will be notified when anyone encounters a possible case of abuse, neglect, or exploitation. Although this is not always the case, it is the response most likely to lead to a criminal prosecution. With that in mind, there are collaborative issues nested in the mere act of responding to a report. Gaining entry is often a problem for protective services workers if the caregiver or perpetrator denies access to the victim or residence. The presence of law enforcement can be helpful in overcoming such obstacles. Although there are certain legal limitations that bind law enforcement when responding to emergency situations, they possess an aura of authority not always extended to APS. Very often the mere fact that law enforcement accompanies the APS worker is enough to gain entry and access to the victim. It may also be an issue of safety for protective services and other professionals responding to allegations of abuse. The environment can be volatile and fraught with the potential for violence. Law enforcement certainly has a role to play in these circumstances.

Other areas in which a collaborative or multidisciplinary response can meet the goals of protecting the victim and holding the offender accountable surround those actions necessary for effective case building. Evidence collection is primarily a law enforcement responsibility. It is time-sensitive and very often involves the victim as part of the crime scene (physical abuse, neglect, and sexual assault are examples). The collection of evidence from the victim may involve photography or possibly intrusive medical procedures. All will require a level of understanding, support, and sensitivity that can be provided by other professionals, such as victim advocates, social workers, or medical personnel. Conducting interviews of both the victim and possible offender should involve a multidisciplinary team of professionals who understand the most effective techniques. This could include a mental health assessment or other forms of health-related issues best handled by those with the proper expertise. Law enforcement needs to conduct a forensic interview that provides information as to what happened, how it happened, and who may have done it. The interview cannot be leading or suggestive in any way. Interviewing the offender does not always necessitate giving Miranda warnings and law enforcement can work effectively with other professionals in an ethical and legal manner to obtain the most effective information. This approach should also mitigate the need for multiple interviews and other inherent problems, such as prior and inconsistent statements.

Some examples of effective collaboration include the victim advocate assisting in gaining the victim's cooperation to photograph the injuries over a period of time, providing assistance in explaining the court process, and answering any questions about the criminal justice system. Health services can provide documentation of injuries or other indicators of abuse or neglect. The judiciary can provide protective orders and assist in securing assets or possible guardianship.

Elder abuse cases often present complex issues for which the criminal justice system lacks adequate training or expertise. This is particularly true of financial exploitation or facility cases, given the complex nature of the evidence. It should also be noted that in cases of financial exploitation, the requirement to protect assets and possibly to recover those taken, may necessitate involving experts from the civil legal or financial community. The ability to draw on a wider community of experts in these diverse areas can lead to better recognition of possible criminal events and result in improved case building. It is also important to include the possibility of expert testimony in complex cases. These experts should be able to address the dynamics of elder abuse and domestic violence, aging, neglect, and financial exploitation. Health care professionals can identify the effects of aging and disease versus those of abuse and neglect. The experts come from the medical community, social services, forensic, accounting, or other areas requiring specialized knowledge of the complex issues involved in elder abuse, neglect, or exploitation cases.

Ultimately, every criminal case has a resolution. The end result should hold the offender accountable for the behavior and protect the victim from further harm. It is important that victims who are physically and emotionally able to do so play a role in the sentencing process. This can include a sentence resulting in prison or probation and can be accomplished with the help of a victim advocate who can assist in presenting the victim's desires to the court. It is also critical that court personnel be sensitive to the needs of victims in this category. It is often necessary that accommodations be made for elders or other vulnerable adults, particularly if they will be required to testify. If the offender receives a prison sentence or probation, another set of professionals in the probation and parole function within each jurisdiction should become involved. It is equally important that they receive training in the dynamics of elder abuse, neglect, and exploitation so that they can adequately monitor the offender. Judges also need to have a complete understanding of the dynamics of this crime so that they can craft the appropriate sentence.

Although offender accountability clearly is a role of the criminal justice system, other systems have direct and indirect responsibilities as well. Relatively few cases of elder abuse and neglect meet the legal standards required to prove a criminal case. For a variety of reasons, including lack of substantial evidence on which to convict, the majority of matters cannot, or should not, be handled by the criminal justice system. This is not to say that abusive conduct is acceptable and should not be sanctioned, discouraged, and interdicted. Instead, other systems pursuing different remedies must respond and act.

How do other systems hold offenders accountable? Protective services receive and investigate allegations. Like law enforcement, they interview alleged victims, witnesses, and perpetrators. They obtain physical evidence, including medical and financial records, and photograph victims and their living environments. When warranted they pursue court orders to exclude abusers from their victims' homes, assist victims to understand how to have orders enforced, and can help identify alternate decision makers, caregivers, and money managers. They can work with civil attorneys to secure the appointment of a guardian or the removal of an abusive or exploitative one.

Health care professionals can make mental health assessments of victims and perpetrators to determine their ability to understand courses of action, their ability to enter into transactions, as well as their susceptibility to undue influence. They also can make recommendations about whether victims can testify or stand trial. They can treat certain conditions to increase some witnesses' abilities to recall events or testify. In fact, treatment of conditions as delirium, urinary tract infections, and hearing loss may result in such a degree of improvement that what had previously appeared to be dementia and confusion is reversed, and the person demonstrates significantly improved mental and communication functioning. Finally, health professionals can assess mental functioning of a perpetrator to determine whether he or she can be held criminally responsible for abusive conduct.

The collaborative effort necessary to affect accountability can be accomplished through a formal team process or may be the result of an informal working relationship established in a particular jurisdiction. In all cases, the issues of validation of the victim's loss and enhancement of their safety, while holding the offender accountable, is critical. Accountability can be both direct and indirect, and may focus on only one aspect of a particular event. Coordination of these actions, however, can be important and beneficial.

For instance, in a financial exploitation case, there are steps that can be taken by both the criminal and civil justice systems that will secure assets, promote victim safety, and hold the offender accountable. The civil justice system also plays a role in offender accountability. Civil attorneys representing abused or exploited clients can file lawsuits against perpetrators for civil damages, recovery of assets and medical costs, and, in some situations, for punitive damages to punish egregious conduct and deter future abuse. Attorneys can obtain civil judgments and garnish wages or attach assets of the abuser to satisfy those judgments. Attorneys, as well as individuals, also can seek civil protective orders to protect against abusive family and household members. A broader discussion of such orders is found later in this chapter. Attorneys can file a variety of lawsuits against abusive and exploitative corporations and businesses, such as nursing homes and board and care facilities, and their employees. Suits have been brought for fraud, unfair business practices, failure to ameliorate pain, inadequate pain management, wrongful death, and other physical harms.

Some of the specific ways in which the accountability goal can be met by other key systems are outlined next:

Civil Justice System

- Bring lawsuits to recover assets and/or to overturn transfers of property or other assets that were obtained through fraud, undue influence, deception, or other unlawful means.
- Issue restraining orders.
- Obtain civil damages from the offender for the physical or emotional injury caused to the victim and/or the victim's family.
- Remove offender from any legal authority over the victim, including revocation of offender's role as the victim's agent under a financial or health care power of attorney or as the victim's guardian or conservator.
- Enjoin dissipation of assets.
- Bring lawsuits to prevent an offender from gaining the assets through a will or other mechanism of inheritance from a victim whose death the offender caused.

Domestic Violence/Sexual Assault Networks

- Provide expert testimony regarding dynamics of abuse and neglect.
- Collaborate with other systems to enhance response to victim needs.
- Provide safety planning (and accountability and safety function).

Protective Services

- Obtain records without subpoenas or search warrants.
- Investigate allegations.
- Report crimes to the criminal justice system.
- Maintain offender registry, if authorized.
- Conduct social work interviews that do not require a Miranda warning.

- Assist other systems in those areas of expertise particular to protective services.
- Provide expert testimony when required.

Health Care

- Provide expert witness testimony.
- Document medical conditions that are risk factors for abuse and neglect.
- Notify criminal justice or protective services of potential abuse and neglect cases.
- Provide expert medical assistance to other systems during the case-building process, such as interpreting medical findings in patient records.
- Determine cause and manner of death when homicide is suspected.
- Conduct research that supports improved system response.
- Identify and treat the offender's medical conditions that lead to abuse.

The previous section highlighted what particular disciplines do to promote perpetrator accountability. In this section, tasks that professionals in every discipline perform as part of their work are considered. Although there are variations as to when and how disciplines perform these functions, each shares in the following functions:

- Can report suspected abuse, neglect, and exploitation. There may be differences in where and to whom reports are made. For example, some may report to law enforcement, the prosecutor's office, or protective services; others may report to regulatory agencies or professional licensing organizations, such as medical or other professional associations, courts, or long-term care facility licensure and certification agencies.
- Document observations, statements, and known sources of information. Many acts of elder abuse involve patterns of behavior rather than a single event. Documenting every contact provides a historical record that may show patterns of conduct, the identity of caregivers, the elder's level of functioning, collateral sources of information, and knowledge of the elder's abilities and limitations. Many states have created special laws or sentencing enhancements for crimes committed against vulnerable and frail adults. Some states limit APS involvement to situations

where the victim is vulnerable. That a perpetrator knew his or her victim was vulnerable may be a critical element for proving lack of victim consent. Evidence, including medical findings, provides critical information in civil, administrative, or criminal proceedings convened to hold offenders accountable.

- Provide information and testimony in various tribunals. Whether as participants in multidisciplinary informal collaborations, formal teams, or as consultants and witnesses, professionals from a variety of systems rely on experts to provide technical information, render opinions on standards of practice, and educate judicial officers, tribunals, and juries.

Facility Investigations

Facility investigations present unique and challenging issues. Abuse and neglect that take place in facilities often can go undetected for an extended period. This results in extremely difficult obstacles in the area of evidence collection and the subsequent conduct of a criminal investigation. Administrative/regulatory investigations often can lead to criminal action against the individuals employed by the facility and its corporate structure. This is one of the major differences between abuse and neglect investigations conducted in the community and those in facilities. It also increases the number of potential offenders involved in a particular case, given the number of employees or family members who may have had contact with the victim. Other challenges surround the complex nature of the medical issues, daily operating procedures of a facility, and the resident records that must be reviewed. It requires an understanding of quality of care standards and the role of employees in the individual's care. These are areas of expertise not often found in local criminal justice agencies. These cases demand a collaborative approach. In many states these investigations are handled by the attorney general's Medicaid Fraud Control Unit, APS, or the Long Term Care Ombudsman Program (in those states where the ombudsman program fulfills the APS role in long-term care facilities). In every instance, the involvement of professionals who have experience in conducting facility investigations should be sought.

The collaborative roles already presented in this chapter are important in facility cases, and each discipline can contribute to the case-building process. Professionals from the medical community can play a critical role in determining the extent of abuse or neglect given the complex medical issues presented by most facility residents. Offender accountability may be the single most important difference in facility cases. The majority of cases of abuse and neglect in community settings involve only one offender. In facility cases there may be more the one offender. Some offenders, such as members of the facility management, may not have direct contact with the victim, but are culpable in the abuse and neglect. For professionals conducting facility investigations, close coordination with noncriminal justice agencies can be productive in the following ways:

- Use the regulatory agencies to show a pattern of abuse and neglect within the facility.
- Use the authority of other agencies to obtain evidence not readily available to law enforcement, such as medical records or records of facility inspections.
- Interview personnel from other agencies; don't just review the records. Their observations can often provide additional insights helpful to a criminal case.

In a number of facility cases, the civil justice system has been used successfully to hold offenders accountable, particularly the parent corporation. These actions range from addressing the failure to report the abuse to protecting those employees that commit the abuse, and are subject to punitive actions on the part of management (Moskowitz, 2003).

These are some of the ways in which systems can provide support to the case-building process and, ultimately, to holding the offender accountable. Experience with collaborative arrangements, formal or informal, have shown that this is the best approach to meeting the accountability goal, as well as the needs of the victim.

Court Orders

Throughout this book, reference has been made to court orders and their importance in enhancing victim safety and holding offenders accountable. In this section, orders are defined, various state and federal weapons restrictions are described, and rules concerning enforcement issues are analyzed. This section is not intended to provide legal advice for the best way to handle any particular case. Across the United States, there is wide variation in the availability of orders, covered relationships and conduct, and specific relief provided. Given the reality that most elder abusers are family members, this segment focuses on domestic violence and stalking orders.

A civil or criminal court can issue court orders. Civil court orders may be named protective orders, restraining orders, or injunctions. Criminal court orders, called criminal court stay-away orders or criminal court protective orders, are issued in charged cases or as a condition of probation after a criminal conviction. The party to be protected through the issuance of the court orders called the *protected party*. The abuser is the *restrained party*. Typically, courts restrain the abuser from certain actions such as coming within a certain distance of the protected party or their residence, or annoying, molesting, stalking, striking the protected party, as well as destroying or vandalizing their property. In many states, these violations are crimes once the order is issued and served on the restrained party.

Once a person is restrained by a court order and made aware of its contents through service of the order, there are certain limitations and restrictions imposed under state and federal law. Many states and federal laws prohibit persons restrained by a domestic violence or stalking court order from possessing firearms while the order is effective. The prohibition applies to short-term, temporary orders, as well as to actual orders issued after a full hearing before a court. State and federal authorities maintain registries of domestic violence and stalking court orders to assist in tracking orders, their terms and conditions, and whether service of the restrained party has been achieved. Many states' registries are linked to the federal court orders data bank.

Under federal law, persons subject to *qualified* protective orders are prohibited from shipping or transporting in interstate or foreign commerce, or possessing in or affecting commerce, any firearm or ammunition that has been shipped or transported in interstate or foreign commerce (18 U.S.C. § 922(g)(8)). Possession of a firearm is prohibited whether or not the order itself specifically prohibits possession of a firearm. The maximum punishment is a 10-year prison sentence (18 U.S.C. § 924(a)(2)). There are certain exceptions for restrained persons required to carry a firearm as a condition of employment. Qualified orders restrain a person "from harassing, stalking, or threatening an intimate partner of such person or child of such intimate partner or person, or engaging in other conduct that would place an intimate partner in reasonable fear of bodily injury" (18 U.S.C. § 922(g)(8)(B)). Intimate partners include current and former spouses, current and former cohabitants, and co-parents, but not dating persons who have not cohabited (18 U.S.C. § 921(a)(32)).

A qualified order is one that restrains a person "from harassing, stalking, or threatening an intimate partner of such person or child of such intimate partner or person, or engaging in other conduct that would place an intimate partner in reasonable fear of bodily injury" (18 U.S.C. § 922(g)(8)(B)). Intimate partners include current and former spouses, current and former cohabitants, and co-parents, but not dating persons who have not cohabited (18 U.S.C. § 921(a)(32)). Under the Violence Against Women Act, initially passed in 1994 and reauthorized in 2000, states are required to enact legislation that gives "full faith and credit" to one another's orders, that is, they fully recognize and enforce orders issued throughout the United States. These orders are sometimes referred to as *foreign orders* and refer to domestic violence and stalking orders issued by courts in other states, the District of Columbia, U.S. territories and insular possessions, and Indian tribal courts. Orders must have been issued by courts with jurisdiction over the parties and subject matter and after the restrained party was given notice (served with the order) of the time and place of the hearing. It is not necessary that the restrained party actually attend the hearing. This means that once a court has jurisdiction to issue and make an order regarding elder domestic violence and has the parties before it, the order is valid throughout the country no matter where the victim may encounter the restrained party.

A Case Example

Herbert has abused Leticia throughout their 40-year marriage. Once the children were grown and married, she filed for divorce and obtained a restraining order, based on the decades of abuse, prohibiting Herbert from contacting her or following her. Herbert was served with the order and was present in court when the judge issued the permanent order. Leticia moved to the other side of the country to be near her oldest daughter. One day she was shocked to find Herbert standing on her porch holding a hunting rifle and yelling at her.

This example raises several issues. The order is valid and enforceable even though Leticia has moved across the country. The order meets the conditions required under the Violence Against Women Act. Under the order, Herbert was prohibited from possessing a firearm for the period during which the order was valid. He was in violation of federal law (18 U.S.C. § 922(g)(8)). Herbert's actions may also violate the law in the jurisdiction where Leticia now lives. Thus, the state where Leticia now lives has the authority to enforce the order in accordance with its law. If the enforcing state directs that its law enforcement officials arrest for violations and provides that the violation is a crime, Herbert could be arrested for local charges. With foreign orders, the issuing state decides who is protected, the terms and conditions to be ordered, and how long the order is valid. The enforcing state determines whether the violation is a crime, penalties for violations, the arrest authority of the responding law enforcement agency, and detention procedures. Additional information about full faith and credit is available from the Full Faith and Credit Project of the Pennsylvania Coalition Against Domestic Violence (phone 800-256-5883, ext. 2).

One of the most frustrating aspects of court orders is that the protected party may not enforce the order and may even "invite" the abuser to return to the victim's home. Law enforcement officials or protective services professionals often learn of the situation when called back to the residence by a new problem. Legally, only courts can make, modify, or revoke an order. The order remains valid and enforceable, notwithstanding the acts of the parties. The abuser as the restrained party is in violation of the order and may be subject to arrest. The protected party is not prohibited from acting in any particular way and cannot violate an order that only protects him or her. Professionals working with such parties can help to educate them to avoid this confounding and frustrating situation (Heisler, 2004).

CONCLUSION

Accountability is a multidisciplinary issue. Through the collaborative efforts of every profession, a victim's well-being and safety can be addressed and the offender held accountable for his or her actions. The criminal justice system is the primary focus of this chapter, but it is only one part of a greater system. That system has overlapping responsibilities and skill sets that enhance any investigation of abuse and neglect. Accountability does not necessarily result in a prosecution or punishment, but it does impart a message on the part of society that abuse and neglect are not acceptable.

CHAPTER TWELVE

Systems Review
and Change Through
Multidisciplinary
Collaborations

INTRODUCTION

Multidisciplinary collaborations, whether informal or formal, may have two significant benefits in addition to the goals of improving efforts to prevent or respond to elder abuse that were discussed in Chapter 6. The two benefits are reviewing and enhancing: (1) the ways in which disciplines or systems provide services, whether preventive or reactive, to older persons, and (2) the availability and function of elder abuse-related services. In reality, systems review looks at the areas in which systems can break down. These might include: (1) identification of victims (which systems should be identifying victims and are they effectively doing so?), (2) reporting and referrals (once systems identify victims, are they making reports and referrals to appropriate agencies?), (3) provision of services (are services meeting the needs of victims?), and (4) coordination of services and the systems providing them (are services seamless and provided without conflict between agencies?).

The first benefit is reached by conducting needs assessments, either informally or formally, of clients and service providers. The second benefit is achieved, again either informally or formally, by using those needs assessments to identify and develop solutions to the problems identified by the needs assessments. These solutions may include training programs; memoranda of understanding, policies, and protocols;

informal or formal collaborations; improved or new services; improved or new statutes and regulations to benefit victims and hold perpetrators accountable; and research. They may involve collaborations with systems or disciplines that are not currently concerned with serving elder abuse victims, but that should have a role in response or prevention. The end result of these efforts should be a seamless response to victims and a consistent message to perpetrators that elder abuse will not be tolerated.

Comprehensive systems review will assess the relationship of systems to the central life domains of older persons, as described in Chapter 7. These domains affect the older person, the intervention and safety strategies available, and all the systems that serve and help to implement these intervention and safety strategies. The failure to look broadly at systems and their impact on older persons will result in incomplete or unsuccessful change. For example, system changes that encourage the criminal justice system to arrest and jail abusive caregivers may not succeed unless the victims are provided with emergency shelter and other services that meet their needs for care. The puzzle analogy described in the Introduction works here as well. The complex nature of elder abuse means that no one system can fully meet the needs of an elder abuse victim. Just as that fact justifies the need for multidisciplinary collaboration, it explains the need for a comprehensive approach to systems review and change.

This chapter discusses the various ways in which multidisciplinary collaborations can accomplish these results, and provides examples of and suggestions for collaborations among various systems for the purpose of systems review and change. It describes the types of multidisciplinary teams formed specifically to cultivate system change and concludes with an illustration of how one of those teams, an elder abuse fatality review team, develops recommendations for system change.

IMPORTANCE OF SYSTEMS REVIEW AND CHANGE

This chapter distinguishes the "case review" function (discussed previously in Chapter 10) from the "systems review and change" function of multidisciplinary collaborations, but case review can and often does lead to systems review and change. Ideally, case reviews inform system review and change efforts. If the two functions are not linked, then case review only benefits the individual client whose case was reviewed and systems change may not be based in reality or may not address highest priority needs first. When staff members of entities that prevent or respond to elder abuse repeatedly see the same or similar issues and problems in the cases they handle, they should address those concerns systemically. Doing so will benefit future clients and enable their organizations to act more effectively and efficiently.

Systems Review

A multidisciplinary systems review, like an internal or external review of a single system, can accomplish many important objectives leading to the ultimate goal of preventing elder abuse or improving services to elder abuse victims. A systems review is, in effect, a "needs assessment" of the systems involved in the review and the services that they provide to elder abuse victims and perpetrators. Like a case review, a multidisciplinary systems review may be conducted by a team or by an informal group of representatives from more than one discipline. Regardless of the level of formality, a systems review can include, but is not limited to, identifying:

- Whether the systems are meeting the needs of their clients
- The role(s) of each system participating in the review
- How the participating systems relate to each other and their clients
- The need for training the workers in the systems
- Gaps in services and service delivery
- Solutions to the problems identified

Each of these steps is discussed next in more detail.

Identifying Whether the Systems Are Meeting the Needs of Victims

Systems review begins by assessing whether elder abuse victims' needs are being met by the systems involved in the review process. This step may occur in a variety of ways, either directly or indirectly.

Direct ways involve asking older persons about their experiences using services or their reasons for not using services. Older persons should also be asked what help they want, which may indicate that current services don't respond to their needs and prompt ideas for creating new services or programs. This process may involve private or semiprivate means such as interviews, surveys or satisfaction questionnaires, and focus groups. A public forum, such as a hearing or town hall meeting, also provides an opportunity for feedback; but some older victims of abuse may be reluctant to speak publicly about their experiences, or they may be unable to attend a public event.

Direct assessments will not reach all victims, however. Some vulnerable elders never use any services because they lack awareness of, or access to, available services. It may not be possible to reach them to ask why they do not use existing services. Other older persons may not be able or willing to participate in interviews, surveys, or focus groups because of language barriers, cognitive impairments, physical disabilities, reluctance to have others inquire about their private life, or the fear of being stigmatized. Others may not use services because of historical discrimination or ridicule by the systems in question, or because of fear of the ramifications of using those systems. For example, many individuals from racial or ethnic minorities may be reluctant to contact law enforcement or other government agencies because of past discrimination or abusive treatment against them or others in their cultural group by those agencies (Ohio Domestic Violence Network, 1999). A closeted gay, lesbian, bisexual, or transgender person may fear being "outed" and humiliated as a result of making a report about an abusive partner (Ohio Domestic Violence Network, 1999).

These problems may require systems conducting a review to use indirect means in lieu of, or in addition to, direct means to determine whether older victims' needs are being met. Indirect means may include asking staff of the systems involved in the review about their experiences in meeting victims' needs. Indirect means may also involve asking representatives of other disciplines who may or should work with elder abuse victims, but who are not part of the systems review, whether they think that victims' needs are being met. Information may be gathered through interviews, surveys, or focus groups. To illustrate, elder law practitioners working in legal services and in private practice could be interviewed about how the systems are addressing cases related to abuse by guardians or conservators. Domestic violence or sexual assault programs could be surveyed about the extent to which they are serving older persons. Focus groups could be held with leaders from populations that have traditionally been underserved or discriminated against by the systems in question, such as minority and ethnic groups and gay/lesbian/bisexual/transgender persons.

Identifying the Role(s) of Each System Participating in the Review

Systems review continues with the development of a complete and current understanding of the goals and roles of each system in relation to the prevention of elder abuse and the responses to elder abuse victims. Participants in the review process may lack information, or they may have outdated information. These deficits may lead to misunderstandings and stereotypes about each other's goals, roles, and activities that inhibit their ability to work together on cases and systems change. To illustrate, Adult

Protective Services (APS) staff often criticize doctors for failing to report suspected elder abuse. They may not realize that some doctors feel that reporting requirements conflict with their ethical principle of maintaining patient confidentiality. On the other hand, doctors express frustration that when they do make reports to APS, they never learn what happened as a result of their report. They may not realize that APS usually is prohibited from disclosing that information to reporters. The failure to understand each system's ethical and legal precepts is a barrier to serving victims and to collaborations between the disciplines.

Chapter 5 discusses the various systems that prevent or respond to elder abuse. That chapter serves as a starting point for understanding the diverse array of organizations that address elder abuse and their wide range of responsibilities. It may also spark new ideas for multidisciplinary collaborations, particularly with systems that are not currently involved with serving elder abuse victims. Nevertheless, it is critical to remember that the chart provides only general descriptions and that system roles and goals may vary widely depending on state statutes, regulations, policies, procedures, and community practices.

Identifying How the Participating Systems Relate to Each Other and Their Clients

After gaining current and accurate information about the goals and roles of each participant in the system review process, participants are ready to focus on the ways in which their systems actually work with each other. This step involves much more than looking at the goals and roles of the participants as set forth in statutes, regulations, policies, or procedures. It also entails analyzing whether, how, and why the systems' roles complement each other, overlap, or conflict—or some combination of those relationships. This step involves determining whether and how the participating systems actually communicate and collaborate with each other. It is helpful to look at the history of relationships between the participating systems. When did they develop and why? Have there been obstacles to collaboration and, if so, why? Have the individual systems changed since any relationship between them was first developed and, if so, how? Are those system changes relevant to the relationship under examination and, if so, how? Do administrators or staff of the various systems involved have regular interaction or opportunities for interaction? If yes, where, when, and why? If no, why not? Are there memoranda of understanding or protocols governing the systems' interactions? If so, are they current, adequate, and actually being followed?

Identifying the Need for Training the Workers in the Systems

One of the key barriers to multidisciplinary collaboration is a lack of understanding of the goals and roles of other disciplines. Accordingly, the review of systems' relationships will likely lead participants to identify many areas where training the workers in those systems would improve services related to elder abuse.

Systems review may make it clear that the workers in one system need additional training about their own system in addition to training about the other systems with which they should or do collaborate. Or the workers in multiple systems may need training about new developments related to elder abuse, such as new statutes or research identifying new risk factors or other dynamics. Obvious areas for training include current information about pertinent systems and the statutes, regulations, policies, and practices that govern those systems; communication and confidentiality issues; the needs of victims; and ways in which system relationships might be improved to better prevent elder abuse or serve victims.

A case discussed earlier in the book to illustrate how systems respond to elder abuse victims also demonstrates the need for training the workers in those systems. When Pearl, an 80-year-old woman with dementia, was sexually assaulted by an employee of the long-term care facility in which she resided, the head of nursing at the facility, despite having witnessed part of the incident, failed to report it to the administrators or to a regulatory agency (see Chapter 8). This situation highlights the importance of training nursing home management and staff about sexual abuse and reporting responsibilities.

Identifying Gaps in Services and Service Delivery

Listening to victims and analyzing systems and the ways in which they relate to prevent elder abuse or serve victims will undoubtedly illuminate gaps in services and programs, especially at times when the economy is bad and services and programs face budget cuts. When multiple victims have common needs that cannot be met by available services, it will become clear that changes in the methods of service delivery or the addition of new services are necessary.

"Walking" victims through the complete process of available services can illuminate gaps and other problems with delivery. This audit of services from a victim's perspective may help providers recognize problems, such as the lack of accessibility to certain services for persons with disabilities, the lack of public transportation to available services, or the lack of materials in large print or in foreign languages that are commonly spoken by older persons in the community. For example, an audit of services might disclose that there is no emergency shelter available to older women. There could be a variety of reasons for this problem. The local domestic violence shelter may have a policy of providing shelter only to women who have young children. The possibility of using available beds in hospitals and long-term care facilities on an emergency basis for elder abuse victims may not have been explored.

It is critical to involve victims in the process of identifying gaps in services; otherwise, precious resources may be wasted developing new services that do not meet their needs. A multidisciplinary team that keeps reviewing cases in which older victims of domestic violence refuse to go to the local domestic violence shelter provides an illustration. The team decides that the problem is that the shelter's bedrooms are on the second floor, and it is too difficult for the older women to walk up the stairs. The team members volunteer their time and resources over several weekends to renovate a storage room on the first floor of the shelter so that it can be used as a bedroom; however, older women still refuse to go to the shelter. Team members start asking the older women why they will not use the shelter and learn that the problem is not the stairs, but rather that the older women do not want to stay in a shelter environment where they will be in close proximity to a number of noisy young children. The older women also indicate that they are afraid to leave their pets in the care of their abusers. As a result, the team works with a local hospital to arrange emergency temporary shelter for older women on weekends when beds are empty. It also works with the local chapter of the Humane Society to arrange emergency temporary shelter for the women's pets.

Service providers can also identify gaps and problems with delivery in their own system and in others. For example, law enforcement officers who investigate elder abuse cases and arrest alleged perpetrators will likely be frustrated if the local prosecutors do not pursue those cases. If the prosecutors do not bring those cases due to the lack of sufficient evidence, a variety of problems may be identified. One problem might be the failure of mandatory reporters or of responding agencies, such as APS or emergency medical services, to report cases to law enforcement quickly enough to enable evidence collection. Another problem might be the lack of training for law enforcement officers on evidence collection in elder abuse cases. If the prosecutors do not pursue elder abuse cases because of a lack of resources for, interest in, or training about elder abuse, however, a far different set of problems will be identified.

A more formal process for identifying gaps in intervention systems is known as a "community resource assessment" (Ohio Domestic Violence Network, 1999) or "community audit." Using information gathered from victims, service providers, and others who are or should be connected to those systems, as discussed previously, this assessment can determine that gaps in systems are related to (1) lack of resources; (2) problems with personnel working in the systems, such as staff that is inadequate in number, untrained, or that lacks understanding of its roles and responsibilities; and (3) problems with systems, such as inadequate policies and procedures, lack of accountability, lack of consensus about intervention goals, and physical or cultural barriers to services (Ohio Domestic Violence Network, 1999).

Identifying Solutions to Problems With Collaborations, Training, and Services

The process of multidisciplinary systems review may shed light on solutions to some of the problems that it identifies. Or the process may simply identify problems. Regardless of the result, programs should consider all possible options and research whether others in similar situations have experienced similar problems. If so, what creative solutions were developed? Did they work as hoped? What were the results? Did victims benefit? What lessons were learned that would make it easier for another program to use or adapt a similar solution? Technology, such as the Internet and listserves, has made it much easier for programs to share ideas. Moreover, there is a growing body of both practice- and research-related literature on elder abuse.

Solutions should be identified thoughtfully. Ideally, victims should be asked what options they would prefer. Once the most appropriate ideas are recognized, they should be developed further and implemented through the systems change process, which is described next.

Systems Change

Systems change can be accomplished either through an informal collaboration or a formal team, and through methods that include, but are not limited to:

- Training programs
- Documents, such as memoranda of understanding, protocols, and policies
- New or additional collaborations
- New or enhanced services
- New statutes and regulations
- Research

Each idea is discussed in more detail next.

Developing Training Programs

One of the most commonly identified problems relates to the need for training representatives of the many disciplines that are or should be involved in preventing or responding to elder abuse. Training programs are often the first cut in times of tight budgets. That approach is shortsighted, however, as training programs help participants stay current and competent, resulting in better and more efficient services to older persons. Even if agency training programs have been cut, opportunities to provide training on elder abuse still exist. Many disciplines require that their workers obtain continuing education credit to retain their jobs or their licenses to practice, and developers of continuing education programs are always interested in new topics. Web-based training and other forms of distance learning offer new opportunities for lower-cost training.

Training programs offer diverse disciplines important opportunities for networking. Various training formats have been found to be useful. Professionals benefit from skill-based training (e.g., learning how to interview older people), information from another system about its services, or information about multiple systems and services presented to a multidisciplinary audience. Trainings can take place in various settings, such as an "in-service" in the workplace, workshops, or conferences, or Web-based training and other forms of distance learning. Training programs may result from the efforts of a multidisciplinary collaboration, or they may serve as a precursor to developing a formal or informal collaboration.

Developing good training programs takes time and resources. Federal and state grant programs, such as those funded by the Older Americans Act, the Violence Against Women Act, or the Victims of Crime Act, may provide financial support. Also, these programs may have already supported the development of national model curricula or other resource materials that state and local program planners can use to avoid "reinventing the wheel." For example, some of these programs have developed materials on serving victims who have disabilities, who are from racial or ethnic underserved populations, or who are gay, lesbian, bisexual, or transgender persons.

Training and programs that use interactive and skills-building exercises are particularly well suited to support the goal of multidisciplinary collaboration. Program planners and presenters may want to consider the following suggestions for developing and implementing training programs:

- Understand the culture of the audience, particularly as it relates to training. For example, law enforcement officers are used to starting their day very early, so they will be more likely to attend and be happier if a training program starts and ends early. Doctors also start their day very early, but it will be important to know if the group of doctors being trained needs to conduct hospital rounds before attending a training program. Some groups do better with certain types of interactive exercises than others. Some judges, for example, dislike role-playing, but they enjoy sharing "war stories" and learning through those examples.
- Members of one discipline do not like to be told how to do their job by someone from another discipline. This means that if members of one discipline are training members of another discipline, then one or more representatives of the discipline that is being trained should lead and actively participate in the program. When training programs involve an audience representing multiple disciplines, there should be significant involvement from each of the disciplines that make up the audience. To illustrate, recent research demonstrates a connection between animal abuse and elder abuse (The Humane Society of the United States & Wisconsin Department of Health and Family Services, 2003). Thus, it would be logical to train APS workers to recognize the signs of animal abuse and to train Human Society and animal control agency workers to recognize the signs of elder abuse. If the two disciplines are trained separately, the training team should include representatives of each discipline and a representative from the discipline comprising the audience should lead the program. If the two audiences are combined, then representatives from each discipline should be actively involved in conducting the training.
- Understand the experience and needs of the audience. Provide information of the appropriate level of complexity for the participants.
- Use the appropriate jargon for the audience. When an audience is multidisciplinary, presenters from one discipline may have to translate their jargon for the benefit of other disciplines.
- Develop and provide practical resource materials that training participants can use on the job.
- Develop training programs that conform to adult learning theories.
- Develop training programs that allow time for and promote activities intended to foster relationship building. Multidisciplinary collaborations are built on positive relationships. If

training participants never have an opportunity to talk to each other during a program, an opportunity to develop or enhance a new partnership may be lost.

Developing Memoranda of Understanding, Protocols, and Policies

The systems review process may well demonstrate that participants would benefit from developing written statements about their respective roles and how will they relate to each other in serving victims of elder abuse. This step can take place through preparation of memoranda of understanding, protocols, or policies. Despite their different names, the three types of documents are usually the same. Their purpose is to memorialize an agreement between two or more entities about the processes they will follow in relation to some undertaking. That undertaking might be a process that the entities will follow for referring cases to each other or when handling cases jointly, an agreement between the entities about the responsibilities they will have as members of a multidisciplinary team or as partners in planning a training program, or an agreement between entities about their roles in implementing a grant project.

The development of memoranda of understanding, protocols, and policies by partners in a multidisciplinary collaboration may also foster system change within each partner organization. The existence of these documents may institutionalize certain practices within an agency, helping to ensure that these practices continue even as the agency experiences leadership changes and staff turnover.

Memoranda of understanding, protocols, and policies can help ensure consistency in the day-to-day work involving elder abuse victims. These documents should be reassessed and, if necessary, revised periodically to keep them current, appropriate, and useful.

The cases discussed previously demonstrate several situations where memoranda of understanding, protocols, or policies could improve the response to older victims. One example is the case of Rosa and Juanita Costilla, in which a 92-year-old woman was neglected by her low-functioning daughter, and APS did not respond until after the hospital that treated Rosa had made two reports within 24 hours (see Chapter 8). This case illustrates that APS and the hospital could develop a protocol for the hospital to follow when making reports to APS. That protocol could provide guidance to help hospital personnel indicate clearly to APS when they think an emergency response is warranted. The case also demonstrates that APS and law enforcement could benefit from establishing policies regarding joint visits to the home of a suspected elder abuse victim. The case of Mildred and Arthur Brown, a couple married for 59 years and with a long history of domestic violence (also discussed in Chapter

8), provides another example. In that case, law enforcement responded to a 911 call from Mildred, who reported that Arthur was hurting her. The officer took Arthur away for a while, but did not refer Mildred to a domestic violence or APS program. This case illustrates the benefit of having protocols to ensure that law enforcement officers provide a victim with information about the local domestic violence and APS programs and to contact those programs themselves whenever they determine that an older person is experiencing domestic violence.

Developing New or Additional Collaborations

The systems review process will probably also reveal the need for new or additional collaborations, whether informal or formal. These collaborations could be for any of the purposes discussed in this chapter: to develop a case review or systems review team; to draft memoranda of understanding, protocols, or policies; to develop and implement training programs; to develop programs and services to fill the needs of victims; and to develop and advocate for legislative and other policy changes.

Several examples of informal collaborations, such as that of APS working with the local chapter of the Humane Society and animal control officers to develop care arrangements for victims' animals, have been discussed previously. Another example would be creating an ad hoc group composed of representatives from the Alzheimer's Association, law enforcement, APS, and other agencies to develop a coordinated response to situations where a person with Alzheimer's disease physically harms a partner or caregiver. By initiating collaborations with organizations that advocate for traditionally underserved populations, service agencies may be able to increase their awareness of how to reach out to and work with those populations, and thus enhance their service delivery and credibility.

Formal collaborations, including multidisciplinary teams, often grow from a systems review process and an informal collaboration. For example, the idea for the fiduciary abuse specialist team (see Chapter 6) was sparked when the APS and Long Term Care Ombudsman Programs in Los Angeles began to see a growing number of financial abuse cases and felt that they lacked the ability to handle them well. The APS program turned to law enforcement officers and others who had expertise investigating financial crimes. The informal collaboration evolved into a formal team as the need to review these challenging cases became routine and the number of disciplines involved with the review process grew (U.S. Departments of Justice, Office of Justice Programs, & Health and Human Services, 2000). Another example is the development of "code enforcement teams" (explained in Chapter 6), such as Operation Spot

Check in Florida and Operation Guardian in California, which were created to conduct unannounced inspections of long-term care facilities after informal systems reviews demonstrated that the regularity of facility inspections by licensure and certification staff allowed facilities to anticipate and prepare for the inspection, sometimes masking the true quality of care provided by the facility (U.S. Departments of Justice, Office of Justice Programs, & Health and Human Services, 2000).

Developing or Enhancing Services

Systems reviews will undoubtedly lead to recognition of the need for more services to fill the many gaps in the response to elder abuse victims. Collaborations generally can do more to create new services and strengthen existing services than individual systems can do on their own. Collaborative efforts offer not only strength in numbers, but also a broader consideration of issues and resources and a wider connection to funding possibilities and political support.

In recent years, several communities that have seen the need for temporary emergency housing for older victims have created "elder shelters." Some communities have developed special support groups for older victims after seeing either that there were no support groups or that older victims would not attend those that did exist because either they were difficult to get to, or they were composed of younger people and the older people felt too uncomfortable with them (U.S. Departments of Justice, Office of Justice Programs, & Health and Human Services, 2000). After seeing that some victims of elder abuse needed a guardian or conservator but had no family or friends willing or able to take on that responsibility, some communities established public guardianship programs to fill that need. In two communities in Florida, "elder justice centers" were established to make the courts more user-friendly to older litigants. Each of these efforts was complex and challenging; each was collaborative in nature and probably would not have succeeded without the support of multiple disciplines.

Developing New Statutes and Regulations

Systems reviews will almost assuredly demonstrate the need to create or strengthen statutes and regulations related to elder abuse. Collaborations are critical to such an effort for several reasons. It is always advisable to bring as many stakeholders as possible to the table to consider and draft legislation, because it is easier to work through issues in the drafting stage than it is in the midst of a legislative session. It is also valuable to demonstrate a groundswell of support for legislation or proposed regulations as early as possible to build momentum. Collaborations also broaden the base of support and fundraising.

The focus of a statutory reform effort may be fairly narrow. For example, a systems review may indicate that a state's statutes governing civil and/or criminal orders of protection or mandatory arrest for domestic violence only cover situations of abuse by a spouse or domestic partner. These statutes do not protect many victims of elder abuse because they do not cover abuse by other family members such as adult children. A collaborative effort involving domestic violence agencies, APS, law enforcement, prosecution, the state bar association, and victim assistance professionals could draft and support statutory amendments to fix this problem.

On the other hand, the focus of a statutory reform effort may be broader. In numerous states, task forces have developed to examine existing statutes and to propose new statutes. In Georgia, for example, a group of advocacy and regulatory agencies collaborated on an initiative to improve the state's statutes related to abuse in long-term care facilities (U.S. Departments of Justice, Office of Justice Programs, & Health and Human Services, 2000). Minnesota and Wisconsin both have taken action to reform their entire protective services systems. These comprehensive efforts have involved task forces composed of representatives from APS, the Long Term Care Ombudsman Program, law enforcement, prosecution, the court system, health care professionals, and other disciplines (see, for example, Wisconsin's Adult Protective Services Modernization Project Web site: http://www.dhfs.state.wi.us/APS/).

Developing Research

The systems review process can lead to research that may, in turn, inform system change. Identifying or seeking to identify problems with a current response to elder abuse may be a tool to engage researchers in analyzing specific services or systems. Researchers may also play important roles in ongoing collaborations by conducting literature searches that help inform practice and policy; analyzing the results of focus groups held with victims, members of disciplines that serve victims, or others; or testing interventions. The need for research and the various elder abuse research agenda that have been developed to date are discussed in the next chapter.

Teams Devoted to Systems Review and Change

As stated at the outset of this chapter, both informal and formal collaborations can implement systems review and change. The work of case review teams and other types of multidisciplinary teams can lead to systems review and change. But there are a few types of multidisciplinary teams that are specifically devoted to the goals of systems review and change. These are the systems review and systems coordination teams that are discussed in Chapter 6. Specifically, they are fatality review teams and coordinated community response teams. Statutory revision task forces, such as those used in Minnesota and Wisconsin, are another example of a formal team devoted to systems review and change.

An Example of Fatality Review

The medical examiner received a report about the death of Chloe, a 60-year-old woman. Chloe was living with her boyfriend when she was admitted to the hospital with sepsis, an infection that had spread throughout her body. Chloe died shortly after admission to the hospital. Her physicians suspected elder neglect because she had lost 40% of her body weight, 50% of her hair was missing from her head, and she was covered with pressure ulcers. Chloe's boyfriend stated that she had been well until one week before admission to the hospital, and she had refused medical help. Chloe died despite multiple measures to save her life. The autopsy revealed that Chloe had pulmonary edema (fluid in the lungs), which was listed as the cause of death. The medical examiner's office made a preliminary finding that an overload of fluid administered by the physicians contributed to Chloe's death.

An elder abuse fatality review team analyzed Chloe's death at the request of the medical examiner's office. This team had two purposes: determining whether any systems changes might prevent similar deaths in the future and helping to determine whether a criminal offense occurred. After hearing from the team members with geriatric expertise, the team concluded that Chloe's malnourished condition actually led to the overload of fluids. The pulmonary edema was unavoidable; it was the result of an aggressive attempt to save Chloe's life rather than medical mismanagement.

With this information, the medical examiner's office and the prosecutor's office, both of which were represented on the team, decided that a criminal offense had occurred. The medical examiner's office ruled that the cause of death was homicide by neglect. The prosecutor's office charged Chloe's boyfriend with homicide.

The team also discussed the possibility that the health care system and the criminal justice system might fail to recognize deaths of other older people that resulted from or were related to elder abuse. The discussion revealed that several of the disciplines represented by team members, including the forensic pathologists in the medical examiner's office, receive virtually no education and training about the physical implications and symptoms of elder abuse and neglect. As a result, the team developed several recommendations that called for training staff of emergency rooms, law enforcement, the medical examiner's office, and the prosecutor's office about medical forensic issues related to elder abuse and neglect.

Many communities, particularly larger urban jurisdictions, have systems review teams and teams that are focused on case reviews or victim safety. There are often strong connections between these teams. Multiple teams may have individual members in common. Or they may have member agencies in common, although different people represent the agencies. For example, frontline workers or supervisors may represent agencies on case review teams, whereas program administrators serve on systems review teams. Either way, these commonalities will help the various teams share appropriate information and coordinate their efforts.

CONCLUSION

As indicated at the beginning of this chapter, case review can and should inform systems review and change. In the same way, systems review and change should inform broader strategies to end elder abuse. That topic is the subject of the last chapter.

Where Do We Go From Here?

CHAPTER THIRTEEN

Strategies to End Elder Abuse

Improving methods of handling cases, protecting victims, holding perpetrators accountable, and reviewing and changing systems through a multidisciplinary approach are all critical to end the problem of elder abuse. Yet that approach alone is not sufficient. Many other strategies are necessary to prevent elder abuse, including improving detection and treatment of the problem, supporting increased funding for elder abuse intervention programs and research, and expanding efforts to protect victim safety and hold perpetrators accountable. These strategies also might include:

- Advocating for social change
- Improving services and remedies for current victims by enhancing funding for services, increasing professional and public awareness, encouraging community involvement, and increasing legal and legislative advocacy
- Helping future victims by expanding knowledge through data collection and research

Concurrent implementation of multiple strategies is necessary to improve the response to current and future victims. For example, social activism is needed to support increased funding and legislative advocacy. Legislative advocacy and increased funding are needed to foster research and improve data collection. The need for multiple strategies can be a boon to multidisciplinary collaboration. In responding to elder abuse, each discipline places a different emphasis on the value of, and has varying levels of expertise in, each of these strategies. Those differences in values and expertise can enable various disciplines to collaboratively develop, but not necessarily collaboratively implement, a more effective plan to end elder abuse. Such multidisciplinary collaborations have other benefits as well. They may result in a broader constituency that offers "strength in numbers." Collaborations also may help to thwart the negative public perception that one discipline or system is simply advocating for increased resources for its own benefit.

As Chapter 1 indicates through its presentation of the historical context of elder abuse, much progress has occurred in the last 10 years. Nonetheless, many of the positive changes have been intermittent. Some communities have made noteworthy advances in their response to elder abuse, whereas others have yet to take action. But even in those communities where improvements have occurred, too often the interest in elder abuse is dependent on the efforts of one person or a few people, and initiatives cease when those people move on. Much more work is needed. Concern for elder abuse victims should be institutionalized in the disciplines and organizations that serve them. This chapter discusses that work, focusing on potential strategies to end elder abuse and ways of implementing them in a collaborative fashion.

NEED FOR STRATEGIC INITIATIVES

There are a variety of reasons why strategic initiatives are so important. Clearly, elder abuse has a devastating impact on its victims, as illustrated by the case examples presented throughout this book and by the work of Lachs and others indicating that elder abuse increases the risk of mortality (Lachs, Williams, O'Brien, Pillemer, & Charlson, 1998).

Another justification for the work is referred to as *the demographic imperative*. As the introduction to this book explained, the exact number of elder abuse victims annually is unknown. Nonetheless, it is safe to assume two things: (1) the problem is growing as evidenced by the increase in incidents of abuse being recognized and reported to authorities, and (2) significant growth of the problem is anticipated because of the growth in the size of the older population (Bonnie & Wallace, 2003, p. 9). As a result of increased life expectancies and the size of the baby boom generation, "by 2030, the population over age 65 will nearly triple to more than 70 million people, and older people will make up more than 20% of the population (up from 12.3% 1990)" (Bonnie & Wallace, 2003, p. 10). Compounding the impact of the growth of the older population is the fact that old age brings physical and cognitive changes that may make a person more vulnerable to elder abuse. Moreover, "some particularly vulnerable groups of older persons will also experience large increases. These include the "oldest old" (age 85+) living alone, older women, older racial minorities living alone and with no living children, and older unmarried persons with no living children and no siblings" (U.S. Department of Justice, Office of Justice Programs, 1998b, p. 3).

The potential social costs of elder abuse pose another reason for working to end it. The term *social costs* refers to the economic costs, both direct and indirect, of a problem to society. Although a recent World Health Organization report indicated that there are "no systematically documented studies of the economic effects of abuse of the elderly" (Waters et al., 2004, p. 13), valuable information can be gleaned from both the methodology and results of social cost analyses of other forms of interpersonal violence.

The report found a range of results in national studies about the social costs of child abuse and domestic violence in the United States. In those studies, the social cost of child abuse ranged from $14 billion to $94 billion, depending on what costs were included. The report found only one national U.S. study of the cost of intimate partner violence. That study looked at a limited range of direct and indirect costs; it concluded that the social cost of intimate partner violence was $12.6 billion (Waters et al., 2004).

Presumably, the social cost of elder abuse also totals billions of dollars. In 1999, Charmaine Spencer, an adjunct professor at the Gerontology Research Centre of Simon Fraser University in Vancouver, Canada, prepared a report on the social and economic costs of abuse in later life for Health Canada (the Canadian equivalent of the U.S. Department of Health and Human Services). Her report suggests dozens of potential tangible and intangible costs associated with elder abuse. She categorized these costs into:

- Health and medical costs (such as hospitalization, mental health services, case management, coroners, premature death, and protocol development)
- Justice costs (including the costs of providing civil and criminal courts, law enforcement, victim assistance, legal services, corrections services, victim compensation)
- Community service costs (such as Adult Protective Services [APS], advocacy, guardianship, Long Term Care Ombudsman Programs, shelter support groups, volunteer services)
- Institutional settings (adequate staffing levels, care costs, legal costs associated with lawsuits over quality of care or staff matters related to elder abuse, criminal records checks, staff training on abuse)
- Labor costs (including premature retirement resulting from abuse, less staff time for equally pressing matters)
- Prevention, education, and research costs (such as conferences and development of training materials)

- Business costs (such as forensic audits, increased insurance claims, and defending lawsuits)
- Taxes and transfers (including loss of revenue to the government)
- Pain, suffering, and other intangibles (such as decreased quality of life, diminished independence, loss of life, pain and suffering, stress) (Spencer, 1999)

ADVOCATING FOR SOCIAL CHANGE

Given the demographic realities and potential costs associated with elder abuse, it may be difficult to understand why the problem has remained largely invisible. Possible explanations include ageism, minimal coverage in the media, and the lack of advocacy by the victims of elder abuse and neglect or their families. Advocacy is needed to change these attitudes and problems.

Different approaches to social activism are inevitable. Some disciplines may choose to focus their efforts on changing statutes related to elder abuse. An example of this type of advocacy is the work of Mothers Against Drunk Driving, which has devoted its efforts to making drunk driving socially unacceptable and to strengthening the statutes against drunk driving. Others may choose to focus on challenging the underlying belief systems that support abusive conduct. The domestic violence movement illustrates this type of advocacy through its efforts to challenge systems that support the belief that men are entitled to obedience from their wives and children. Other disciplines may advocate for social change by working with the media to publicize stories of elder abuse to the public. Still other disciplines, such as the judiciary, may not be able to participate in advocacy efforts because of ethical or legal prohibitions against such activities, but they may be able to play a role in ending elder abuse through professional education or participation in certain types of multidisciplinary collaborations.

Ageism

Robert Butler, who coined the term *ageism* in 1968, defines it as:

> a process of systematic stereotyping of and discrimination against people because they are old, just as racism and sexism accomplish this with skin color and gender. Old people are categorized as senile, rigid in though and manner, old-fashioned in morality and skills.... Ageism allows the younger generations to see older people as different from themselves; thus they subtly cease to identify with their elders as human beings. (Butler, 1975, p. 12)

Ageism may be an underlying factor in many of the causes of elder abuse. Ageism may also partially explain our society's historical lack of interest in and response to elder abuse. Our society tries to ignore older people and the fact that millions of them are abused each year. Even worse, our society sees the elderly population as a costly drain on the nation's resources. Our society does not devote resources to problems that it does not want to see. The result is a message to both victims and perpetrators that says that our society will tolerate elder abuse.

Minimal Coverage in the Media

Historically, the media has paid little attention to the problem of elder abuse. Coverage of the problem has increased dramatically in the last few years, but all too often reporters fail to identify that a problem involves elder abuse, fail to suggest appropriate resources for help and additional information, or fail to correctly and adequately present the definitions and dynamics of elder abuse as related to the story. Advocacy efforts could proactively educate the media to recognize and develop stories about elder abuse; they could also react to incorrect or insufficient stories. As an example, recently the five partner organizations of the National Center on Elder Abuse collaborated to write a letter to syndicated columnist "Dear Abby" after she provided an insufficient response to a reader who was a victim of elder abuse. Advocates can also support media coverage of this problem by providing background information and resources for investigative reports. Recent examples include the *St. Louis Post-Dispatch* series on institutional abuse in Missouri and *The Washington Post* series on assisted living problems in Virginia. Additional suggestions for working with the media are provided in the "Increasing Public Awareness" section of this chapter.

Lack of Advocacy by the Victims of Elder Abuse and Neglect

Most of the social movements of the last 50 years—civil rights, women's rights, domestic violence and sexual assault victims' rights, other crime victims' rights, and gay rights—have resulted from self-advocacy by the persons who were the victims of discrimination or crime. Policymakers and media representatives often ask why elder abuse victims are not advocating for improved intervention programs. The answer to the question is that many older victims either cannot or will not advocate for themselves. Elder abuse victims may die or be rendered physically or mentally incapable of self-advocacy as a result of their abuse. Some victims may have been incapable of protecting and advocating for themselves before their abuse. Others may fear retaliation from their abusers if they speak out about what has happened to them. Some may not realize that their experiences constitute elder abuse. And others may be too ashamed about what has happened to them to speak openly of their experiences.

Policymakers and media representatives also ask why other people are not advocating on behalf of elder abuse victims. The answers may be found in several of the other issues discussed in this chapter: ageism, lack of public and professional awareness, lack of media attention, and lack of community involvement. The situation has begun to change in the past few years, however, and advocacy efforts by family members of victims and by aging services and other organizations have grown. Advocacy efforts by family members of victims of institutional abuse and abuse or exploitation by guardians have sparked Congressional hearings and investigative reports by the U.S. General Accounting Office (now known as the U.S. Government Accountability Office) and by the media.

Advocates need to encourage victims and their family members to share their stories with policymakers and the media and to support their efforts in doing so. Strategies that have proved successful include having victims or family members present their stories at legislative hearings and at policy conferences or on videotapes that can be used repeatedly.

IMPROVING SERVICES AND REMEDIES FOR CURRENT VICTIMS

To improve services and remedies for current victims of elder abuse, it is necessary to increase funding for services, increase professional awareness, increase public awareness, involve the community, and conduct legal and legislative advocacy.

Advocating for Increased Funding

The means of ending elder abuse discussed in this chapter cannot be accomplished without resources. Only the federal government has the resources and ability to support development of a national, comprehensive, collaborative approach to the problem of elder abuse. But the efforts of the federal government alone will never be sufficient; they must be supplemented by financial resources from state and local governments. These resources could be used to conduct outreach programs, provide services to victims, support training programs or multidisciplinary teams, or enhance efforts to hold perpetrators accountable. Some examples of successful efforts to obtain funding at the local, state, and federal levels are provided next.

Local advocacy efforts have resulted in funding from local government authorities or from local agencies, such as area agencies on aging, for the purposes already set forth. To illustrate, the Office of the Ventura County (California) District Attorney, in conjunction with several other local agencies and service providers, has obtained funding from the local area agency on aging and from state agencies to conduct a community outreach program, develop a multidisciplinary team, conduct training, and prosecute cases (U.S. Departments of Justice, Office of Justice Programs, & Health and Human Services, 2000, pp. 25–26). Other programs have obtained funding after advocating for the imposition of surcharges on filing fees for local services (such as registering deeds or filing court cases).

Advocacy efforts at the state level have led to some of the same results. This type of advocacy can occur through the statutory and appropriations processes. It can also occur as a result of advocacy aimed at the leadership of funding agencies. The Nevada Elder Abuse Prevention Council provides an example of effective advocacy. Led by the state attorney general and the Division for Aging Services, the council includes representatives of several state and local agencies and advocacy organizations, as well as some federal agency representatives. The council has conducted its activities, which include the development of an action plan, protocols, a guide for mandatory reporters, consumer brochures, videos, training materials, and training programs, with funds from the state legislature, the Division of Aging Services, and sanction money received from nursing facilities (U.S. Departments of Justice, Office of Justice Programs, & Health and Human Services, 2000, pp. 81–82). Programs in other states have used sanctioned money from regulatory actions and from penalties awarded in court cases to support elder abuse programs and services. In California several years ago, the county social services departments, which house the APS programs, banded together with advocates and successfully lobbied to double the state's funding level for APS.

The authorization of, and appropriation for, training programs about violence against older women and women with disabilities in the Violence Against Women Act reauthorization also illustrates a funding success. When the bill was enacted, funding for those programs was not appropriated. The multidisciplinary Violence Against Women taskforce successfully spent the next year advocating for the funds to be included in the next year's Department of Justice appropriation. If the Elder Justice Act (see later discussion) is enacted, advocates will have to ensure that Congress provides the required funding for its programs in agency appropriations.

Advocacy for funding from private foundations, other charitable organizations, and corporations is also necessary. For example, a multidisciplinary team may apply for a foundation grant or try to obtain funding from the local chapter of the United Way or a similar agency. Corporations often devote financial or in-kind resources to a cause after they are educated about the need for their help. It is important that efforts to end elder abuse seek support from government agencies and from nongovernment agencies to enhance their stability and accomplishments.

Increasing Professional Awareness

Much more could be done to provide education about elder abuse to the members of disciplines that work with older persons. At the current time, the core curricula for educating doctors, nurses, dentists, psychologists, other health care professionals, and social workers usually do not contain information about recognizing and reporting elder abuse (Institute of Medicine, 2002). The same can be said of law schools. Neither law enforcement academies nor training programs for other first-responders provide much, if any, content on elder abuse. Members of these disciplines generally learn about elder abuse only if they happen to have a case involving an older victim or attend a continuing education program that addresses the topic.

Yet opportunities abound to provide education about elder abuse as part of the core curricula for these disciplines. For example, medical students could learn about elder abuse during emergency room and geriatrics rotations. At the Baylor College of Medicine, students doing geriatric rotations are required to make a home visit with an APS worker and to attend meetings of the multidisciplinary team and fatality review team in which the medical school participates. Law professors could teach about elder abuse cases as part of their classes on elder law, trusts and estates, family law, health care law, criminal law, torts, civil procedure, and more. Elder law cases could be included in clinical programs (Eisenberg, 1991). Social work professors could teach about elder abuse cases and services; they could also require students to make home visits with APS workers, attend multidisciplinary team meetings, and do more to gain exposure to the problems experienced by elder abuse victims. Instructors at law enforcement academies and other programs for first-responders, such as emergency medical services, could incorporate elder abuse into their basic and advanced classes.

All of the various disciplines could do more to encourage their educators to address elder abuse in professional training programs. For example, including elder abuse as a topic in the accreditation, licensure, and certification requirements of various disciplines may encourage the teachers in those disciplines to address the subject (Institute of Medicine, 2002).

There are also extensive opportunities to include elder abuse in continuing education programs for every discipline that is, or should be, involved in working with older victims. Continuing education programs may provide more opportunities than professional training core curricula for content on elder abuse and for multidisciplinary collaboration in the development and presentation of that content. For example, continuing legal and medical education programs could address the benefits of screening all older persons for abuse and how to conduct such screening. Continuing judicial education classes could include information about the development of protection orders in cases involving elder abuse. Judges and court staff could learn about legal resources available in the community to which they could refer apparent victims of elder abuse and about the ways in which elder abuse victims may need to be accommodated in the courtroom (Stiegel, 1995). Continuing education programs for members of any discipline could include information about promising practices in handling elder abuse cases from experts in their own discipline, allowing professionals to learn about and replicate useful practices developed in other communities.

Increasing Public Awareness

As was the case with child abuse and domestic violence, enhancing public awareness of elder abuse is an important step toward ending the problem. The work of the participants at the National Policy Summit on Elder Abuse, conducted in 2001 by the National Center on Elder Abuse with the support of the U.S. Administration on Aging and the Office for Victims of Crime at the U.S. Department of Justice, supports that theory. Tied for first among the summit's top 10 recommendations was a call to "mount a national education and awareness effort" (NCEA, 2002). The recommendation stated that "high national priority must be given to raising America's awareness about elder abuse and neglect. To inform the public at large, as well as policy makers, including legislators, justices, and state and local leaders, the federal government should" implement nine action steps, including these:

- "Action Step 2—Develop a campaign to educate policy makers on elder abuse issues, and engage the support of key legislators to increase funding for elder abuse public awareness."
- "Action Step 3—Educate the media about elder abuse to encourage greater attention and sensitivity in news coverage."
- "Action Step 8—Declare National Elder Abuse Awareness Month."
- "Action Step 9—Dissemination prevention education and public information." (NCEA, 2002, pp. 4–5)

The National Association of Adult Protective Services Administrators, now known as the National Association of Adult Protective Services Advocates, has also called for a national public awareness campaign (National Association of Adult Protective Services Administrators, 2003).

The federal government has yet to devote resources to the initiatives suggested by the summit participants, but many states and communities have undertaken public awareness efforts. These have included development of media campaigns, such as billboards and public service announcements; dissemination of information about elder abuse to older persons through methods such as placemats used for home-delivered meals and inserts in pharmacy bags containing prescriptions; and establishment of elder abuse awareness months and colored ribbon campaigns. Anecdotal reports indicate that these efforts have had some success, resulting in increased number of reports to APS and other agencies, improvements in system responses, and enhanced funding or other support.

Educating the media about elder abuse is an important step in enhancing public awareness of the problem. Such a strategy must be both proactive and reactive. Being proactive involves feeding stories about elder abuse to reporters or assisting reporters who are producing such stories by participating in interviews and providing additional information. It may involve inviting reporters to attend, or even present at, key education programs and meetings. Being reactive may necessitate individual or collaborative responses to inaccurate, incomplete, or inappropriate portrayals of elder abuse by the media. This may entail writing letters intended to educate media representatives and the public when the media provides misinformation about elder abuse. It also may involve taking steps to counter negative or incorrect media images about elder abuse when they are used in advertisements or in movies. For example, in recent years, a large corporation developed several product advertisements that were perceived by advocates as promoting elder abuse or treating the problem as a joke. Elder abuse advocates protested to the company about these ads, resulting (the second time this occurred) in the company withdrawing them and issuing letters of apology.

Involving the Community

The problem of elder abuse is pervasive, complex, and multifaceted. Development of a federal response with provisions for better funding of the myriad systems that prevent and respond to elder abuse, research, and increased community awareness will help a great deal, yet still be insufficient to end the problem. The involvement of community organizations, including faith-based groups, nonprofit agencies, other civic and public service groups, and local foundations, could go far in benefiting victims of elder abuse. These organizations could help to implement effective intervention strategies based on the needs of their own communities. They are in the best position to know their community's strengths and weaknesses, including the availability or lack of local resources, and to identify the needs of older persons in the population.

The case of Mattie, an 83-year-old woman, provides an example of the critical role that community organizations can play. Mattie had become more frail and unable to manage her household, which was now in a state of disrepair. She continued to go to church, but her personal hygiene and general cleanliness had declined. A young woman from the neighborhood was stealing Mattie's Social Security check from her mailbox each month. The pastor and church members observed these problems and tried to convince Mattie to accept help so that she could continue to live in her house. Mattie refused. One of her neighbors, also a member of Mattie's church, reported her situation to APS. After the report, several church members went to Mattie's home and convinced her to move out temporarily and stay with one of them while they performed a major clean-up of her house. Mattie understood the significance of the problem after an APS worker visited her. She accepted help from her neighbors, who cleaned her home and her clothes. The neighbors developed a schedule to check on Mattie regularly and to bring her food periodically. This community intervention supplemented the work of APS and allowed Mattie to live in her home safely and independently.

Federal and state governments could fund programs to train community organizations to identify and intervene in cases of elder abuse. These groups could help to provide some of the specific resources needed for individual interventions. This approach will not eradicate elder abuse or replace existing social services, but it will supplement those services. Federal and state recognition of the seriousness of elder abuse could spur community organizations to make this issue a priority for their members.

Legal Advocacy

Another important step toward the goal of ending elder abuse is legal advocacy for victims. Lawsuits against abusers in the civil courts can impact individual victims. In the criminal courts, prosecutions can hold perpetrators accountable. But legal advocacy may also have broader systemic and societal impact.

Decisions in civil and criminal cases may influence decisions in subsequent civil and criminal cases, even those that occur in other jurisdictions, if they are included in case reporters. These legal precedents are intended to ensure consistency in application of the law from case to case.

Civil or criminal actions brought against a corporation, such as a nursing home or a nursing home chain, may ultimately result in better care for all the residents of the home or the chain's homes. These lawsuits, of which there are a growing number, generally involve actions against the managerial staff or owners of the facility or the chain, rather than actions against the nursing aides and other low-level staff who may actually have committed the abuse or neglect. For example, the Medicaid Fraud Control Units, which exist in almost every state, have brought criminal prosecutions against "owners, managers, controlling individuals, and corporate entities" (Connolly, 2002, p. 430). A California district attorney's office prosecuted the owners, corporate entities, and/or operators of a nursing home (Connolly, 2002, p. 430). In addition, some U.S. attorneys' offices have brought civil actions against nursing home chains under the federal False Claims Act for failure to provide quality care. The first of those cases settled for monetary damages, the imposition of an independent temporary monitor to oversee operations and recommend improvements, the implementation of care improvement protocols by the chain, and letters of apology to the families of three victims. In this case, the U.S. attorney's office consulted with medical experts to develop the care improvement protocols (Connolly, 2002, p. 430). This case provides an example of the benefits of multidisciplinary collaboration in legal advocacy.

Different types of multidisciplinary collaboration also may support legal advocacy. Other disciplines may serve as witnesses or expert witnesses in legal actions. They may bring issues to the attention of civil and criminal lawyers. Legal actions may be encouraged and supported by the deliberations of multidisciplinary teams, as was demonstrated by the case of Chloe in the previous chapter.

Legislative Advocacy

Chapter 1 discusses the federal legislative activity that has occurred since elder abuse was recognized as a problem. Although some advances have been made, much more legislative advocacy is needed at the state and federal level to further the progress made to date. This advocacy must focus on improving statutes related to elder abuse and on increasing funding for programs and services to victims. Multidisciplinary collaborations can play an important role in legislative advocacy on substantive issues at the local, state, and federal levels (funding initiatives were discussed previously).

Advocacy at the State Level

Significant legislative action has occurred in the states, particularly in the last few years, as some states have expanded their mandatory reporting statutes, strengthened or enacted new civil remedies, and enhanced or created new criminal statutes and penalties (Heisler & Stiegel, 2002; Stiegel, 2000). That state focus on elder abuse has been sporadic, however. Some states have seen a lot of legislative activity, whereas others have seen very little. As a result, the response to elder abuse, particularly by APS and the criminal justice system, varies widely from state to state.

New civil or criminal remedies are needed to protect the lives and property of victims and hold perpetrators accountable. States need to do more to require training of various disciplines about elder abuse, because without mandates such training may not occur. Enhancing or enacting civil and criminal statutes on elder abuse could encourage civil lawyers and prosecutors to pursue legal actions against perpetrators. Statutory changes may be necessary in many states to enable the development of elder abuse fatality review teams or other types of multidisciplinary teams and to allow disciplines to share otherwise confidential information and develop a more collaborative response to victims. Legislative action may be necessary to foster special handling of elder abuse cases by the courts, prosecutor's offices, or law enforcement agencies. Examples of special handling might include expedited hearings in elder abuse matters, "vertical prosecution" of elder abuse cases, and specially trained elder abuse prosecutors or law enforcement officers in their respective agencies. States legislatures could require and fund improved data management systems and collection efforts by APS programs, the courts, and law enforcement agencies (Heisler & Stiegel, 2002).

Multidisciplinary collaborations have already suggested and promoted legislative changes in some states. For example, when the nation's first elder abuse fatality review team developed in Sacramento, California, it was advised that California's law governing child abuse and domestic violence fatality review teams did not govern its efforts. The team drafted proposed legislation authorizing elder abuse fatality review teams, found a sponsor for it, and advocated successfully for its enactment. In other states, bar associations and advocates for elder abuse victims have worked together in support of legislative changes to enhance civil remedies for elder abuse or to require that the courts heard elder abuse cases in expedited fashion.

Advocacy at the Federal Level

Much more advocacy is needed at the federal level. Federal legislation on issues such as racial and age discrimination, child abuse, and domestic violence have changed societal attitudes about and systems' responses to those challenging problems. The same action is necessary to address elder abuse.

The Elder Justice Act, S. 2010, which was introduced in the 109th Congress (after failures to enact similar bills in both the 107th and 108th Congresses), could lead to significant improvements in society's response to elder abuse. By enacting and funding the Elder Justice Act, Congress will accomplish the following critical steps:

1. [B]ring a comprehensive approach to preventing and combating elder abuse, neglect, and exploitation, a long invisible problem that afflicts the most vulnerable among the aging population of the United States.

2. [R]aise the issue of elder abuse, neglect, and exploitation to national attention, and to create the infrastructure at the Federal, State, and local levels to ensure that individuals and organizations on the front lines who are fighting elder abuse, neglect, and exploitation with scarce resources and fragmented systems have the resources and information needed to carry out their fight.

3. [B]ring a comprehensive multidisciplinary approach to elder justice.

4. [S]et in motion research and data collection to fill gaps in knowledge about elder abuse, neglect, and exploitation.

5. [S]upplement the activities of service providers and programs, to enhance training, and to leverage scarce resources efficiently to ensure that elder justice receives the attention it deserves as the Nation's population ages.

6. [E]xamine the many different laws and practices relating to elder justice in different States and jurisdictions to ascertain which among those laws and practices are the most effective.

7. [P]romote the development of an effective adult fiduciary system, including an adult guardianship system, that protects individuals with diminished capacity, maximizes their autonomy, and develops effective resources and an elder rights system.

8. [R]ecognize and address the role of mental health, disability, dementia, substance abuse, medication mismanagement, and family dysfunction problems in increasing and exacerbating elder abuse, neglect, and exploitation.

9. [C]reate a short- and long-term strategic plan for the development and coordination of elder justice research, programs, studies, training, and other efforts nationwide.

10. [P]romote collaborative efforts and diminish overlap and gaps in efforts in developing the important field of elder justice. (Hatch & Lincoln, 2005)

The multidisciplinary national Elder Justice Coalition, with members from national, state, and local organizations and individual members, is advocating for enactment and appropriation of the Elder Justice Act.

Enactment of the Elder Justice Act is critically important to the progress of the field, but it does not provide the only opportunity for legislative advocacy at the federal level. There are other federal statutes that relate to elder abuse in some way, including, but not limited to:

- The Older Americans Act, which authorizes the National Center on Elder Abuse, legal services for older persons, the Long Term Care Ombudsman Program, state and local programs for elder abuse prevention, and many other aging services
- The Social Security Act, which governs the Social Security, Medicare, Medicaid, and Social Services Block Grant programs and, thereby, relates to representative payees, long-term care facility licensing and certification, Medicaid Fraud Control Units, and funding of state APS programs
- The Violence Against Women Act, which supports services for victims and programs to train law enforcement officers, prosecutors, judges, and others about abuse, domestic violence, dating violence, sexual assault, and stalking against older persons and persons with disabilities
- The Family Violence Prevention and Services Act, which supports domestic violence programs and shelter services
- The Victims of Crime Act, which supports services and compensation for victims of crime
- Many statutes governing federal crimes and civil violations that are committed against elder abuse victims

When these or other pertinent statutes are reauthorized, which happens periodically, there are opportunities to add or amend existing provisions related to elder abuse victims and programs. For example, when the Violence Against Women Act was reauthorized in 2000, the training programs mentioned previously were added to the statute. The state and local elder abuse prevention programs were included in the Older Americans Act reauthorization of 2000 (42 U.S.C. §3001 *et. seq.*, as amended). Of course, existing statutes may also be amended at any time through the enactment of new statutes affecting current provisions. For example, when the Medicare Prescription Drug, Improvement, and Modernization Act of 2003 (P.L. 108–173) was enacted, it included a provision to establish a federal pilot program on criminal background checks of nursing home staff.

The 2000 reauthorization of the Violence Against Women Act provides an illustration of the importance of multidisciplinary collaboration in federal legislative advocacy. A national taskforce composed of dozens of advocacy groups addressing domestic violence and sexual assault developed the reauthorization provisions and advocated for their enactment. Without their support, the provisions related to older women and women with disabilities might not have become law.

HELPING FUTURE VICTIMS BY EXPANDING KNOWLEDGE THROUGH DATA COLLECTION AND RESEARCH

Data Collection

Invariably, one of the first questions asked by legislators, policymakers, potential funders, and media representatives is "how many older persons are victims of abuse?" Unfortunately, little data at the federal, state, or local level are collected about the incidence (number of times that a problem occurs during a certain time period) and prevalence (percentage of a defined population that experiences a problem) of elder abuse. When data are collected, there are usually substantial methodological and definitional flaws in the process. The lack of data in general, and reliable data in particular, poses significant challenges to the development of policy about, resources for, and social awareness of elder abuse. The inability of service providers and advocates to provide comprehensive, accurate, supportable data results in minimization and neglect of the problem.

Collaborative efforts between researchers, program administrators, and practitioners are needed to fix the problems with data collection. To demonstrate the opportunities for collaboration and change, this chapter briefly discusses the types of data that are currently collected and the problems that occur.

Data From State APS Programs

As discussed in the Introduction to this book, there are substantial methodological and definitional problems with collection and comparison of data from the state APS programs (these problems were discussed in some detail in the Introduction and will only be recapitulated briefly here). These problems include "the lack of consistent definitions, as well as compatible data collection systems in the states." Even if APS data were more consistent and comparable, they would not provide an accurate picture of the extent of the problem because only a small percentage of elder abuse incidents are ever reported to APS (NCEA, 1998). Confounding the matter further is the fact that several state APS programs only respond to cases of domestic elder abuse, whereas others respond to both domestic and institutional abuse (Teaster, 2002).

Congress appropriated $1 million for the 1998 National Elder Abuse Incidence Study, which is the only national incidence study of elder abuse conducted to date. The study had serious methodological problems, which resulted in missing the most isolated and vulnerable elders who were at greatest risk of abuse (Cook-Daniels, 1999; Otto & Quinn, 1999).

Data Regarding Abuse and Neglect of Long-term Care Facility Residents

Efforts to collect data about abuse and neglect of residents of long-term care facilities face generally the same methodological and definitional problems as data collection about domestic abuse, but the problems are amplified by the range of facilities considered to be "long-term care facilities" and the array of data sources. There are several potential national sources for data related to nursing homes: reports of abuse made to Long Term Care Ombudsman Programs, reports of abuse made to APS in states where APS investigates nursing homes, deficiency citations by regulatory agencies for resident abuse, and reports from the state nurses aide registries (Hawes, 2003). Another source of information are the state Medicaid Fraud Control Units, which investigate and prosecute cases of resident abuse and neglect. There are no comparable national sources for data related to residential care homes, however, because of the lack of federal regulations governing those facilities (Hawes, 2003).

Despite this broad array of data sources, "there is no definitive evidence about prevalence" of elder abuse in long-term care facilities for a variety of reasons (Hawes, 2003, pp. 469–470), including these:

- Reports are made to myriad agencies, "each of which uses different definitions, investigative protocols, and standards of proof." (Hawes, 2003, p. 470)
- There is difficulty distinguishing "abuse from the effects of chronic diseases found among many elderly, particularly those at risk for abuse and neglect because of their functional limitations." (Hawes, 2003, p. 471)
- There is significant underreporting of resident abuse and neglect, due to underreporting by health care professionals, residents and their family members, and long term care ombudsmen; unreliable reporting by the nurses aide registries, and underreporting

in the OSCAR (Online Survey Certification and Reporting System) database administered by the Centers for Medicare and Medicaid Services. (Hawes, 2003)

Crime Data

The federal government collects data on violent crime through the National Crime Victim Survey, the FBI Uniform Crime Reports, and the FBI National Incident-Based Reporting System (Acierno, 2003). The usefulness of these criminal justice system statistics in providing information about elder abuse is significantly flawed; however, there are problems with each instrument.

- The FBI's Uniform Crime Reports system does not ask about elder abuse; it tracks only a limited group of violent crimes that are reported to the police. The report does not provide data on the age of the victim or relationship between the victim and perpetrator (Acierno, 2003).
- The National Crime Victim Survey, conducted by the Bureau of Justice Statistics at the U.S. Department of Justice, randomly contacts between 80,000 and 100,000 U.S. citizens age 12 and over to ask if they have experienced crime, whether reported or unreported to law enforcement. The survey does gather limited information about victim age and relationship to perpetrator, but it does not ask specific questions about elder abuse (Acierno, 2003).
- The FBI's National Incident-Based Reporting System provides only limited information about elder abuse because it only counts crimes that were reported to law enforcement (Acierno, 2003).

Data Collection by the State Courts

Data collection by the state courts provides more examples of the problems with data on elder abuse. Although many guardianship or conservatorship cases heard by courts involve elder abuse, there are no known court systems that collect data on these cases. Indeed, many court systems do not even distinguish in their data collection between cases involving guardianships of minors and guardianships of adults (U.S. General Accounting Office, 2004). Criminal courts usually do not track the ages of the victims or perpetrators in cases nor the relationship between the victims and perpetrators. Thus, opportunities to gather data about elder abuse cases in the criminal courts are lost. In civil courts, the situation is the same; generally, data are not collected about the ages or relationships of the parties involved.

The difficulty of developing reliable data on the extent of elder abuse has been recognized and discussed for decades. Over the years, numerous recommendations have been made on ways to overcome the problems discussed previously. Those recommendations have usually been offered as part of broader research agendas (to avoid redundancy?) and are discussed in the next section.

Research

Research on elder abuse is imperative to increase knowledge about the extent of the problem, foster better understanding and recognition of the problem, and support the development and implementation of effective interventions. Numerous recommendations for research have been developed by multidisciplinary groups of experts. Each of those groups has also explicitly or implicitly recognized the importance of involving practitioners in any research initiatives.

The National Research Council, part of the National Academy of Sciences, established the Panel to Review Risk and Prevalence of Elder Abuse and Neglect to develop a research agenda on elder abuse (Bonnie & Wallace, 2003, p. 2). The multidisciplinary panel, composed of researchers and practitioners, analyzed the existing research on elder abuse and identified the following problems: "(1) unclear and inconsistent definitions, (2) unclear and inadequate measures, (3) incomplete professional accounts, (4) lack of population-based data, (5) lack of prospective data, (6) lack of control groups, and (7) lack of systematic evaluation studies" (Bonnie & Wallace, 2003, p. 2). Two of the seven reasons cited for these problems by the panel of experts were: "little funding and few investigators" and "*inadequate links between researchers and service agencies*" (emphasis added) (Bonnie & Wallace, 2003, p. 2).

Increasing Knowledge About the Extent of the Problem

The National Research Council panel developed several recommendations for research on the extent of the problem. These included (1) development of operational definitions and validated and standardized measurement methods for the elements of elder abuse; (2) population-based surveys; (3) the design and fielding of national prevalence and incidence studies of elder abuse, including "both a large-scale, independent study of prevalence and modular add-ons to surveys of aging populations"; (4) development of new methods of sampling and identifying elder abuse victims in the community to improve occurrence estimates; and (5) new study sampling and detection methods to measure the occurrence of elder abuse in long-term care facilities and hospitals (Bonnie & Wallace, 2003, pp. 3–6).

In one landmark national collaboration effort, the National Policy Summit on Elder Abuse brought together 80 national, state, and local experts in elder abuse, APS, law enforcement, and other relevant disciplines to develop a national action agenda (Aravanis, 2002). The summit participants called on Congress to enact a national elder abuse law that would, among other things, "establish a grant program to fund research and data collection on elder abuse prevalence, elder and family needs, and promising interventions that would inform policy making" (National Center on Elder Abuse, 2002, p. 2).

The National Center on Elder Abuse issued "A Research Agenda on Abuse of Older Persons and Adults with Disabilities" in the late 1990s. Derived from the responses of APS program administrators and workers and other disciplines, the agenda also offered recommendations for research on the scope of the problem (Wolf, 1999a).

Fostering Better Understanding and Recognition of the Problem

Experts from various disciplines have repeatedly urged that research be conducted on the nature and consequences of elder abuse. Such research would inform efforts to determine the extent of the problem. It would also enhance the ability of professionals to recognize when an older person is a victim of elder abuse.

The National Research Council panel also promulgated several recommendations on this issue. They included: (1) "basic research on the phenomenology of elder mistreatment"; (2) longitudinal investigations on "the clinical course, antecedents, and outcomes of the various types of elder mistreatment occurrence..., including follow-up studies of the clinical, social, and psychological outcomes of elder mistreatment cases detected"; (3) studies on "risk indicators and risk and protective factors for different types of elder mistreatment"; (4) risk factors, including "the clinical course of elder mistreatment"; and (5) research to "improve and develop new methods of screening for possible elder mistreatment in a range of clinical settings" (Bonnie &Wallace, 2003, pp. 2–5).

The National Center on Elder Abuse Research Agenda also suggested numerous issues that could be studied to raise the level of understanding and recognition of the problem. Several of the questions, including these, were similar to the recommendations made by the National Research Council panel: (1) "What is the trajectory of abuse over time?" (2) "What are the risk factors for elder abuse, neglect, and exploitation?" (3) "What is the relationship between undue influence, incompetence, and diminished capacity and elder abuse?" (4) "What is the relationship between elder abuse and depression?" and (5) "Is there a relationship between suicide and elder abuse?"

Supporting the Development and Implementation of Effective Interventions

The calls for research on the effectiveness of interventions in elder abuse cases have been longstanding, widespread, and consistent. Practitioners recognize that their involvement with victims may have good or bad consequences. They want to maximize use of interventions that lead to positive outcomes and minimize use of interventions that lead to negative outcomes. For research to have real-world impact, it is essential that practitioners be involved in the design of research on interventions.

The National Research Council panel issued the following recommendations related to interventions: (1) "Research is needed on the process of designating cases as incidents of mistreatment in order to improve criteria, investigative methods, decision-making processes, and decision outcomes"; and (2) "Research on the effects of elder mistreatment interventions is urgently needed. Existing interventions to prevent or ameliorate elder mistreatment should be evaluated, and agencies funding new intervention programs should require and fund a scientifically adequate evaluation as a component of each grant" (Bonnie & Wallace, 2003, pp. 5–6).

The National Policy Summit on Elder Abuse also called for the government to establish a national elder abuse research and program innovation institute that would, among other things, support research on intervention methods (NCEA, 2002).

The National Center on Elder Abuse Research Agenda, which was largely developed by practitioners, offered many ideas for research on interventions. The participants designated the following issues as high priority: (1) "What are the best practice standards for conducting APS work (potential national guidelines)?" (2) "What is effective training for new APS employees?" (3) "What happens to those clients who refuse interventions?" (4) "How are outcomes defined and measured?" and (5) "Are there (should there be) differences in investigation techniques/interventions for different populations (older adults [persons with developmental disabilities, persons with mental illness]) and types of abuse/neglect?" (Wolf, 1999).

Interventions in family violence, including elder abuse, were the topic of another research agenda developed by a multidisciplinary expert panel for the National Research Council and Institute of Medicine. This panel's recommendations do not specifically relate to elder abuse, but most of them provide useful guidance to researchers on that subject.

Of importance, the panel recognized the importance of collaboration in research efforts, stating that:

> The lack of collaboration between researchers and service providers has impeded the development of appropriate measures and study designs in assessing the effectiveness of programs. It has also discouraged research on the design and implementation of service interventions and the multiple pathways to services that address the causes and consequences of family violence. (Chalk & King, 1998, p. 10)

CONCLUSION

There have been vital advances in the response to elder abuse, particularly in the last few years. The formation of multidisciplinary collaborations and teams across the United States is a positive change. Public and professional awareness is increasing. Involvement of other disciplines beyond social services has helped to advance the field, to help make victims safer, and to hold perpetrators accountable. Legislators, other policymakers, and the media are becoming more aware of and interested in the problem of elder abuse. The Centers for Disease Control and Prevention and academic medical centers are becoming aware of elder abuse as an important line of study. Funding for research and program development is beginning to increase, and for the first time there is hope for significant increases in funding for elder abuse work if the Elder Justice Act is enacted and appropriated.

Just as a puzzle is not complete until all of the pieces are in place, the full solution for addressing elder abuse has still not been developed. Much more remains to be done; however, the progress of the past decade demonstrates that multidisciplinary collaboration is essential for the picture to be completed. Work on the issue of elder abuse is not only challenging and intellectually stimulating, but it offers almost unlimited opportunity to make a difference in the manner and discipline of one's choice. Whether at the local, state, or national level, anyone can play an important role. Whether one serves and advocates for individual victims; advocates for social change; enhances professional or public awareness; develops intervention programs; investigates, prosecutes, litigates, or judges cases; provides medical care to victims; conducts research; promotes and participates in community involvement; or fulfills any other role related to elder abuse intervention, the work will always be satisfying and it will make a difference in the lives of older persons. The rewards will be even greater when the work is done in collaboration with others who share the same goal of ending elder abuse.

It is not the critic who counts: not the man who points out how the strong man stumbles or where the doer of deeds could have done better. The credit belongs to the man who is actually in the arena, whose face is marred by dust and sweat and blood, who strives valiantly, who errs and comes up short again and again, because there is no effort without error or shortcoming, but who knows the great enthusiasms, the great devotions, who spends himself for a worthy cause; who, at the best, knows, in the end, the triumph of high achievement, and who, at the worst, if he fails, at least he fails while daring greatly, so that his place shall never be with those cold and timid souls who knew neither victory nor defeat.

Theodore Roosevelt, 1910, April 23, Citizenship in a Republic,
speech at the Sorbonne, Paris, France

APPENDIX A

Timeline of Significant National Events in the Elder Abuse Field

Year	Significant National Event
1960s	Sen. Moss report titled "Nursing Home Care in the United States: Failure in Public Policy" is released and a series of hearings held. The National Council on the Aging conducted the earliest study of adult protective services. The 1961 White House Conference on Aging recommends a collaborative approach to elder abuse.
1970s	Burston identifies the phenomenon of "granny battering." Passage of Title XX of the Social Security Act includes funds for APS.
1980	U.S. Senate Committee on Aging holds hearings and publishes a report titled "Elder Abuse: An Examination of a Hidden Problem." Bill is introduced, but not passed, titled "Prevention, Identification and Treatment of Adult Abuse."
1981	All states have an APS service system.
1983	First Texas APS conference.
1985	Rep. Claude Pepper issues a report titled "Elder Abuse: A National Disgrace."
1986	"Elder Abuse and Neglect: Causes, Diagnosis, and Intervention Strategies" is written by Tomita and Quinn.

(continued)

Year	Significant National Event
1988	Pillemer and Finklehor publishes their random sample study of elders in Boston. Dr. Rosalie Wolf forms the National Committee for the Prevention of Elder Abuse. The National Center for State Long Term Care Ombudsman is created.
1989	The first National Center on Elder Abuse is establised by the U.S. Administration on Aging. The National Association of Adult Protective Services Administrators is created.
1990	Congressional Committee on Aging drafts a report titled "Elder Abuse: A Decade of Shame."
1991	Congressional subcommittee drafts a report titled "Protecting America's Abused Elderly: The Need for Congressional Action."
1992	AARP holds a national forum addressing the needs of older battered women.
1994	The Administration on Aging funds six national demonstration projects to address the needs of older battered women.
1997	National Center on Elder Abuse and Archstone Foundation conference titled "Understanding and Combating Elder Abuse in Minority Communities."
1998	The National Center on Elder Abuse partnership changes to include the National Association of State Units on Aging, the National Association of Adult Protective Services Administrators, the American Bar Association Commission on Legal Problems of the Elderly, the Clearinghouse on Abuse and Neglect of the Elderly at the University of Delaware, the National Committee for the Prevention of Elder Abuse, and the Institute on Aging in San Francisco. Lachs et al. study finds that older adults who were mistreated were three times at greater risk of dying within the next decade than nonabused elders. The National Elder Abuse Incidence Study is published.
1999	The National Clearinghouse on Abuse in Later Life, a project of the Wisconsin Coalition Against Domestic Violence, is created.
2000	Department of Justice sponsors a roundtable titled "Elder Justice: Medical Forensic Issues Relating to Elder Abuse and Neglect." American Society on Aging devotes an issue of *Generations* to elder abuse. The departments of Justice and Health and Human Services holds a national symposium.

(continued)

Year	Significant National Event
2001	National Policy Summit on Elder Abuse is sponsored by the National Center on Elder Abuse.
2002	The first national health care conference on elder abuse is held. The Violence Against Women Act authorizes funds to train justice personnel on elder abuse and abuse against people with disabilities. The Elder Justice Act is drafted and introduced.
2003	National Center on Elder Abuse was re-funded, with the National Association of State Units on Aging, the National Association of Adult Protective Services Administrators, the American Bar Association Commission on Law and Aging, the Clearinghouse on Abuse and Neglect of the Elderly at the University of Delaware, and the National Committee for the Prevention of Elder Abuse as partners. The "Response to the Abuse of Vulnerable Adults: The 2000 Survey of State Adult Protective" is published by the National Center on Elder Abuse. The National Research Council publishes "Elder Mistreatment: Abuse, Neglect, and Exploitation in an Aging America." The FBI sponsors a four-day symposium on family violence, including elder abuse. The *Violence Against Women* journal devotes an issue to domestic abuse in later life. The Elder Justice Act is reintroduced to Congress.
2004	The Department of Justice sponsors second medical forensics roundtable.

References

Abrams, W., Beers, M., Berkow, R., & Fletcher, A. (Eds.). (1995). *The Merck manual of geriatrics* (2nd ed.). Whitehouse Station, NJ: Merck.

Acierno, R. (2003). Elder mistreatment: Epidemiological assessment methodology. In R. J. Bonnie & R. B. Wallace (Eds.), *Elder mistreatment: Abuse, neglect, and exploitation in an aging America* (pp. 261–302).Washington, DC: The National Academies Press.

Albright, A., Brandl, B., Rozwadowski, J., & Wall, M. (2003). *Building a coalition to combat domestic abuse in later life.* Madison, WI: National Clearinghouse on Abuse in Later Life.

Alpert, E. J., Tonkin, A. E., Seeherman, A. M., & Holtz, H. A. (1998). Family violence curricula in U.S. medical schools. *American Journal of Preventive Medicine, 14*(4), 273–282.

Anetzberger, G. J. (1998). Psychological abuse and neglect: A cross-cultural concern to older Americans. In *Understanding and combating elder abuse in minority communities* (pp. 141–151). Long Beach, CA: Archstone Fondation.

Anetzberger, G. J. (2001). Elder abuse identification and referral: The importance of screening tools and referral protocols. *Journal of Elder Abuse & Neglect, 13*(2), 3–22.

Anonymous. (2002). Protecting older Americans: A history of federal action on elder abuse, neglect, and exploitation. *Journal of Elder Abuse & Neglect, 14*(2/3), 9–85.

Ansello, E. F. (1996). Causes and theories. In L. Baumhover & S. C. Beall (Eds.), *Abuse, neglect, and exploitation of older persons* (pp. 9–29). Baltimore: Health Professions Press.

Aravanis, S. C. (2002). A profile of the national policy summit on elder abuse: Perspective and advice on replication. *Journal of Elder Abuse & Neglect, 14,* 58–69.

Baladerian, N. (2004). *Interview skills to use with abuse victims who have developmental disabilities.* Los Angeles: Arc Riverside.

Balaswamy, S. (2002). Rating of interagency working relationship and associated factors in protective services. *Journal of Elder Abuse & Neglect, 14*(1), 1–20.

Berger v. United States, 295 U.S. 78, 88 (1935).

Bergeron, R. (2001). An elder abuse case study: Caregiver stress or domestic violence? You decide. *Journal of Gerontological Social Work, 34*(4), 47–63.

Bernatz, S. I., Aziz, S. J., & Mosqueda, L. (2001). Financial abuse. In M. D. Mezey (Ed.), *The encyclopedia of elder care* (pp. 264–267). New York: Springer.

Bernet, W. (1997). Case study: Allegations of abuse created in a single interview. *Journal of the American Academy of Child and Adolescent Psychiatry, 36*(7), 966–970.

Blakely, B. E., & Dolon, R. (1991). The relative contributions of occupation groups in the discovery and treatment of elder abuse and neglect. *Journal of Gerontological Social Work, 17*(1/2), 183–199.

Blakely, B. E., & Dolon, R. (2000). Perceptions of adult protective services workers of the support provided by criminal justice professionals in a case of elder abuse. *Journal of Elder Abuse & Neglect, 12*(3/4), 71–94.

Block, C. R. (2003). How can practitioners help an abused woman lower her risk of death? In *Intimate partner homicide* (U.S. Department of Justice, National Institute of Justice, Publication No. 250, pp. 2–7). Washington, DC: U.S. Department of Justice.

Blondell, R. D. (1999). Alcohol abuse and self-neglect in the elderly. *Journal of Elder Abuse & Neglect, 11*(2), 55–75.

Blum, B. (1999, August). *Targeting America's seniors.* Paper presented to the U.S. Senate Committee on Commerce, Science, and Transportation, Washington, DC.

Bonnie, R. J. & Wallace, R. B. (Eds.). (2003). *Elder mistreatment: Abuse, neglect, and exploitation in an aging America.* Washington, DC: The National Academies Press.

Bozinovski, S. D. (1995). *Self-neglect among the elderly: Maintaining continuity of self.* Unpublished doctoral dissertation. University of Denver, Colorado.

Brandl, B. (2000). *From a web of fear and isolation to a community safety net.* Madison, WI: National Clearinghouse on Abuse in Late Life.

Breaux, J., & Hatch, O. (2002). The elder justice act, S. 333. *Journal of Elder Abuse & Neglect, 14*(2/3), 1–6.

Brill, N. (1976). *Teamwork: Working together in the human services.* Philadelphia: Lippiencott.

Brock, K. (2003). *When men murder women: An analysis of the 2001 homicide data.* Washington, DC: Violence Policy Center.

Brown, A. (1989). A survey on elder abuse at one Native American tribe. *Journal of Elder Abuse & Neglect, 1*(2), 17–37.

Brownell, P., Berman, J., & Slamone, A. (1999). Mental health and criminal justice issues among perpetrators of elder abuse. *Journal of Elder Abuse & Neglect, 11*(4), 81–94.

Burgess, A., Dowdell, E., & Prentky, R. (2000). Sexual abuse of nursing home residents. *Journal of Psychosocial Nursing, 38*(6), 10–18.

Burston, G. R. (1975). Granny battering. *British Medical Journal* (3), 5983, 592.

Butler, R. (1975). *Why survive? Being old in America.* New York: Harper & Row.

California District Attorneys Association. (1985). *Ethics and responsibility for the California prosecutor.* Sacramento, CA: Author.

California District Attorneys Association. (2001). *Domestic violence prosecutor orientation guide.* Sacramento, CA: Author.

California Welfare and Institutions Code. §§ 15610.55, 15633.

Campbell, J. C. (1995). *Assessing dangerousness: Violence by sexual offenders, batterers, and child abusers.* Thousand Oaks, CA: Sage.

Campbell, J. C., Webster, D., Kozoil-McLain, J., & Block, C. R. (2003). Assessing risk factors for intimate partner homicide. In *Intimate partner homicide* (U.S. Department of Justice, National Institute of Justice, Publication No. 250, pp. 14–19). Washington, DC: U.S. Department of Justice.

Chalk, R., & King, P. (1998). *Violence in families: Assessing prevention and treatment programs.* Washington, DC: National Research Council and Institute of Medicine.

Cohen, D. (1998). Homicide-suicide in older persons. *American Journal of Psychiatry, 155,* 390–396.

Cohen, D. (2000). An update on homicide-suicide in older persons: 1995–2000. *Journal of Mental Health and Aging, 6*(3), 195–197.

Connolly, M.-T. (2002). Federal law enforcement in long-term care. *University of Maryland Journal of Health Care Law and Policy,* 230–293.

Cook-Daniels, L. (1997). Lesbian, gay male, bisexual, and transgendered elders: Elder abuse and neglect issues. *Journal of Elder Abuse & Neglect, 9*(2), 35–49.

Cook-Daniels, L. (1999). Interpreting the National Elder Abuse Incidence Study. *Victimization of the Elderly and Disabled, 2*(1), 1–2.

Cote, M. (2002, March). A matter of trust and respect. *CAMagazine.com.* Retrieved July 28, 2004, from http://www.camagazine.com/index.cfm/ci_id/6798/la_id/1.htm

Crawford v. Washington, 124 S. CT. 1354 (2004).

Crichton, S., Bond, J., Harvey, C.D.H., & Ristock, J. (1999). Elder abuse: Feminist and ageist perspectives. *Journal of Elder Abuse & Neglect, 10*(3/4), 115–130.

Davies, J., & Lyon, E. (1998). *Safety planning with battered women: Complex lives/difficult choices.* Thousand Oaks, CA: Sage.

DeBecker, G. (1997). *The gift of fear.* New York: Dell Publishing.

DeVoe, E. R., & Faller, K. C. (2002). Questioning strategies in interviews with children who may have been sexually abused. *Child Welfare, 81*(1), 5–31.

Dimah, K. P. & Dimah, A. (2003). Elder abuse and neglect among rural and urban women. *Journal of Elder Abuse and Neglect, 15*(1), 75–93.

Dolon, R., & Hendricks, J. E. (1989). An exploratory study comparing attitudes and practices of police officers and social work providers in elder abuse and neglect cases. *Journal of Elder Abuse & Neglect, 1*(1), 75–90.

Dombo, E. A. (1995). *Widening the circle: Sexual assault/abuse and people with disabilities and the elderly.* Madison: Wisconsin Coalition Against Sexual Assault.

Dunlop, B., Rothman, M. B., Condon, K. M., Hebert, K. S., & Martinez, I. L. (2000). Elder abuse: Risk factors and use of case data to improve policy and practice. *Journal of Elder Abuse & Neglect, 12*(3/5), 95–122.

Dychtwald, K., & Flower, J. (1990). *Age wave: How the most important trend of our time will change your future.* New York: Bantam Books.

Dyer, C. B., & Goins, A. M. (2000). The role of interdisciplinary geriatric assessment in addressing self-neglect of the elderly. *Generations, 24*(2), 23–27.

Dyer, C. B., Connolly, M.-T., & McFeely, P. (2003). The clinical and medical forensics of elder abuse and neglect. In R. J. Bonnie & R. B. Wallace (Eds.), *Elder mistreatment: Abuse, neglect and exploitation in an aging America* (pp. 339–381). Washington, DC: The National Academies Press.

Dyer, C., Hyer, K, Felt, K., Lindeman, D., Busby-Whitehead, J., Greenberg, S., et al. (2003). Frail older patient care by interdisciplinary teams: A primer for generalists. *Gerontology and Geriatric Education, 24*(2), 51–62.

Dyer, C. B., Hyman, D. J., Pavlik, V. N., Murphy, K. P., & Gleason, M. S. (1999). Elder neglect: A collaboration between a geriatrics assessment team and adult protective services. *Southern Medical Journal, 92*(2), 242–244.

Dyer, C. B, Pavlik, V. N., Murphy, K. P., & Hyman, D. J. (2000). The high prevalence of depression and dementia in elder abuse or neglect. *Journal of the American Geriatric Society, 48*(2), 205–208.

Dyer, C. B., Silverman, E., Nguyen, T., & McCullough, L. (2002). Ethical patient care. In M. Mezey, C. Cassell, M. Bottrell, K. Hyer, J. Howe, & T. Fulmer (Eds.), *A case book for geriatric health care teams* (pp. 151–165). Baltimore: Johns Hopkins University Press.

18 U.S.C. § 921(a)(32) , 2000.

18 U.S.C. § 922(g)(8), 2000.

18 U.S.C. § 922(g)(8)(B), 2000.

18 U.S.C. § 924(a)(2), 2000.

Eisenberg, H. B. (1991). Combating elder abuse through the legal process. *Journal of Elder Abuse & Neglect, 3*(165–196).

42 U.S.C. § 3001 *et seq.* 2000.

Francis, D., & Young, D. (1992). *Improving workgroups: A practical manual for team-building.* San Francisco: Jossey-Bass Pfeiffer.

Gelles, R. J. (1983). An exchange/social control theory. In D. Finkelhor, R. J. Gelles, G. T. Hotaling, & M. A. Straus (Eds.), *The dark side of families: Current family violence research* (pp. 151–165). Beverly Hills, CA: Sage.

Godkin, M., Wolf, R., & Pillemer, K. (1989). A case-comparison analysis of elder abuse and neglect. *International Journal of Aging and Human Development, 28*(3), 207–225.

Greenberg, J. R., McKibben, M., & Raymond, J. A. (1990). Dependent adult children and elder abuse. *Journal of Elder Abuse & Neglect, 2,* 73–86.

Griffin, L. (1994). Elder maltreatment among rural African-Americans. *Journal of Elder Abuse & Neglect, 6*(1), 1–27.

Hafemeister, T. (2003). Financial abuse of the elderly. In R. J. Bonnie & R. B. Wallace (Eds.), *Elder mistreatment: Abuse, neglect, and exploitation in an aging America* (pp. 382–445). Washington, DC: The National Academies Press.

Hagan, S. P. (2001). Profiling the rapist. In *Investigation and prosecution of sexual sssault* (pp. 113–137). Sacramento: California District Attorneys Association.

Hall, D. (1998). Victims of stalking. In J. R. Meloy (Ed.), *The psychology of stalking* (pp. 113–137). San Diego, CA: Academic Press.

Harris, S. (1996). For better or for worse: Spouse abuse grown old. *Journal of Elder Abuse & Neglect, 8*(1), 1–33.

Harshbarger, S. (1989). Prosecutor's perspective on protecting older Americans: Keynote address. *Journal of Elder Abuse & Neglect, 1*(3), 5–15.

Hart, B. (1988). Beyond the duty to warn: A therapist's duty to protect battered women and children. In K. Yllo & M. Bograd (Eds.), *Feminist perspectives on wife abuse* (pp. 234–248). Newbury Park, CA: Sage.

Hawes, C. (2003). Elder abuse in residential long-term care settings: What is known and what information is needed? In R. J. Bonnie & R. B Wallace (Eds.), *Elder mistreatment: Abuse, neglect, and exploitation in an aging America* (pp. 446–500). Washington, DC: The National Academies Press.

Hawley, D., McClane, G. E., & Strack, G. B. (2001). A review of 300 attempted strangulation cases, part III: Injuries in fatal cases. *The Journal of Emergency Medicine, 21*(3), 317–322.

Heath, J. M., Dyer, C. B., Kerzner, L. J., Mosqueda, L., & Murphy, C. (2002). Four models of medical education about elder mistreatment. *Academy of Medicine, 77*(11), 1101–1106.

Heisler, C. J. (2004). Domestic abuse court orders: An overview. *Victimization of the Elderly and Disabled, 6*(5), 65–78.

Heisler, C. J., & Brandl, B. (2002a). Agency policy considerations and training issues for victim and worker safety. *Victimization of the Elderly and Disabled, 5*(1), 1–16.

Heisler, C. J., & Brandl, B. (2002b). Safety planning for professionals working with elderly and clients who are victims of abuse. *Victimization of the Elderly and Disabled, 4*(5), 76–78.

Heisler, C. J., & Quinn, M. J. (2002). The legal response to elder abuse and neglect. *The Public Policy and Aging Report, 12*(2), 8–14.

Heisler, C. J., & Stiegel, L. A. (2002). Enhancing the justice system's response to elder abuse: Discussions and recommendations of the "improving prosecution" working group of The National Policy Summit on Elder Abuse. *Journal of Elder Abuse & Neglect, 14*(4), 31–54.

Hendricks-Matthews, M. K. (1997). A survey of family-violence curricula in Virginia medical schools and residencies at university medical centers. *Academy of Medicine, 71,* 154–156.

Hickey, T. (1979). *Neglect and abuse of the elderly: Implications of a developmental model for research and intervention.* Ann Arbor. University of Michigan, School of Public Health.

Hickey, T., & Douglass, R. (1981). Neglect and abuse of older family members: Professionals' perspectives and case experiences. *The Gerontologist, 21*(2), 171–176.

Hofford, M., & Harrell, A. (1995). *Family violence: Interventions for the justice system* (Program Brief, U.S. Department of Justice, Office of Justice Programs, NCJ 144532). Washington, DC: U.S. Department of Justice.

Holt, M. G. (1993). Elder sexual assault in Britain: Preliminary findings. *Journal of Elder Abuse & Neglect, 5*(2), 63–71.

Hudson, M., Beasley, C., Benedict, R., Carlson, J., Craig, B., & Mason, S. (1999). Elder abuse: Some African American views. *Journal of Interpersonal Violence, 14*(9), 915–939.

Hudson, M., & Carlson, J. (1999). Elder abuse: Its meaning to Caucasians, African Americans, and Native Americans. In T. Tatara (Ed.), *Understanding elder abuse in minority populations* (pp.187–204). Philadelphia: Brunner-Routledge.

The Humane Society of the United States & Wisconsin Department of Health and Family Services. (2003). *Creating safer communities for older adults and companion animals.* Madison: Wisconsin Department of Health and Family Services.

Institute of Medicine. (2002). *Confronting chronic neglect: The education and training of health professionals on family violence.* Washington, DC: The National Academies Press.

Iserson, K. V. (1984). Strangulation: A review of ligature, manual, and postural neck compression injuries. *Annals of Emergency Medicine, 13*(3), 179–185.

Jasinski, J. L., & Dietz, T. L. (2003). Domestic violence and stalking among older adults: An assessment of risk markers. *Journal of Elder Abuse &Neglect, 15*(1), 3–18.

Jay, R. (1999). *Building a great team.* Englewood cliffo, NJ. Prentice-Hall.

Johnson, K. D. (2003). *Financial crimes against the elderly* (Guide no. 20). Washington, DC: U.S. Department of Justice, Office of Community Oriented Policing Services.

Kahan, F. S., & Paris, B. E. (2003). Why elder abuse continues to elude the health care system. *Mount Sinai Journal of Medicine, 70*(1), 62–68.

Katz, S., Ford, A. B., Moskowitz, R. W., Jackson, B., & Jaffe, M. (1963). Studies of illness in the aged. The index of ADL: A standardized measure of biological, psychosocial function. *Journal of the American Medical Association, 185,* 914–919.

Katzenbach, J. & Smith, D. (1993). *Wisdom of teams: creating the high performance organization.* New York: Harper Business.

Kohlman-Thomson, L. (1972). *Kohlman Evaluation of Living Skills (KELS).* Bethesda, MD: American Occupational Therapy Association.

Korbin, J., Anetzberger, G., & Austin, C. (1995). The intergenerational cycle of violence in child and elder abuse. *Journal of Elder Abuse & Neglect, 7*(1), 1–15.

Kosberg, J. I., & Nahmiash, D. (1996). Characteristics of victims and perpetrators. In L. Baumhover & S. Colleen Beall (Eds.), *Abuse, neglect, and exploitation of older persons* (pp. 31–49). Baltimore: Health Professions Press.

Lachs, M. S., Williams, C. S., O'Brien, S., Hurst, L., & Horowitz, R. (1997). Risk factors for reported elder abuse and neglect: A nine-year observational cohort study. *The Gerontologist, 37,* 469–474.

Lachs, M. S., Williams, C. S., O'Brien, S., Hurst, L., Kossack, A., Siegal, A., et al. (1997). ED use by older victims of family violence. *Annals of Emergency Medicine, 30*(4), 448–454.

Lachs, M. S., Williams, C. S., O'Brien, S., Pillemer, K. A., & Charlson, M. E. (1998). The mortality of elder mistreatment. *Journal of the American Medical Association, 280,* 428–432.

LaFave, W. R., & Scott, A. W. (1986). *Criminal law* (2nd ed.). Eagan, MN: West.

Larkin, H. (2001). The sexual assault medical examination: Things you should know before trial. In *Investigation and prosecution of sexual assault* (III-1–III-16). Sacramento: California District Attorneys Association.

Lawton, M. P., & Brody, M. (1969). Assessment of older people: Self-maintenance. *The Gerontologist, 9,* 179–186.

Le, Q. (1997). Mistreatment of Vietnamese elderly by their families in the United States. *Journal of Elder Abuse & Neglect, 9,* 51–62.

Line, W. S, Jr., Stanley, R. B., Jr., & Choi, J. H. (1985). Strangulation: A full spectrum of blunt neck trauma. *Annals of Otology, Rhinology, & Laryngology, 94*(1), 542–546.

Lithwick, M., Beaulieu, M., Gravel, S., & Straka, S. (1999). The mistreatment of older adults: Perpetrator-Victim relationships and interventions. *Journal of Elder Abuse & Neglect, 11*(4), 95–112.

Longress, J. (1994). Self-neglect and social control: A modest test of an issue. *Journal of Gerontological Social Work, 22*(3/4), 3–20.

Los Angeles County Area Agency on Aging. (2001). *Los Angeles fiduciary abuse specialist team handbook.* Santa Monica, CA: WISE Senior Services.

Malphurs, J. E., & Cohen, D. (2001). A State-wide case control study of spousal homicide-suicide in older persons. *American Journal of Geriatric Psychiatry, 9*(1), 49–57.

Matlaw, J. R., & Spence, D. M. (1994). The hospital elder assessment team: A protocol for suspected cases of elder abuse and neglect. *Journal of Elder Abuse & Neglect, 6,* 223–227.

McClane, G. E., Strack, G. B., & Hawley, D. (2001). A review of 300 attempted strangulation cases, part II: Clinical evaluation of the surviving victim. *The Journal of Emergency Medicine, 21*(3), 311–315.

Meloy, J. R. (1998). The psychology of stalking. In *The psychology of stalking* (pp. 1–23). San Diego, CA: Academic Press.

Menio, D., & Keller, B. (2000). CARIE: A multifacted approach to abuse prevention in nursing homes. *Generations, 24*(2), 8–32.

Montgomery, R.J.V. (1989). Investigating caregiver burden. In K. Mankides & C. Cooper (Eds.), *Aging, stress, and health* (pp. 201–208). New York: John Wiley and Sons.

Moon, A. (2000). Perceptions of elder abuse among various cultural groups: Similarities and differences. *Generations, 24*(2), 75–80.

Moon, A., & Benton, D. (2000). Tolerance of elder abuse and attitudes toward third-party intervention among African-American, Korean-American, and white elderly. *Journal of Multicultural Social Work, 8*(3/4), 283–303.

Moskowitz, S. (2001). Filial responsibility statutes: Legal and policy considerations. *Journal of Law and Policy, 9*(3), 709–736.

Moskowitz, S. (2003). Golden age in the golden state: Contemporary legal developments in elder abuse and neglect. *Loyola Law Review, 36*(2), 589–666.

Mouton, C., Rovi, S., Furniss, K., & Lasser, N. (1999). The associations between health and domestic violence in older women: Results of a pilot study. *Journal of Women's Health & Gender-Based Medicine, 1*(9), 1173–1179.

Muelleman, R. L.,& Feighny, K. M. (1999). Effects of an emergency department-based advocacy program for battered women on community resource utilization. *Annals of Emergency Medicine, 33*(1), 62–66.

Muram, D., Miller, K., & Cutler, A. (1992). Sexual assault of the elderly victim. *Journal of Interpersonal Violence, 7*(1), 70–76.

Nahmiash, D. (2002). Powerlessness and abuse and neglect of older adults. *Journal of Elder Abuse and Neglect, 14*(1), 24.

National Adult Protective Services Association. (2004). *Ethical principles and best practices guidelines.* Boulder, CO: Author.

National Association of Adult Protective Services Administrators. (1993). *A national study of involuntary protective services to adult protective services clients.* Richmond, VA: Author.

National Center on Elder Abuse. (1998). *National elder abuse incidence study.* Washington, DC: Author.

National Center on Elder Abuse. (n.d.). *Frequently asked questions: Definitions.* Retrieved August 29, 2004, from http://www.elderabusecenter.org

National Center on Elder Abuse. (2002). National action agenda, 2002: Call to action to protect America's most vulnerable elders. *Journal of Elder Abuse & Neglect, 14*(4), 3–10.

National Clearinghouse on Abuse in Later Life. (2003). *National domestic abuse in later life resource directory.* Madison, WI: Author.

National Clearinghouse on Abuse in Late Life & Wisconsin Coalition Against Domestic Violence. (2003). *Anticipate: Identifying victim strengths and planning for safety concerns.* Madison, WI: Author.

National District Attorneys Association. (1977). *National prosecution standards.* Chicago: Author.

Neufeldt, V. (Ed.). (1995). *Webster's New World Dictionary.* New York: Simon and Schuster.

Nerenberg, L.(1995). *Building partnerships: A guide to developing coalitions, interagency agreements, and teams in the field of elder abuse.* San Francisco: Institute on Aging.

Nerenberg, L. (1996). *Financial abuse of the elderly.* Washington, DC: National Center on Elder Abuse.

Nerenberg, L. (2000a). Developing a service response to elder abuse. *Generations, 24*(2), 86–92.

Nerenberg, L. (2000b). Forgotten victims of financial crime and abuse: Facing the challenge. *Journal of Elder Abuse & Neglect, 12*(2), 49–73.

Nerenberg L. (2000c). *Helping hands: The role of adult protective services in preventing elder abuse and neglect.* San Francisco: Institute on Aging.

Nerenberg, L. (2003). *Multidisciplinary elder abuse prevention teams: A new generation.* Washington, DC: National Center on Elder Abuse.

Nievod, A. (1992). Undue influence in contract and probate law. *Journal of Questioned Document Examination, 1*(1), 14–26.

Ohio Domestic Violence Network. (1999). *THEMIS–A manual for legal advocates.* Columbus, OH: Author.

The old increasingly being bilked by the people they must rely on. (1991, December 16). *The New York Times,* p. A1.

Otiniano, M., & Herra, C. (1998). Hispanic elder abuse. In B. Brandl, & L. Cook-Daniels (Eds.), *Understanding and combating elder abuse in minority communities* (p. 194). Long Beach, CA: Archstone Foundation.

Otto, J. M. (2002). Program and administrative issues affecting adult protective services. *The Public Policy and Aging Report, 12*(2), 3–7.

Otto, J., & Quinn, K. (1999). The national elder abuse incidence study: An evaluation by the National Association of Adult Protective Service Administrators. *Victimization of the Elderly and Disabled, 2*(1), 4–15.

Pavlik, V. N., Hyman, D., Festa, N., & Dyer, C. B. (2001). Quantifying the problem of abuse and neglect in adults: Analysis of a statewide database. *Journal of the American Geriatrics Society, 49,* 45–48.

Payne, B. K. (2001). Understanding differences in opinion and "facts" between ombuds-men, police chiefs, and nursing home directors. *Journal of Elder Abuse & Neglect,* 13(3), 61–77.

Payne, B. K., Berg, B. L., & Byars, K. (1999). A qualitative examination of the similarities and differences of elder abuse definitions among four groups: Nursing home direc-tors, nursing home employees, police chiefs, and students. *Journal of Elder Abuse & Neglect,* 10(3/4), 63–85.

People v. Heitzman, 9 Cal. 4th 189, 37 Cal. Rptr. 2d 236, 886 P. 2d 1229 (1994).

People v. Hill, 17 Cal. 4th 800, 72 Cal Rptr. 2d 656 (1998).

Pfeiffer, E. (1989). Why teams? In E. L. Siegler, K. Hyer, T. Fulmer, & M. Mezey (Eds), *Geriatric interdisciplinary team training* (pp. 14–16). New York: Springer Publishing.

Phillips, L. (1986). Theoretical explanations of elder abuse: Competing hypotheses and unresolved issues. In K. Pillmer & R. Wolf (Eds.), *Elder abuse: Conflict in the family* (pp. 197–217). Dover, MA: Auburn House.

Phillips, L., de Ardon, E., & Briones, G. (2000). Abuse of female caregivers by care recipients: Another form of elder abuse. *Journal of Elder Abuse & Neglect,* 12(3/4), 123–144.

Pillemer, K. (1986). Risk factors in elder abuse: Results from a case control study. In K. A. Pillemer & R. S. Wolf (Eds.), *Elder abuse: Conflict in the family* (pp. 239–263). Dover, MA: Auburn House.

Pillemer, K., & Finkelhor, D. (1988). The prevalence of elder abuse: A random sample sur-vey. *The Gerontologist, 28,* 51–57.

Pillemer, K., & Finkelhor, D. (1989). Causes of elder abuse: Caregiver stress versus problem relatives. *American Journal of Orthopsychiatry, 59*(2), 179–187.

Pillemer, K., & Moore, D. W. (1988). Abuse of patients in nursing homes: Findings from a survey. *The Gerontologist, 29,* 314–320.

Pittaway, E., & Westhues, A. (1993). The prevalence of elder abuse and neglect of older adults who access health and social services in London, Ontario, Canada. *Journal of Elder Abuse & Neglect, 5*(4), 77–93.

Podnieks, E. (1992a). Emerging themes from a follow-up study of Canadian victims of elder abuse. *Journal of Elder Abuse & Neglect, 4*(1/2), 59–111.

Podnieks, E. (1992b). National survey on abuse of the elderly in Canada. *Journal of Elder Abuse & Neglect, 4*(1/2), 5–58.

Poythress, E. L., Harrel, R., Booker, J., & Dyer, C. B. (2001). Physicians and elder mistreat-ment: Development and function of the TEAM institute. *Victimization of the Elderly and Disabled, 4,* 1–10.

Poythress, E. L., Vogel, M., Pavlik, V. N., Hyman, D., Parker, M., Tremaine, B., et al. (2001, November). Outcomes of geriatric assessment and intervention in elder mistreatment. Paper presented at the meeting of the Gerontological Society of America, Chicago.

Qualls, S., & Czirr, R. (1988). Geriatric health teams: Classifying models of professional and team functioning. *The Gerontologist, 28,* 3372–3376.

Quinn, M. J. (2000). Undoing undue influence. *Journal of Elder Abuse & Neglect, 12*(2), 9–17.

Quinn, M. J. (2001). Friendly persuasion, good salesmanship, or undue influence. *Elder's Advisor, 2,* 449–456.

Quinn, M. J., & Heisler, C. J. (2002). The legal response to elder abuse and neglect. *Journal of Elder Abuse & Neglect, 14*(1), 61–77.

Ramsey-Klawsnik, H. (1991). Elder sexual abuse: Preliminary findings. *Journal of Elder Abuse & Neglect, 3,* 373–390.

Ramsey-Klawsnik, H. (1993b). Questions and answers: Elder sexual abuse. *Illness, Crisis and Loss, 2*(4), 92–96.

Ramsey-Klawsnik, H. (2000). Elder abuse offenders: A typology. *Generations, 24*(11), 17–22.

Ramsey-Klawsnik, H. (2003). Sexual abuse within the family. *Journal of Elder Abuse & Neglect, 15*(1), 43–58.

Rathbone-McCuan, E., & Hashimi, J. (1982). *Isolated elders: Health and social intervention.* Rockville, MD: Aspen.

Reis, M., & Nahmiash, D. (1997). Abuse of seniors: Personality, stress, and other indicators. *Journal of Mental Health and Aging, 3*(3), 337–356.

Reis, M., & Nahmiash, D. (1998). Validation of the indicators of abuse (IOA) screen. *The Gerontologist, 38*(4), 471–480.

Reulbach, D. M., & Tewksbury, J. (1994). Collaboration between protective services and law enforcement: The Massachusetts model. *Journal of Elder Abuse & Neglect, 6*(2), 9–21.

Sanchez, Y. (1999). Elder mistreatment in Mexican American communities: The Nevada and Michigan experiences. In T. Tatara (Ed.), *Understanding elder abuse in minority populations* (pp. 67–77). Philadelphia: Brunner-Routledge.

Saxena, S., Brody, A. L., Maidment, K. M., Smith, E. C., Zohrabi, N., Katz, E., et al. (2004). Cerebral glucose metabolism in obsessive-compulsive hoarding. *American Journal of Psychiatry, 161,* 1038–1048.

Schechter, S. (1987). *Guidelines for mental health practitioners in domestic violence cases.* Denver: National Coalition Against Domestic Violence.

Schimer, M. R., & Anetzberger, G. J. (1999). Examining the gray zones in guardianship and involuntary protective services laws. *Journal of Elder Abuse & Neglect, 10*(3/4), 19–38.

Seaver, C. (1996). Muted lives: Older battered women. *Journal of Elder Abuse & Neglect, 8*(2), 3–21.

Sharps, P., Campbell, J. C., Gary, F., & Webster, D. (2003). Risky mix: Drinking, drug use, and homicide. In *Intimate partner homicide* (U.S. Department of Justice, National Institute of Justice, Publication no. 250, pp. 8–13). Washington, DC: U.S. Department of Justice.

Singer, M. T. (1992). Undue influence and written documents: Psychological aspects. *Journal of Questioned Document Examination, 1*(1), 4–13.

Spangler, D., & Brandl, B. (2003). *Golden voices: Support groups for older abused women.* Madison, WI: National Coalition for Abuse in Later Life.

Spencer, C. (1999). *Exploring the social and economic costs of abuse in later life.* Unpublished report.

Steinmetz, S. K. (1977). *The cycle of violence.* New York: Praeger.

Steinmetz, S. K. (1988). *Duty bound: Elder abuse and family care.* Newbury Park, CA: Sage.

Stiegel, L. A. (1995). *Recommended guidelines for state courts handling cases involving elder abuse.* Washington, DC: American Bar Association.

Stiegel, L. A. (2000). The changing role of the courts in elder abuse cases. *Generations, 24*(2), 59–64.

Strack, G. B. McClane, G. E., & Hawley, D. (2001). A review of 300 attempted strangulation cases, part I: Criminal legal issues. *The Journal of Emergency Medicine, 21*(3), 303–309.

Straus, M. A., Gelles, R. J., & Steinmetz, S. (1980). *Behind closed doors: Violence in the American family.* New York: Anchor Press/Doubleday.

Sutton, W. (1976). *Where the money was: The memoirs of a bank robber.* New York: Viking Press.

Tatara, T. (1993). Understanding the nature and scope of domestic elder abuse with the use of state aggregate data: Summaries of the key findings of a national survey of state APS and aging agencies. *Journal of Elder Abuse & Neglect, 5*(4), 35–57.

Teaster, P. B. (2002). *A response to the abuse of vulnerable adults: The 2000 Survey of State Adult Protective Services.* Washington, DC: National Center on Elder Abuse.

Teaster, P. (2006). *The 2004 survey of adult protective services: Abuse of adults 60 years of age and older.* Washington, DC: National Center on Elder Abuse.

Teaster, P. B., & Nerenberg, L. (2000). *A national look at multidisciplinary teams.* Washington, DC: National Center on Elder Abuse.

Thomas, R. W., & Heisler, C. J. (1999). Law enforcement and adult protective services: Critical collaboration in elder maltreatment. *Victim Advocate 1*(2), 13–15.

Tjaden, P. (1997). The crime of stalking: How big is the problem? *National Institute of Justice Research Review.* Washington, DC: U.S. Department of Justice.

Tjaden, P., & Thoennes, N. (1998). Stalking in America: Findings from the national violence against women survey (National Institute of Justice & Centers for Disease Control Research Brief). Washington, DC: U.S. Department of Justice.

Tomita, S. K. (1999). Exploration of elder mistreatment among the Japanese. In T. Tatara (Ed.), *Understanding elder abuse in minority populations* (pp. 119–139). Philadelphia: Brunner-Routledge.

U.S. Census Bureau. (2004?). *Demographic data 2000.* Retrieved July 28, 2004, from http://www.census.gov

U.S. Congress, Select Committee on Aging. (1981). *A report: Elder abuse (an examination of a hidden problem).* Washington, DC: U.S. Government Printing Office.

U.S. Department of Health and Human Services, Office of Disease Prevention and Health Promotion. (2000?). *Healthy people 2000.* Retrieved July 28, 2004, from http://www. healthy people.gov

U.S. Department of Justice, National Institute of Justice. (1993). *Project to develop a model anti-stalking code for states* (NCJ 144477). Washington, DC: U.S. Department of Justice.

U.S. Department of Justice, National Institute of Justice. (1996). *Domestic violence, stalking, and anti-stalking legislation: An annual report to Congress under the Violence Against Women Act* (NCJ 160943). Washington, DC: U.S. Department of Justice.

U.S. Department of Justice, National Institute of Justice & Centers for Disease Control and Prevention. (2000). *Extent, nature, and consequences of intimate partner violence.* Washington, DC: U.S. Department of Justice.

U.S. Department of Justice, National Institute of Justice, Center for Policy Research. (1997). *Stalking in America.* Washington, DC: Office of Justice Programs.

U.S. Department of Justice, Office of Justice Programs. (1998a). *Focus group on crime victimization of older persons: Recommendations to the Office of Justice Programs.* Washington, DC: U.S. Department of Justice.

U.S. Department of Justice, Office of Justice Programs. (1998b). *Stalking and domestic violence: The third report to Congress under the Violence Against Women Act.* Washington, DC: U.S. Government Printing Office.

U.S. Department of Justice, Office of Justice Programs & U.S. Department of Health and Human Services. (2000). *Our aging population: Promoting empowerment, preventing victimization, and implementing coordinated interventions* (NCJ 186256). Washington, DC: U.S. Department of Justice.

U.S. General Accounting Office. (1991). *Elder abuse: Effectiveness of reporting laws and other factors* (GAO/HRD-91-74). Washington, DC: U.S. Government Printing Office.

U.S. General Accounting Office. (2002). *Nursing homes: More can be done to protect residents from abuse* (GAO-T-HEHS-02-312). Washington, DC: U.S. Government Printing Office.

U.S. General Accounting Office. (2004). *Guardianships: Collaboration needed to protect incapacitated elderly people.* Washington, DC: U.S. Government Printing Office.

U.S. Senate, Special Commission on Aging, 102nd Congress. (1991). *An advocate's guide to laws and programs addressing elder abuse: An information paper.* Washington, DC: U.S. Government Printing Office.

Viano, E. (1980). Victimology: An overview. In J. L. Kosberg (Ed.), *Abuse and maltreatment of the elderly: Causes and interventions.* (pp. 1–18). Littleton, MA: John Wright PSG.

Vladescu, D., Eveleigh, K., Ploeg, J., & Patterson, C. (1999). An evaluation of a client-centered case management program for elder abuse. *Journal of Elder Abuse & Neglect, 11*(4), 5–22.

Waters, H., Hyder, A., Rajkotia, Y., Basu, S., Rehwinkel, J. A., & Butchart, A. (2004). *The economic dimensions of interpersonal violence.* Geneva, Switzerland: Department of Injuries and Violence Prevention, World Health Organization.

Websdale, N. (1999). Lethality assessment tools: A critical analysis. Retrieved July 28, 2004, from the National Online Resource Center on Violence Against Women Web site: http://www.vaw.umn.edu

Wolf, R. S. (1999a). *A research agenda on abuse of older persons and adults with disabilities.* Washington, DC: National Center on Elder Abuse.

Wolf, R. S. (1999b, February). *The criminalization of elder abuse.* Paper presented at the Pan American Congress '99, Symposium on Social Policy II, Elder Abuse, San Antonio, Texas.

Wolf, R. S. (2000a). Elders as victims of crime, abuse, neglect, and exploitation. In M. B. Rothman, B. D. Dunlop, & P. Entzel (Eds.), *Elders, crime, and the criminal justice system: Myth, perceptions, and reality in the 21st century* (pp. 19–42). New York: Springer.

Wolf, R. S. (2000b). Introduction: The nature and scope of elder abuse. *Generations, 24* (2), 6–12.

Wolf, R. S., & Pillemer, K. A. (1997). The older battered women: Wives and mothers compared. *Journal of Mental Health and Aging, 3*(3), 325–336.

Zona, M., Palarea, R. & Lane, J., Jr. (1998). Psychiatric diagnosis and the offender victim typology of stalking. In J. Meloy (Ed.), *The psychology of stalking: Clinical and forensic perspectives* (pp. 69–84). San Diego, CA: Academic Press.

Zorza, J. (Aug./Sep., 2001). The problem with proxy measures: The inaccuracy of the conflict tactic scales and other crime surveys in measuring intimate partner violence. *Domestic Violence Report,* 83–90.

Index

Vulnerable Older Adults

Health Care Needs and Interventions

Patricia M. Burbank, DNSc, RN, Editor

"It has been said that one measure of a society is the care it provides to its most vulnerable members. By taking on this challenge, Burbank and her colleagues have opened the door to addressing the needs of the most vulnerable among our older population."

—**Mathy Mezey,** RN, EdD, FAAN

Based on the concept that vulnerability in the older populace encompasses those who are at increased risk for physical and psychosocial health problems, this book takes a closer look at vulnerability and how it affects five specific populations within the elderly: those incarcerated in prisons; the homeless; gay, lesbian, bisexual, and transgender people; those who are HIV positive or living with AIDS; and the frail.

Physical and psychosocial health care issues and needs are addressed as well as interventions and resources that can be implemented to care for these very specific populations and their requirements for successful physical and mental health care. The unique challenges of hospice care in prisons, the lack of services that cater to homeless older people, and the overall attitude towards helping elderly gay, lesbian, bisexual, or transgender people are some of the increasingly important issues covered.

Unique Features Include:

- Summary of the latest research and theoretical approaches to give health professionals a concise picture of health care needs of these older adult populations
- Interdisciplinary approach to care, cultural considerations, and neglect and abuse
- Discussion of strategies and resources for caring for older adults with dementia for each vulnerable population

2006 · 304pp · 0-8261-0208-5 · hardcover

11 West 42nd Street, New York, NY 10036-8002 • Fax: 212-941-7842
Order Toll-Free: 877-687-7476 • Order On-line: www.springerpub.com